Brattleboro Vt. Sept. 12th

My dear Noble.

It is warm and
summery this afternoon, and such
an agreeable atmospheric contrast, to the two
chilly days which have preceded it,
that I feel thawed into a sufficiently
genial mood to attempt to write
you.   Yours of the 7th came duly
(like other letters) to my hand, and (unlike
other letters) to my heart. I believe I
can say to you that it was and is not
lost upon me.   Of course I cannot
answer it. It is a comfort to know
that you dont want to have me do so.
I have thought a great deal about the
few words which we said that night
about expression, and am much chagrin-
-ed at the scarcity of that commodity
which I discover in my inventory of

mental possessions. I believe that a
when the crisis comes at which I
wish to pour out my offering of molten
passion at the feet of my Adorissima,
~~but~~ I shall be obliged stupidly to stare
in her face, and refer her to "Romeo &
Juliet" for ~~the~~ proper and truthful ex-
-pression of my condition! — Perhaps
you will let me make Charles speak to
Seraphael for me. —

      — "Sir, I can but thank
you, and that means more than I
can say; But I cannot think why you like
me. It is most exquisite but I do not
understand it." —

      I have finished "Charles Auchester."
That is to say, I have read through its
pages. I can never "finish it." I am
sure that "A thing of beauty is a joy forever,"
must have been said expressly for
such a book. I know and trust that
it will never cease to remain with,

and be, in a manner, a part of me.

Lieut. Grant has, at last, by dint of a good deal of patience and some profanity, worried through "Counterparts". He elegantly gives it as his opinion that it is "a d— witching thing, but does not amount to much, after all!" Hence I have commenced it under inauspicious circumstances impressions!

I will send you up the "Life of Chopin" when I have read it,—if you like. No new demonstrations or disclosures have transpired in regard to our disposition or destinations while here. I expect to visit Midd. sometime ~~when~~, unknown as yet when.

Tell me how the Freshman look and how "horse-shedding" prospers, how Allie is flourishing, and College news generally.

Ever yours
E.W. Higley

VERMONT'S PROPER SON

The Letters of Soldier and Scholar
Edwin Hall Higley, 1861 - 1871

Edited with Contextual Narrative

by Richard A. Hanks

Coyote Hill Press

Published by Coyote Hill Press, Riverside, California

Layout & Design by Robin S. Hanks

First Edition, 2014

Printed in the United States

ISBN: 978-0-9912641-1-7 All rights reserved.

Front Cover Photograph of a Federal cavalry column along the Rappahannock River, VA, 1862. National Archives photo no. 111-B-508.

Front Cover Image of Edwin Hall Higley courtesy of Groton School Archives.

Contents

Dedication

This work is dedicated to my wife Robin who has my everlasting appreciation for the numerous hours given to layout and design of this publication. It is only through her extraordinary artistic talents and unwavering support that this book could be possible.

Acknowledgements

There are many who gave generously of their time and knowledge to create this book. My earnest gratitude to Curator Brenda Focht and Archivist Kevin Hallaran of the Riverside Metropolitan Museum, who solicited my involvement in this project and whose comments and scrutiny of the manuscript, improved the work. I am grateful to friend and Archivist Bill Bell for his reading of the manuscript and Riverside librarian Ruth McCormick for her assistance in accessing needed information. My thanks to museum intern Taylor Libolt for his initial transcriptions. I am also indebted to Joan Hall for reading the manuscript and her tireless work on the index.

Along the way other archivists and librarians graciously assisted my search for materials that would enhance the stories of Edwin Hall Higley and Calvin Day Noble. These include Curator Danielle Rougeau of the Middlebury College, Vermont Archives, Archivist Douglas Brown of Groton School, Librarians Elaine McHale and Suzanne Levy of the Fairfax County, Virginia Historical Society, Michael Yockey and Francesca M. McCrossan of the Swedenborgian House of Studies in Berkeley, Charlie Waddell and the Herndon, Virginia Historical Society, and the Library of Congress, Prints & Photographs Division. My sincere appreciation for the help of Ruth Breindel, Managing Editor of the *New England Classical Journal*, Holly Reed of the National Archives & Records Administration and Civil War collector Francis Guber.

Preface

To the historian or anyone whose passions run to the details of human agency, an archives is a magical place. By its nature, and the common practice of budgets, the secrets of an archives are often undiscovered or simply obscured; manpower limiting what can be arranged for public use. But often enough, collections reveal nuggets from the past that surprise and often delight us. Archives become laboratories for understanding the human condition.

The letters of Edwin Hall Higley took a circuitous route to the neat shelves of the Riverside Metropolitan Museum in Riverside, California. Circumstance and ill health brought them in the person of Calvin Day Noble, close friend of their author. They span the years of 1861 to 1871. It is a testament to his sense of friendship with Higley that the valued correspondence traveled from Vermont through the Midwest and Massachusetts before accompanying Noble to Southern California.

Day Noble (his preference) came at a time when Riverside was in its infancy in 1874. He was a former journalist and minister of the Swedenborgian faith. He chose Riverside, like so many others, for the dry heat of the area, to relieve the debilitation of tuberculosis, or consumption as it was called. While never completely abandoning his ministerial beliefs, he turned to education, opening the private Dovenook school in Riverside while also tending to his fruit trees. Dovenook and its instructors, including Noble's wife Hannah, who he called Pansy, offered students Latin, German, French, Drawing, and Music; "higher branches of high school years that were missing from public education," wrote Riverside historian, Tom Patterson.[1] Students at Dovenook included Samuel Cary Evans, Jr., his brother Pliny, Charles Benedict, Robert Bettner and A.C. Fulmor. An impression must have been made since some time after Noble's death on July 12, 1885 the letters were turned over to Samuel Evans, Jr. by Pearl and Miriam Noble, Day's daughters. Acquisition of the Evans collection in 2000 brought the letters to their current home.

While the record on Calvin Day Noble is sparse, he represents, in many respects, the character of those attracted to the colony in Southern California on the edge of a desert. And, like all others who settled this area, he brought his past with him. That past included an enduring friendship for a fellow scholar, art enthusiast and intellectual traveler and a rare glimpse into the trials and hopes expressed in a dear friend's letters. All but one of the letters examined in this work were penned by Edwin Higley but they also tell us something about Calvin Noble as well, and a fidelity to a pursuit of life with purpose.

Higley's letters while in service during the Civil War are printed in full and presented in italics. The transcriptions are offered as close to the original as possible, which includes misspellings and other grammatical errors. In particular, Higley often omitted apostrophes for words showing possessive case.

[1] Tom Patterson, "Dovenook's unique role in Riverside education," *Riverside Press Enterprise*, October 19, 1980.

Introduction

When reading through a collection of letters such as those of Edwin Higley, one becomes acutely aware at some point that these words were not meant for you. They are the property of their creator and their recipient, in this case Calvin Day Noble. You also quickly understand that this is a one-sided conversation. Noble's letters to Higley, if they even still exist, have not been located. However, Noble's attitudes or concerns are often evident in Higley's responses. One can also find the voice of Noble in his published work extant in the Riverside collection. With these realizations you begin to appreciate that you are witness to the private world of these two men; their hopes, fears, actions and justifications which guided their inter-action in a society long past. They were scholars in a time when that level of scholarship was rare, juxtaposed against the violent maelstrom that was the American Civil War. For Higley, in his letters, he confided to his friend the vicissitudes of his reality and the solace and refuge he found in the beauty and tenderness gifted to him by his education in music, literature and the classical instruction which made up his personality.

Both men were born into the romantic age of the Victorian era. Vermont in the mid-19th century was a settled area, steeped in puritan values and traditions stemming from its colonial roots— the first state to join the new republic following the Revolution. Honor, family, duty and the aesthetic expression of emotion, as a recognition of the inner-self, guided adherents of this period. Although outside the religious pale of staid Christian belief, Transcendentalists such as Ralph Waldo Emerson and Henry David Thoreau inspired the hearts and intellects of young men such as Higley and Noble. To the transcendentalist, wrote Jerry Phillips and Andrew Ladd, "a farmer at work in the corn fields, a poet thinking through the logic of a certain metaphor, a scientist bent on discovering the natural cause behind the diversity of song birds, and a reformer committed to struggling against social injustices—all these individuals are involved in revealing the 'higher laws' of the world that cannot be perceived by the senses."[2]

Ironically, historians point to the 1860s and the Civil War as the end to the classic era of romanticism but for Higley and Noble the imprint had been made. The intuitive rejection of the sterile world of reason, given birth by the Age of Enlightenment, was nurtured in their youth and matured as they entered college. Phillips and Ladd wrote that, for the romantic, there is a preference for emotion over reason; belief in the self and potential of the individual and "a predilection for the artist in particular" and "creative spirit" in general. This is innately represented in the lives of these two men. For Higley it was the lure of music. An accomplished keyboardist, he is fascinated with the romantic composers of his day, particularly Felix Mendelssohn; a love shared by Noble. Romanticism inspired their sense of duty and honor and may have been the spirit of Higley's desire to assist a nation in defining the principles which govern it—it is a search for nobility in life.

As Higley and Noble reached adulthood, America was seeking to delineate its own literary path through writers such as Emerson, Emily Dickinson, and James Fenimore Cooper. While stirred by American authors, Higley and Noble also found favorites among the newest and brightest emerging from Europe in the themes of romantic novelists such as George Sand, or Elizabeth Sara Sheppard ("A thing of beauty is a joy forever,") and the "sad, rippling foamy tones" of the ballad-like expressions of Charles Kingsley.

The two men, however, pursued expression in different ways and followed divergent life paths. During the war, Noble remained among the halls of Middlebury College, while Higley clung to whatever culture he could find amid the killing fields of Virginia.

Calvin Day Noble

Calvin Day Noble descended from a long line of Congregational Church stalwarts. His father, grandfather and great-grandfather had all been members of its clergy. Born in Rochester, Vermont on August 13, 1840, he was left an orphan by the age of six. He lived on a farm until the age of 14 when he found employment as a typesetter in a printing-office. He prepared for Middlebury at the Burr Seminary in Manchester, Vermont and graduated with honors from Middlebury in 1864 ("philosophical oration, the second honor of his class,") according to a family history.[3] He became the assistant editor of the *Vermont Record* of Brattleboro and the *Brandon Record*, before leaving within the year to work as the literary editor for the *Houston Telegraph*. While a Vermont editor, he published the personal accounts of Edwin Higley's experiences in Confederate prison camps. In Texas, his health began to fail from the debilitating onset of tuberculosis and he moved to Cleveland, Ohio.

While attending Middlebury College, he lived on the farm of his maternal grandfather James Jewett and through his grandfather's influence converted to the teachings and doctrines of Emanuel Swedenborg. Once in Cleveland, his attraction to this "higher world" found form in the mystery of the new religion. Swedenborgianism, or the New Jerusalem Church, doctrinally deviates little from mainstream Protestant faiths. It practices the sacraments of baptism and communion, believes in the existence of heaven and hell and good works and the divinity of Christ. The church is more in line with Universalist belief, however, seeing the divine Christ as a whole, inclusive of the Father and Holy Ghost.

It is the personal experiences of Swedenborg at the age of 57, however, which attracted spiritualists to the faith. A scientist born in 1688, Swedenborg claimed a personal communing with Christ who "initiated him into the spiritual sense of the Scriptures;" an interaction with angels and spirits which would continue until his death in 1772. He wrote prolifically about his principles but did not try to establish a church while he was alive and it was not until 1787 that one was formally organized in London. His doctrines, however, had been introduced as early as 1784 into the United States. Ironically, a preparatory school for the Church was incorporated in June 1866 at Waltham, Massachusetts, the home of Hannah Phinney, who Day Noble married on Christmas Eve in 1870.[4] Noble actively took up the ministry in Cleveland in 1867, erecting a house of worship he called the Chapel of the Morning Star, and preaching there for three years.

In the same year as his marriage, Noble accepted a position ministering to two separate congregations in Chicago, while the resident preacher was away in Europe. His health continuing to decline, Noble left behind his full pastoral duties in the spring of 1874, and moved his wife Hannah, who he affectionately called Pansy, and their two small children to his wife's hometown of Waltham. He began searching for a new home where he might regain his health, visiting communities in the South but finally settled on the idea of Southern California. Pansy and the children remained in Waltham, when, in the fall of 1874, Noble left by train for Riverside. He records for Vermont editors his long train and steamer trip to the southland where Pansy and the children joined him six months later. Both died within three months of each other in 1885. Illness and circumstance cost Noble certain life choices and the companionship of his dear friend, Edwin Higley, but the memories live in the letters he carried, which revive the history of both men.[5]

Edwin Hall Higley

Edwin Hall Higley was born in Castleton, Vermont on February 15, 1843 to a line rooted in Vermont history. His great-grandfather brought the family from Connecticut to Castleton in 1779. His grandfather Erastus joined the Congregational Church in

1817, becoming a deacon in 1834, and set a course for much
of the family. Edwin's father, uncle and a brother became
Congregational or Presbyterian ministers. He was named
after a friend of his father's and fellow theologian, Reverend
Edwin Hall who was president of Castleton Seminary and later
Auburn Theological Seminary.[6] Religious piety for many of the
Higleys was excited by the Great Awakening of the mid-1700s
and particularly the vigorous and hypnotic preaching of George
Whitefield. Higley's great-great-grandfather was converted by
Whitefield. These "New Lights," such as Whitefield, replaced the
sobriety of original Puritanism with a God of personal, emotional
revivalism.[7]

Hervey Owen Higley, n.d.
Photo courtesy of Middlebury College Archives.

Hervey Higley, Edwin's father, had been ordained in 1829
after attending the Andover Theological Seminary and earlier
received a strong classical education at Castleton Seminary
and Middlebury College where, as a distinguished scholar,

he graduated in 1825 with the "valedictory honor." The tie to Castleton Seminary and Middlebury College was a strong one for the Higley family. Besides Edwin's father, his uncle Nelson and two brothers, Henry, and Alfred all received degrees from the institution. Scholar Allen Ward wrote that Hervey Higley developed a love for classical languages such as Latin and Greek which aided him at Andover and as a theologian. Edwin remembered that, "a knotty page of Latin was always sure of a graceful translation at any call, and his Greek testament was a portion of his daily reading." Faith and a respect for knowledge created an intellectual atmosphere which nurtured the curiosity and creativity of Edwin and his siblings as they grew up.[8]

According to Ward, "Edwin Hall Higley practically embodied the geography, history, and culture of New England and was linked to many of the major people, places and events in the first 300 years of the American national experience." Reverend Sherrard Billings remembered the family at a 1922 dedication of a plaque to Edwin Higley in Groton, Massachusetts. The ancestors of Edwin Higley "trained their children in ways of straight thinking, as well as straight living. . . . They were officers of the militia, deputies of the General Assembly and members of all important committees."[9] The family ties, in part, ran to the original Pilgrim family of Brewster which was appropriated as a first name by succeeding Higleys. Higley's great-grand uncle, Brewster III, who moved the family to Castleton during the Revolutionary War, fought in the critical campaign against British General John Burgoyne in 1770 and may have been with Ethan Allen and Benedict Arnold when Fort Ticonderoga fell to American rebels in 1775. He would be one of the largest landowners in the Castleton area. Brewster's son (Brewster IV) and brother of Erastus, Higley's grandfather, was a member of the Continental Army who fought with Washington at Trenton and endured the privations of Valley Forge.[10]

Edwin Higley and his older sister Emma possessed a dual love of music and education. Called her "natural gift" and "her genius" by a family chronicler, Emma Higley was the instructor of vocal music at Middlebury College for twenty years; "a teacher of fine ability" who joined the faculty in 1871.[11] Her brother refers to her fondly at times in his letters and she will be the first he turns to when faced with the burden of decision.

With the firing on Fort Sumter on April 12, 1861and Lincoln's call for volunteers, Edwin Higley immediately stepped forward and became involved in the formation of a local company of Vermonters ready to march at a moment's notice. "We all cried and all made speeches," one Middlebury writer quotes Higley as saying. Much hinged, however, on their families accepting their choice. Edwin wrote to Emma from his room at Middlebury: "… I feel pretty comfortable, seated in my cushioned arm chair with my slippers on, and my lamp casting a cheerful light on several very cheerful things about the room. . . . There is here a good deal of war feeling however. And I want you to get your mind ready to hear that I have enlisted. For I am really thinking very seriously on the subject. It does not seem to me that religious young men ever had a more open opportunity for good than by going into camp and exerting their influence. . . . I played my melodeon this morning for the Methodists, their player being absent. These verses I wrote and read at D. U. the other night . . . ."

Good night
Ned

When wrong is gathering for the fight.
We do not fear to raise our hands.
And battle boldly for the right.
Nor does it seem so brave a deed
To stand amid the cannon's peal,
And, in our country's hour of need,
To bare our bosoms to the steel.
Paler, perchance, may be the brow,
The throbbing pulse may beat more high,
But yet, the truth is simple, now,
'Tis sweet, for native land, to die!'

Thank God! That when the tempest sweeps
And towering mountains loom before,
We need but climb the rugged steeps,
To stand beside the shining shore![12]

The misgivings of his family surely did not come as a surprise to
Higley and he met their arguments head on. It "isn't so," wrote
Higley that "there are plenty of men." Lincoln called for 400,000
volunteers but only 150,000 had responded.[13] The Vermont
cavalry unit remained understaffed. While acknowledging that
military camp life was corrupting, he wrote that "men of religious
principles are wanted, needed here." He was enlisting along
with two classmates, Henry Dwight Smith and John Williamson.[14]
Smith, he said, "is easily influenced," but "he will associate
with us and we can do him good; . . . so if ever I wish to do any
good in a religious point of view, I could never have a better
opportunity." As for his physical stamina: "it is the testimony of
those who know that slightly-built persons bear the labors of a
campaign easier than those who are more rugged and larger. . . ."
He dismissed the idea of damaging his college career by such as
interruption, writing that he and Williamson "have no other idea
than we shall come back (if we come back at all) and finish our
course."[15]

"As to you at home, you have no need of me; Henry and Allie
can take care of the farm and you.[16] So all you have to give up
is the opposition of your own feelings or affection for me, and
ought you not to give up this, if I will, the rest?" He had prayed
"candidly" on the subject. Higley did not want to look back in
fifty years, he wrote, "to this, the greatest struggle for truth and
liberty that the world ever saw, and say that I was a young, strong
man, and the country called loudly for troops, and yet I was
engaged in obtaining a classical education and couldn't go."[17]

On October 2, 1861 his classmates gathered at Addison House
on the Middlebury campus to say goodbye to the three youthful
soldiers. In reply to a farewell address Higley said, in part:

"Classmates, there is a divinity which shapes our ends. I think there is more work for me to do after the war is over; I do not go with the expectation of never coming back. I rely on God; if he wills that I survive the conflict, well; if not, 'tis well—I am ready to die. If any praise is due for this act of mine, give it not all to me; my mother deserves it."

Edwin Hall Higley, 1861.
Photo courtesy of Middlebury College Archives.

Higley gave a partial reading of his mother's letter that night. She was not disposed to say that "all" his arguments were "bosh—but are true, noble and worthy of you." She had a good deal of sympathy for his feeling that fifty years on, he would be ashamed that none of the men of his family stood up when the country was faced with peril. "Though you know very little of the hardships before you, doubtless you can bear them as well as others," his mother said. "If you feel it your duty to go, I should be sorry to stand in your way; Go, and may God bless you, keep you, and bring you safely back."

"I go classmates, feeling I am attended by my mother's blessing," Higley told the gathering.[18]

Only 18, Edwin Higley left his sophomore year behind and enlisted on September 30, 1861. Made orderly sergeant of Company K of the First Vermont Cavalry, he was elevated to the rank of 2nd lieutenant in July 1862. His honor would be tested, first by accusations of cowardice on the battlefield, which unleashed a passionate and successful effort to have the charges refuted. He then faced the indignities of a prisoner of war.

Released and mustered out of the service as a brevet captain of Company K and later Battalion major, on May 15, 1865, he returned to Middlebury, graduating in 1868 with a Bachelor of Arts degree. He earned a Master of Arts in 1871. In 1901, the college awarded him a Doctor of Laws degree.

Following his passion for music and composition, he attempted to make a living as a music teacher in Charlestown, Massachusetts. While teaching in Charlestown, Higley married Jane Shepard Turner of Middlebury on June 2, 1870. The Higleys had only one child, an adopted daughter named Margaret Edna. In 1872 he accepted a professorship to teach Greek and German at Middlebury College; a position he held for ten years until moving to today's prestigious Groton School in Massachusetts in 1884. He was a member of the American Philological Society and Poet (1872) and Orator (1886) and President, in 1887, of the Associated Alumni of Middlebury College. In 1890 he was also President of the Middlebury Phi Beta Kappa Society. His literary works included *Exercises in Greek Composition* and *The Pilgrims and their Psalm Tunes*, in addition to musical compositions and reviews.[19]

Edwin Hall Higley died on May 15, 1916. A Groton student of Professor Higley wrote that "the dominant impression of Mr. Higley, was solidity, a solidity of body and mind and character a sort of four-squareness that couldn't be upset."[20] The following letters in this work by the soldier and scholar Edwin Higley attest to his standards of honor and self-sacrifice.

NOTES:

[1] Edwin Hall Higley, "Centennial Verses," *Middlebury College, Centennial Anniversary, 1800-1900*, (University Press, John Wilson and Son, Inc., 1901), 218-219.

[2] Jerry Phillips and Andrew Ladd, *Romanticism and Transcendentalism, 1800-1860*, (New York: Infobase, 2006), 34.

[3] Lucius M. Boltwood, *History and Genealogy of the Family of Thomas Noble of Westfield, Massachusetts with Genealogical Notes of other families by the Name of Noble*, (Hartford, CT: Privately Printed, 1878), 180.

[4] *New-Church Messenger*, (July 29, 1885), Swedenborgian House of Studies Library (Berkeley, California: Pacific School of Religion), 56. Nicholas Weber, "Swedenborgians," *New Advent Catholic Library*, Vol. 14. (New York: Robert Appleton Company, 1912). 17 Dec. 2013 , http://www.newadvent.org/cathen/14355a.htm.

[5] *New-Church Messenger*, (July 29, 1885), 56; *New Jerusalem Messenger*, volume XX, no. 1 (January 4, 1871), 8.

[6] Allen M. Ward, "Edwin Hall Higley, An American Classicist: The Intersections of Geography, Biography, and History," *New England Classical Journal*, vol. 33, no. 1, (The Classical Association of New England, 2006), 86.

[7] Ibid., 78.

[8] Hervey Higley married Sarah Gerrish Little September 29, 1829. Their children were Emma Little (1834), Henry Post (1839), Edwin Hall (1843) and Alfred Erastus (1844). Hervey had been a trustee of Castleton Seminary and a superintendent of schools for Castleton. See: Allen M. Ward, "Edwin Hall Higley, An American Classicist, 82, 86-87; Mary Coffin Johnson, *The Higleys And Their Ancestry: An Old Colonial Family* (New York: D. Appleton and Company, 1896), 250.

[9] Reverend Sherrard Billings, *An Address in Memory of Major Edwin Hall Higley, L.L.D., Groton School Chapel, June 4, 1922, on the occasion of the unveiling of a tablet to Major Higley*, Archives, Groton School, Groton, Massachusetts, 3-4.

[10] Mary Coffin Johnson, *The Higleys And Their Ancestry*, 249-253; Allen M. Ward, "Edwin Hall Higley, An American Classicist, 59-62, 66.

[11] Mary Coffin Johnson, *The Higleys And Their Ancestry*, 254-255.

[12] W. Storrs Lee, *Father Went to College: The Story of Middlebury* (New York: Wilson-Erickson, 1936), 133-136.

[13] Higley is referring to Lincoln calling for 400,000 volunteers on July 4, 1861.

[14] **John Williamson** was enrolled at Middlebury College from 1860-1862 before joining the 1st Vermont Cavalry where he rose to the rank of 1st lieutenant. He was a member of the Chi Psi Fraternity. During the winter of 1863-1864, he was made Provost Marshal of the 3rd Cavalry Division on the staff of General Judson Kilpatrick where George Benedict wrote that he "proved himself as capable as he was brave in battle." He was wounded June 15th by a gunshot wound to the thigh while skirmishing near Malvern Hill, Virginia. Taken to the Chesapeake General Hospital at Fortress Monroe, he died from his wounds on June 20, 1864. Higley and Williamson were both officers in Company K of the First Vermont Cavalry and would often be tent mates through their first two years.

Henry Dwight Smith attended Middlebury College 1860-1861 after which he enlisted in Company K of the 1st Vermont Cavalry and served until 1864. He did not return to the college and moved to Chicago, Illinois. See: Edgar J. Wiley, *Catalogue of the Officers and Students of Middlebury College in Middlebury, Vermont and of Others Who Have Received Degrees, 1800-1915*, compiled by Edgar J. Wiley (Middlebury, VT: Middlebury College, 1917) 221-222; George Grenville Benedict, *Vermont in the Civil War: A History of the Part Taken by the Vermont Soldiers and Sailors in the War for the Union, 1861-5*, Volume II, (Burlington, VT: The Free Press Association, 1888), 649.

[15] Lee, *Father Went to College*, 136-137.

[16] Higley's brothers, 21-year-old Henry and 16-year-old Alfred. Both received their secondary education at Castleton Seminary as had the rest of their family. Henry went on to Theological seminary and was ordained in 1865. He led Congregational and Presbyterian flocks in Indiana, Wisconsin and California before returning to Vermont. He died in Castleton in 1912. Alfred graduated from Middlebury College in 1868, the same year Edwin completed his studies after his return. Alfred, perhaps because he was the youngest, maintained the Higley farm and took a keen interest in the church, becoming a deacon like his father and a trustee of Castleton Seminary. Changing conditions with Vermont's agrarian outlook may have pushed Alfred to different employment and in 1890 he worked for the U.S. Arsenal in Watertown, Massachusetts and curator of college buildings and grounds for Middlebury College from 1897 to 1905. See: Wiley, *Catalogue of the Officers and Students of Middlebury College*, 199, 231 and Ward, "An American Classicist," 86-87.

[17] Lee, *Father Went to College*, 138.

[18] Johnson, *The Higleys And Their Ancestry*, 259.

[19] Wiley, *Catalogue of the Officers and Students of Middlebury College*, 231-232. See also: "Edwin Higley," Middlebury History Online, Middlebury College Vermont, http://middhistory.middlebury.edu/edwin-hall-higley-professor-of-greek-and-german/.

[20] Wiley, *Catalogue of the Officers and Students of Middlebury College*, 231-232; In Billings, An Address in Memory, 4.

—PART ONE—
HIGLEY GOES TO WAR

Chapter One: 1861

Brattleboro, Vermont was a rendezvous point for area men wishing to enlist in the Union army. It was one of several recruiting stations throughout the state. Edwin Higley officially enlisted on September 30, 1861. Although born in Castleton, Higley had a residence in Brattleboro.[1] The various companies of the 1st Vermont Cavalry then assembled at Camp Ethan Allen in Burlington, Vermont. Joseph Collea wrote that the companies were assigned alphabetical designations as they arrived in Burlington—the "last to detrain from Addison County became Company K" (Higley's company).[2] The 1st Vermont Cavalry trained for the next two months in Burlington and was mustered into United States service on November 19th under the command of 50-year-old Lemuel Platt, a Vermont physician responsible for organizing the regiment.

Upon receiving orders to report to Washington, D.C., the regiment broke camp on December 14th and boarded trains for the nation's capital, filling 153 cars with 966 men, officers and accompanying horses.[3] Higley wrote about the trip. "We college boys rode in the passenger cars nearly all the way to New York, but from there on we rode in an open freight car…. And so we slept on the dirty floor with nothing over us and with the cold wind sweeping over us through the open-work-door."[4] They

1

arrived in Washington, D.C. on December 18, 1861 and were then ordered to Annapolis, Maryland on Christmas Day where they encamped next to the 5th New York Cavalry. The New Yorkers had christened the site Camp Harris after their commander Ira Harris. George Benedict wrote that "the two regiments were often side by side, in camp, in the field and in battle, in subsequent years, and formed a fast friendship which outlasted the war."[5] With no military experience, Platt resigned in February 1862 and command was given to Captain Jonas P. Holiday of the 2nd U.S. Cavalry.[6]

Higley's passion for music would not be interrupted by civil

Troops drilling around Washington, D.C., ca. 1861.
Library of Congress, LC-DIG-ppmsc-03310.

conflict. He brought along a melodeon, "a portable reed organ with suction bellows," which rested across his lap as he played. While playing the keyboard, "his elbows pressed levers that pumped the suction bellows, which drew air over the reeds."[7] He writes that there was almost always a crowd attracted by the instrument in the evening hours in camp.[8] Writer W. Storrs Lee cites a letter by Higley describing how the strains of a Beethoven march would invite the interest of lighthearted soldiers enjoying stories in their Sibley tents or huddled around nearby fires holding off the frigid darkness. As the first intonations met their ears, "flaps opened, and a scattering of men sauntered toward the oddest shelter in the encampment, a board shack roofed with canvas. They thrust open the door, [sagging] on its leathern [sic] hinges, and grouped themselves around Higley and his melodeon." The talented keyboardist switched from the newly popular "Swanee River" to favorites such as "Just Before the Battle, Mother" and "Tenting Tonight" as the chorus of gathered soldiers joined in ragged unison.[9] The need for available space within the tents and the fear of taking his melodeon "into a tent full of heathens," pushed Higley to part with his prized music machine. "I have sent the melodeon and haven't had time yet to miss it."[10] His desire for a keyboard would occupy his thoughts in the future and he often discovered available pianos in Virginia homes, either occupied or abandoned, which soothed his musical needs.

Higley's regiment remained in Annapolis until March 9, 1862 when they "hastily" left for Washington, D.C. On March 27th they were ordered to join the army of Nathaniel Banks in the Shenandoah Valley. Two days later they crossed the Potomac at Harpers Ferry, Virginia—the "sacred soil of the old Dominion," Higley wrote, "and we are in strange quarters indeed.... Our horses are sleeping in some of the finest mansions that I ever saw. The mantles of variegated marble are some of them broken up on the floor....I have thought[s] of the maple sugar often during the past week."[11]

3

Brattleboro, Vt. Sept. 12ᵗʰ [1861]

My dear Noble,

      *It is warm and su*m*mery this afternoon and such an agreeable atmospheric contrast to the two chilly days which have preceded it, that I feel thawed into a sufficiently genial mood to attempt to write you. Your of the 5ᵗʰ came duly (like other letters) to my hand, and (unlike other letters) to my h*ea*rt. I believe I can say to you that it was and* is *not lost upon me. Of course I cannot an*sw*er it. It is a comfort to know that you dont want to have me do so.*

  I have thought a good deal about the few words which we said that night about expression, and am much chagrined at the scarcity of that commodity which I discover in any inventory of mental possessions. I believe that when the crisis comes at which I wish to pour out my offering of molten passion at the feet of my Adorissima,¹² I shall be obliged stupidly to stove in her face,

4

and refer her to "Romeo & Juliet" for the proper and truthful expression of any condition! —Perhaps you will let me make Charles speak to Seraphall[13] for me. —

--"Sir, I can but thank you, and that means more than I can say; But I cannot think why you like me. It is most exquisite but I do not understand it." —

I have finished "Charles Auchester." That is to say, I have read through its pages. I can never "finish it." I am sure that "A thing of beauty is a joy forever," must have been said expressly for such a book. I know and trust that it will never cease to remain with and be, in a manner, a pa<u>rt of</u>, me.

Lieut. Grout[14] has, at last, by dint of a good deal of patience and some profanity, worried through "Counterparts." He elegantly gives it as his opinion that it is" a d--- witching thing, but does not amount to much, after all!" Hence I have commenced it under inauspicious ~~circumstan~~ impressions!

I will send you up the "Life of Chopin" when I have read it, —if you like. No new demonstrations on disclosures have transpired in regard to our disposition or destinations while here. I expect to visit Midd. sometime —unknown as yet when.

Tell me how the Freshmen look and how "horseshedding"[15] prospers, how Allie is flourishing, and College news generally.

Ever yours,
E.H. Higley

I enclose a photograph for the society. You may say to its members, if you like, that my heart is with them as they meet in the pleasant Hall; that the interest, with which I ever regard them, is unabated and my affection unaltered; that I think of them ever as the champions of open-handed, open-hearted brotherhood, and that as such I am proud to think that my homely phiz[16] will find a niche upon their walls.

NOTES:

[1] It is unknown why Higley kept a home in Brattleboro but he compares his quarters in the field in the fall of 1863 to the "'front porch' of my Brattleboro residence, . . . subtracting the residue of the residence therefrom." See: Letter, Higley to Noble, Evans Collection, Riverside Metropolitan Museum, October 5, 1863 in this work.

[2] Joseph D. Collea, *The 1ˢᵗ Vermont Cavalry in the Civil War: A History* (Jefferson, NC: McFarland & Company, Inc., 2010), 10.

[3] See: Benedict, *Vermont in the Civil War*, Volume II, 539.

[4] Transcriptions of Higley Correspondence, January 18, 1862, Middlebury College Archives, Middlebury, Vermont. The person who produced these crudely typed transcriptions is unknown but evidence suggests that these were excerpts of letters sent home during the war, although they are not extant in the collection of letters which were obtained by the Riverside Metropolitan Museum. Higley does refer specifically to Noble in the excerpt for July 21, 1864: "...I shall wish to send or say many things to you, O, Noble; my heart's friends, of whom I have so frequent thoughts, and whose weekly message I so greatl[y] miss." If they are diary entries, as some have suggested, there are considerable gaps in sequence and odd that Higley would address Noble in first person in a diary entry. There are obvious anomalies in these transcriptions particularly with some dates. However, passages used in this work, have been vetted against other sources to verify the date, sequence and chronology of information given in the transcriptions. Higley does mention a journal kept during his time as a prisoner of war in 1864 (August 8, 1864), and he may have referred to that journal when writing of his experiences for Noble. Noble did publish accounts of Higley's imprisonment as a newspaper editor in 1865. Hereafter cited as Transcriptions of Higley Correspondence.

[5] Benedict, *Vermont in the Civil War*, Volume II, 541.

[6] Robert F. O'Neill, *Chasing Jeb Stuart and John Mosby: The Union Cavalry in Northern Virginia from Second Manassas to Gettysburg,* (Jefferson, N.C.: McFarland and Company, Inc., 2012), 136.

[7] Ward, "Edwin Hall Higley, An American Classicist," 79.

[8] Transcriptions of Higley Correspondence, February 3, 1862.

[9] W. Storrs Lee, *Father Went to College*, 140-141. The letters Lee refers to have not been located and it is impossible to tell how much of Lee's account is factually based on the actual words of Higley either from the missing correspondence or the transcriptions of letters housed at the Middlebury College archives. Robert Matteson, writing in 1937 about the collections at Middlebury, stated that one of the prize collections was a "trunk" filled with diaries and letters written by E. H. Higley. These letters and diaries, which may have been used for Lee's book as well, are no longer in the Middlebury archives. At the time of this writing, their whereabouts, if they still exist, are unknown. See: Matteson, *Middlebury Campus*

newsletter, vol. XXXIV, no. 19 (March 3, 1937), 4.

[10] Transcriptions of Higley Correspondence, February 3, 1862 and March 12, 1862. Higley had the melodeon sent to him when the regiment was in winter quarters and returned it to his Vermont home in the spring as warmer weather signaled a return of military action. See: Billings, *An Address in Memory*, 6.

[11] Transcriptions of Higley Correspondence, March 29, 1862. On the march to Winchester, Virginia, regimental commander Jonas Holliday excused himself and while standing alone at the Shenandoah River, committed suicide with a pistol shot to the head. Reported to be "nervous and excitable" in the days preceding the incident, no exact reason for his suicide has been offered. Lt. Colonel George Kellogg assumed command of the regiment at that time. See: Collea, *The 1st Vermont Cavalry*, 29-30.

[12] Italian expression for a greatly adored one.

[13] **"Seraphall" or Seraphael** is the lead character in the romance novel *Charles Auchester* written by Elizabeth Sara Sheppard (under the pseudonym of E. Berger) in 1853 and published initially in England. Sheppard wrote the book when she was only 16 years of age. She died in Brixton, England at the age of 32 on March 13, 1862. According to George Upton, the book is a memorial to the composer Felix Mendelssohn who is represented by Saraphael. See Upton's introduction to *Charles Auchester in Two Volumes, Vol. I* (Chicago: A.C. McClurg and Company, 1891), 5-9. Sophie Fuller wrote that "Sheppard's ethereal Mendelssonian character Chevalier Seraphael commands adoring devotion in all who meet him or hears his music." See *The Idea of Music in Victorian Fiction*, Sophie Fuller and Nicky Losseff, (eds.), (Burlington, Vermont: Ashgate Publishing Company, 2004), 31.

[14] It is the editor's opinion that this is **Luman M. Grout (1823-1913)** who was a recruiting officer at Brattleboro, Vermont at the time Higley enlisted. Grout was a veteran of the Mexican American War and "one of a very few, in the state, who had any practical knowledge of military tactics. He and Edward Sawyer, worked together to prepare the 5th Vermont Infantry and according to a news account, Grout next helped drill a Company I of the 1st Vermont Cavalry of which Sawyer was captain. Although it appears that Higley enlisted at Brattleboro, he was assigned to a different company. Grout was elected captain of Company A of the 8th Vermont Infantry after enlisting on November 13, 1861. See the *St. Albans Messenger*, September 22, 1910, p. 7.

[15] Term coined by James Fenimore Cooper in his last full-length work, *Ways of the Hour*, published in 1850, a year before Cooper's death. In this so-called sociological novel, it refers to circuit riding lawyers who used barns or horse sheds as a quiet place to prepare and perhaps falsely influence witnesses before trial.

[16] Shortening of Physiognomy; a slang term for a facial expression.

Chapter Two: 1862

Following the disastrous rout of Union forces under Irvin McDowell at First Bull Run on July 21, 1861, Lincoln gave command of the newly formulated Army of the Potomac to General George Brinton McClellan whose demeanor was described by one historian as "imperious arrogance."[1] McClellan was a superb organizer at a time when the Union army needed organizing but would prove overly cautious in battle and prone to over-estimating the strength of his Confederate opposition. Urged by Lincoln to move against the rebels, McClellan devised a plan to transport his 100,000 man army down the Potomac River and Chesapeake Bay to Fortress Monroe at the tip of the Virginia peninsula and from there begin a march northwest up the neck of land between the York and James Rivers to the Confederate capital at Richmond.[2]

Higley and his regiment would be continually involved in skirmishes with Confederate units, primarily cavalry, throughout the spring

General George Brinton McClellan and wife, 1862. Library of Congress, LC-DIG-cwpb-05665.

and summer of 1862. The 1st Vermont Cavalry was assigned to the Department of the Shenandoah under Massachusetts politician, Major General Nathaniel Banks. The Shenandoah Valley stretches northeast roughly 200 miles from Roanoke, Virginia in the south to Winchester, Virginia in the north, created by the river which gave the valley its name and is bordered by the Blue Ridge Mountains to the east and the Allegheny Mountains to the west. The valley is separated in the middle by the 50-mile Massanutten Mountain range with the only through access being a pass at New Market to the tighter Luray Valley on its eastern side that ran from Conrad's Store to Front Royal along a narrow pike.

It was Banks' job to help protect the capital, while 4,200 men under Thomas "Stonewall" Jackson were tasked with engaging Banks to ensure none of his divisions could be used to reinforce McClellan's efforts on the peninsula, some 220 miles to the southeast. To lose the valley, Jackson said, was to lose Virginia and possibly the war.[3] Banks had 25,000 men in Virginia's Shenandoah Valley with another 15,000 men under Charles Fremont just to the east in the forested Alleghenies of today's West Virginia. The 1st Vermont Cavalry joined Banks' command following the Battle of Kernstown on March 23, 1862 where the army of Jackson was badly mauled. On April 19th the 1st Vermont saw its baptismal action with a daring cavalry charge to secure a vital bridge at Mt. Jackson as Banks chased Jackson's forces up the Valley with the 1st Vermont in the lead.[4] Higley recalled the attack in correspondence to Noble, saying that the suspense of waiting for the first shots was the hardest part of battle. However, he quickly transitions to a more pleasant discovery, that of a piano in an abandoned plantation house although puzzled by the circumstances. "It is strange that these people are so foolish as to leave their homes in imaginary dread of the vandals as they call us....But this taking of the oath of allegiance is what troubles them. Like cross children they are mad and won't eat and so are courting starvation."[5]

The 1st Vermont Cavalry was assigned to an infantry column following the clash at Mt. Jackson in an unsuccessful attempt to flank Jackson as he moved south, up the valley. They rejoined Banks' main force at New Market by way of the pass at Luray. Higley expressed sympathy for the "poor infantry fellows… trudging along on foot" under the weight of heavy knapsacks. While accompanying the infantry, Higley noted the stark change from the warm reception they had received from the citizens of Burlington and New York. "Here," he said, "are no waving flags, or handkerchiefs or smiling faces.

General Nathaniel P. Banks, ca. 1861.
Library of Congress, LC-USZ62-119420.

Almost all the men have been pressed into the army and no one is left here except a few invalids and the women and children and they all think that we are going to butcher and burn everything which we come to." Near New Market, Virginia, Higley noted "nothing there but crying women and grinning negroes."[6]

On April 24th, the Federal cavalry brigade, including the 1st Vermont, under command of General John P. Hatch, began for Harrisonburg and Staunton only to be blocked by an unfordable river and a burnt bridge on the Staunton Road near Mt. Crawford and returned to Harrisonburg. On April 27th, companies A, D and K were part of a reconnaissance in force around the southern tip of Massanutten Mountain. Their 12 mile march brought them to the outskirts of the hamlet of McGaheysville. Company D of the Vermonters charged a body of Confederates, putting the rebels to flight. Private Stephen Morse, however, was taken prisoner when he was unhorsed after the animal suffered a fatal shot. Corporal John Chase was shot through the bowels and died the next day; the first man of the regiment to die from a hostile bullet, according to George Benedict.[7] Company K was sent into the woods to reconnoiter, searching for the enemy. Higley wrote that, "we dashed into the woods where we supposed that they were lying in wait for us but we soon found that they had retreated further than we thought. We kept right on at a tearing pace over a narrow, rugged road. When the first four or five of us rushed around the bushes into view the enemy started to charge on us but we raised our sabres [sic] and with wild cheers we rushed upon them and then they made a grand advance in the opposite direction."[8]

Jackson was reinforced in late April by a division under Richard Ewell allowing Jackson a chance to march west and engage Fremont's forces which threatened Staunton aside the Virginia and Central Railroad while Ewell, at Conrad's Store, on the east side of the Massanutton, kept an eye on Banks' operations. On May 8th, Jackson successfully defeated the advance brigade of Fremont's army at the Battle of McDowell pushing the Yankees farther west to Franklin. With Union forces now blunted west of the Alleghenies, Jackson returned to the Shenandoah prepared to deal a blow to Banks whose forces had been reduced by a Federal decision to shift a division from Banks to Irvin McDowell who had 35,000 troops in front of Fredericksburg to the east. The strategy was for McDowell to drive south in support of McClellan as

General John Porter Hatch, ca. 1861.
Library of Congress, LC-USZ62-113168.

11

he moved up the Virginia peninsula toward Richmond. His manpower thinned and fearing rebel reinforcements and with his supply and communication lines overly extended, an apprehensive Banks withdrew north to New Market on May 5th and on May 11th relinquished the valley to his opposition by moving further north to Strasburg.

Banks positioned his now reduced ranks at three points just to the north end of the Massanutton Mountain: 1,500 men at Winchester which was his main supply depot, 1,000 more twenty-five miles southeast at Front Royal and 6,500 men nineteen miles to the south at Strasburg to stop any rebel attack north along the main valley roadway. Front Royal was a key strategic point. The north and south forks of the Shenandoah River joined just a mile and a half north of the village with the Manassas Gap Railroad passing over the South Fork of the river; an east-west rail link used to move Union troops. Cavalry, including the 1st Vermont and Higley, were at Strasburg and would act as rear guard when Banks began his final evacuation of the valley. On May 23rd, Colonel Charles Tompkins[9] assumed command of the regiment and two days later was ordered to destroy stores and supplies which could not be loaded and removed before the rebels seized the area. On the day Tompkins took command, Jackson and Ewell overwhelmed the garrison at Front Royal with Union losses put at 904 either killed or captured.[10]

The Confederates had flanked Banks and now had superior numbers but fatigue and bad roads hampered their chances of quickly surging northwest to strike at Winchester, the key point of the Federal triangular defense. News of the disaster at Front Royal rapidly put in motion efforts at Strasburg to move all possible supply and ambulance wagon trains north to Middletown and after that Winchester, to join Banks' main force as his entire army began its hasty retreat to the Potomac. The column was twice cut off by Confederates with great loss and confusion to Union forces.

Higley, riding with Colonel Tompkins, wrote of the dangerous escape with a certain casual abandon. "We have had a terribly

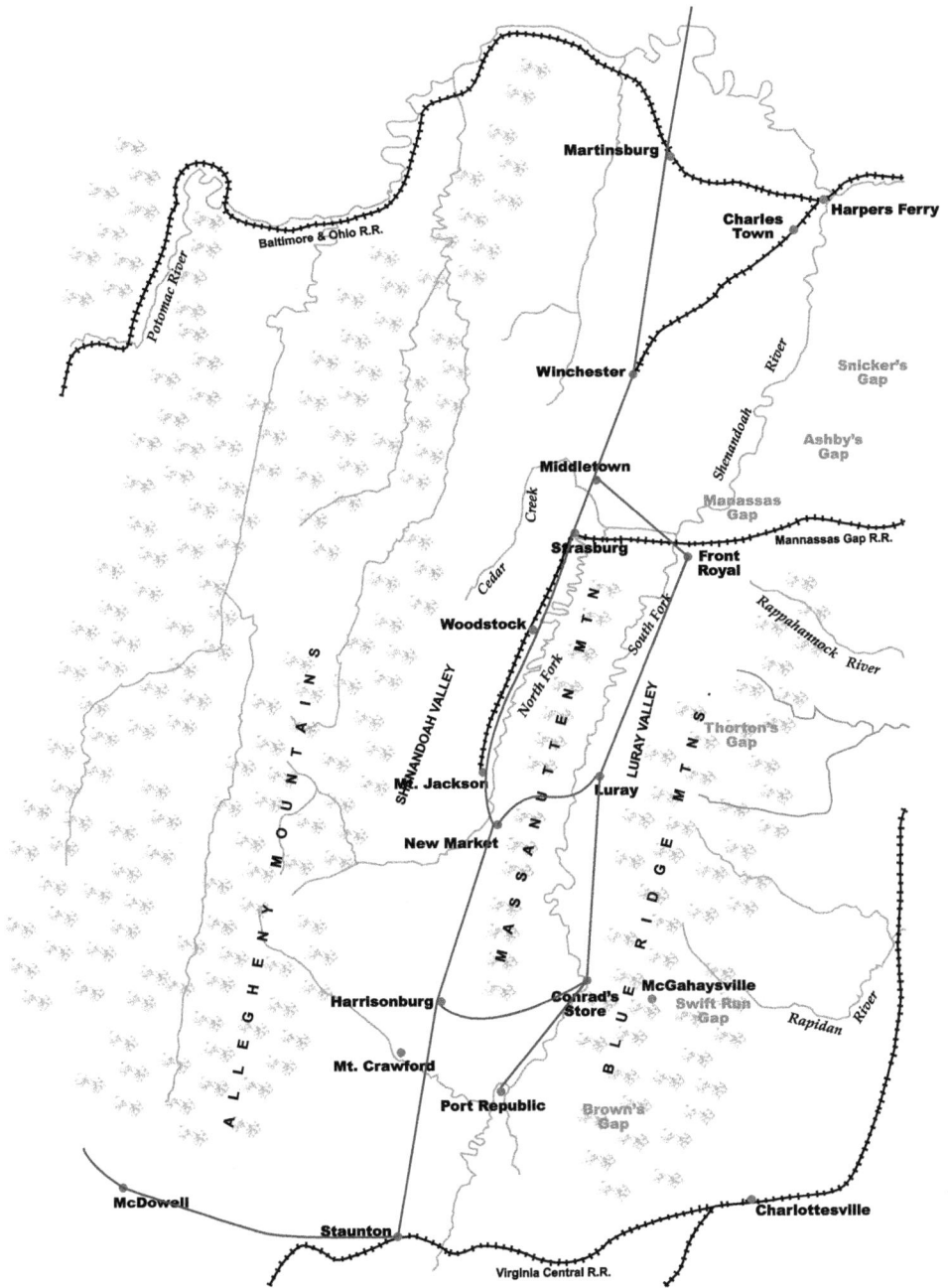

Shenandoah Valley in 1862.
Map Illustrated by Robin Hanks.

exciting time for the last two days," Higley penned on May 26th, the same day Union forces crossed the Potomac to relative safety. In his description of the flanking tactics of Ewell and Jackson at Front Royal, he wrote that "we found that the rascals had crossed the mts. and had cut off our regiment from the rest of the command. Five of our companies cut their way through with terrible loss. The rest of our regiment wholly unconscious of this came on and just as we crossed Cedar Creek [just north of Strasburg] we were welcomed with a brisk cannonading. The shells came whizzing by our heads in a most uncomfortable manner and had to retreat. All our tents and baggage was taken, and the teamsters captured."[11]

Colonel Charles Tompkins.
National Archives photo no. 111-B-1858.

Banks' losses during this 50-mile running battle included 200 men killed, and 700 missing along with 55 wagons.[12] News of his retreat created panic in the north and particularly Washington where false reports of Jackson crossing the Potomac heightened anxiety. Lincoln's efforts to cut Jackson off and destroy his army would prove unsuccessful. Instead of supporting McClellan, Lincoln ordered McDowell to move west from Fredericksburg while a regrouped Fremont would move south along the Alleghenies and Banks would again move south into the Valley to hem in the Confederates. However, Jackson effectively eluded Lincoln's trap through a combination of forced marches, harassment by rebel cavalry, muddy roads and timid Union generalship.[13]

As Banks prepared to re-enter Virginia as part of Jackson's pursuit, Higley, and the 1st Vermont were assessing damage to the regiment at Williamsport where the army crossed on May 26th. On June 3rd he managed a "few lines in an old barn which a couple of us have taken to from complete submersion," as severe storms hammered the area. While in camp at Williamsport the lost stores of the regiment were replaced and their weaponry was upgraded from the dangerously erratic Savage revolvers to a Colt model. Four companies, D, E, I and Higley's Company K became carbineers, receiving Sharpe's carbines instead of revolvers and dubbed "heavy cavalry." The other companies of "light cavalry" carried sabers and revolvers.[14]

The regiment crossed the Potomac and re-entered Virginia on June 13th. On June 19th Company K and Higley, along with three other companies under command of Lieutenant Colonel Kellogg, were part of a scouting expedition near Snicker's Ferry. On June 22nd, they were near Middletown, an area known for its "fine English cherries." A few days later Higley tells of a chance encounter during that mission, with more alluring members of the enemy--young ladies of the secessionist persuasion. The soldiers and these belles of rural Virginia discovered each other in a grove of cherry trees. "They invited us to climb the trees and throw down the little twigs for them to pick," wrote Higley. "We did so and had quite a pleasant time with them. They kindly expressed the wish that the rebels would get us before we got out of the orchard. And we in turn informed them that we were ready and willing to shoot any number of their secesh friends, but we parted very good friends."[15]

Higley wrote around this time from Fort Blenker, later Fort Reynolds, part of Washington's extensive networks of defensive forts. Blenker guarded the Four Mile Run valley and the approach to Alexandria, Virginia. Although on notice to move "at a moments notice," there was time for leisure. "On the whole, we are living like princes now." That lifestyle is now enhanced by a young black servant, Higley noted: "a little 'shade' some three and a half feet high who has followed me from Winchester." This was not unusual for officers to enlist the services of escaped slaves who rallied to Union forces. "The breakfast which my contraband aide-de-camp . . . is now cooking will consist of sweet potatoes roasted in the ashes, coffee, beef steak fried, and soft bread. . . .I weigh over a hundred and fifty-eight which is more than I weighed at home."[16]

Marshall House in Alexandria, Virginia, ca. 1861.
Library of Congress, LC-DIG-cwpb-01463.

On their possible fate in the Shenandoah, he wrote that, "I wouldn't wonder if we should be driven out of Virginia again as we haven't yet enough troops here but there will be a great battle before we leave this time."[17] As Higley penned his thoughts on June 26th, Major General John Pope, whose western successes along the Mississippi River precipitated his promotion to the east, was receiving his instructions to re-align Union forces around the nation's capital creating a new army—the Army of Virginia. His orders were "to protect Washington from 'danger or insult' and to 'render the most effective aid to relieve General McClellan and capture Richmond.'"[18]

The forces under Banks, including the Vermont cavalry, were now in the 2nd Corps of Pope's Army of Virginia which also included Yankee troops under Fremont and McDowell. During the restructuring of the Army of Virginia, Jackson was able to move his forces from the Shenandoah south and assist Lee in pushing McClellan from the gates of Richmond in what was called the Seven Days campaign. Pope soon realized that he would get little or no help from McClellan as he started his push south toward the rebel seat of government.

Very shortly after the interlude in the cherry orchard, Higley and the 1st Vermont were back in the saddle scouting the Shenandoah Valley again, near the northern edge of the Massanutton Mountain, in preparation for Banks' move from east of the Blue Ridge; a reconnaissance in force as far south as the Luray Courthouse. That reconnaissance switched on July 10th to the east of the Blue Ridge with a focus on Culpeper, Virginia. The main task given General Hatch and the cavalry brigade was to disrupt the communication lines between Richmond and the Shenandoah Valley and destroy the Orange and Alexandria railroad from Gordonsville to Charlottesville. Hatch, however, proved unequal to the task, taking a week to move forty-three miles. An added embarrassment for Hatch was the destruction of the wrong bridge—taking out the significant Rapidan Bridge rather than a smaller railroad span. Despite Pope's misgivings about the leadership capabilities of Hatch, he urged the cavalry commander to push toward Gordonsville and again attack the Confederate rail lines. Hatch took it upon himself to cancel the mission and return to Culpeper on July 19th after Union videttes ran into enemy resistance seven miles outside of Gordonsville. Benedict wrote that "disgusted by his want of energy, General Pope relieved him of command, and sent General John Buford, who was a brave and good soldier, to take his place."[19] To blunt the advance of Pope's army, Lee sent Jackson back north once McClellan's retreat to the Chesapeake and withdrawal back to Washington was effected.

Buford on August 2nd moved in force against Orange Court House, which lay on the main road between Culpeper and Gordonsville. The fight was joined with the Vermonter carbineers (companies A, D, E, I and K) acting as skirmishers, along with the 5th New York Cavalry which ran into Confederate pickets five miles north of the village. Pressing ahead they drove the enemy back into the town. A rebel flanking counterattack turned the Yankees and threatened to send them into full retreat. Captain

General John Buford.
Library of Congress, LC-DIG-cwpb-06372.

William Wells assisted by Captain Josiah Hall successfully rallied those fleeing soldiers and signaled their reserve squadron of Vermont troopers to "Charge." The squadron careened into the village where a mounted sabre fight became an entangled melee on the streets of the small town. "Confusion reigned as companies intermingled, and men became separated from their comrades," described one writer.[20] Only a handful of Federal troopers were hurt or killed while the rebels lost upwards of 70 men before being driven from the village. With Pope's army scattered from Culpeper west to the Blue Ridge at Sperryville, Jackson attacked Banks' corps at Cedar Mountain just a few miles south of Culpeper on August 9th. After initial Union success, Confederate reinforcements under A.P. Hill gave Jackson the edge and the victory in this first major action of Pope's campaign. The 1st

Vermont however, was not involved in this fight having been sent that day northeast to Woodville. Higley records that he "narrowly escaped being cut off," which may have referred to the fight at Orange Courthouse. More distressing was the loss of a college fraternity pin.[21]

Orange and Alexandria RR at Culpeper, August 1862.
Library of Congress, LC-DIG-cwpb-01078.

With McClellan moving the Army of the Potomac back to the confines of Washington via the waterways of the Chesapeake and Potomac River, Lee shifted his main forces northeast to the Rappahannock River consolidating with Jackson. While Pope waited for reinforcements from the reticent McClellan, Lee acted, dividing his forces and having Jackson, with the help of rebel cavalry under Jeb Stuart, move west and clockwise, flanking Federal lines and threatening Union rail links in Pope's rear. The depleted cavalry of Pope failed to discover the movement allowing Jackson to march unopposed to Manassas junction on August 26th. Jackson's 24,000 man foot- cavalry had covered more than fifty miles in two days; "one of the war's great marches," according to historian James McPherson. There Jackson's men either consumed or destroyed the main supply base of Pope's army.[22]

Outside of Manassas, Jackson dug in while Lee and James Longstreet followed with the bulk of the Army of Northern Virginia. Pope pulled his scattered forces back to a defensive line along the Rappahannock River on August 20 and 21. An initial clash exposed Jackson's entrenchments. An overtaxed Union cavalry, including the 1st Vermont, were left to guard vital fords across the Rappahannock such as Waterloo Bridge which they reached on August 23rd and skirmished with Confederate infantry, losing two men. Stuart's cavalry, having crossed a day earlier, attacked Pope's

General John Pope, ca. 1862.
Library of Congress, LC-DIG-cwpb-06342.

headquarters the same day. Forced marches massed Pope's army near Manassas where the Second Battle of Bull Run began on August 29th. Benedict wrote that during the second day of fighting on August 30th, the regiment was behind the left wing of the infantry "and was occasionally under fire from the shells which came over the latter."[23] Higley mentions the severity of the shelling in a letter on September 26th: "At the time the brigade was being formed in line of battle and our regiment had come on the line the shells came too thick for the other regiments of the brigade to stand and they ran down under the cover of the hill."[24] "A year later Higley remembered with greater detail, the sound and fury of the battlefield in a letter to Noble. "A year ago and more, we were here when the hot shell were bursting around us," he recalled, "and the shouts and crashing of the angry armies were filling the air. But then our blood was up to fever heat and it was with clenched hands, furrowed brows, and burning cheeks that we went back over Bull Run Creek. But now all that is gone. The air is heavy with stillness and nothing but the mournful wrecks of that day remain."[25]

Bull Run, Va., Federal cavalry at Sudley Ford, March 1862.
Library of Congress, LC-DIG-cwpb-00955.

The Second Battle of Bull Run ended as had the first a year earlier with a Confederate victory and opened the way for the South's first invasion of northern territory which culminated in the Battle of Antietam on September 17th. George Benedict noted the paucity of accounts about the 1st Vermont in the official records for the clash at Bull Run. "Exceedingly deficient," said Benedict; "a bare allusion to the 'severe service' of the cavalry."[26] The battered 1st Vermont was not part of Antietam, the war's bloodiest day, but instead kept to patrol duties in northern Virginia. By October 6th, the regiment was back at Fort Scott near Alexandria which would be their winter quarters.

Although immersed in a "pile of Orders" daily, Higley writes Noble that a visit would allow for some sightseeing since the capitol dome is nearing completion. His longing for the intellectual stimulation provided by his good friend is obvious. Not only does he worry about the fraternal conditions at Middlebury and reports that his friend Ezra Brainerd has "become profane and intemperate" but disparages the "blundering incapacity and carelessness" of Pope and turns nostalgic for the former cautious command of McClellan.

Capitol dome under construction, ca. 1862.
National Archives photo no. 111-BA-1480.

Higley had been promoted to the rank of 2nd lieutenant on July 16, 1862 and was the acting Adjutant of the regiment at the time he wrote the next two letters to Noble.[27] His fellow collegian from Middlebury, John Williamson, was elevated to 1st lieutenant on the same day.

Near Fort Scott Va. Nov. 1st 1862

My dear friend Noble,

I have so long deferred writing to you that I almost fear that I am intruding addressing you at this late day. But it seems that there is no one now, to whom I can look for college news and bro<u>th</u>erly sympathy besides yourself. I dont mean that I am in any particular sorrow or affliction, which calls for sy<u>mpath</u>y, but I was just beginning to prize so highly the value of your influence, and musical, poetical and artistic taste in general, that I never think of you without thinking that I lost one of my greatest privileges in losing your companionship. For if I should escape the varied dangers of disease, bullets, etc. and should come back to College Halls it will not be until you have finished your course there.

I saw Converse[28] the other day, and in rehearsing some of his XΨ[29] experiences he let fall some things in regard to Brainerd,[30] which have made me feel gloomy ever since. That Brainerd, who used to be so humble and earnest in his piety, should have become profane and intemperate, seems almost too sad to believe.

I never meant to be so bigoted in society feeling but if this be true I shall warn my brother who shall go next year to Mid. to shun that influence as he values his soul. Our regiment is still lying here like a dismounted Chevalier in the tournament. If it takes as long to recostruct [reconstruct] the whole grand Army, I do not wonder at the seeming inactivity which I presume you are impatient of. We got into such a continual series of successive mishaps by Popes[31] blundering incapacity and carelessness, that I have a great deal of respect for McClellans[32] much abused bump of caution.

You will find enclosed a photograph which I perhaps ought to apologize for sending to you as it is not very satisfactory to me. But you remember the story of the old lady who rejected a mirror saying that "it made her look like a fright." And so I will not criticize.

There is some hope and less belief in military circles here that our Brigade will be among the number which will compose Gen. Bank's proposed expedition to Texas.[33] I wish it might be so, as whoever goes with Banks is sure of success: and Texas presents a more lenient climate for winter than we shall find here.

The new Vermont Brigade is encamped but a short distance from us. If you dont teach this winter you can't take a better time to visit Washington than at the close of the present term. The Capitol is nearly completed, and our camp is but a short ride from Long Bridge.[34]

You will find me immersed part of every day in a pile of Orders, Despatching [sic] morning Reports, Muster Rolls, etc, etc. But yet time enough to greet you warmly and show you around through the various forts and batteries which compose the "Difenses [sic] of Washington."

If you don't come, the next best thing you can do is send me a piece of yourself in the shape of a copy of some of the poems which you read occasionally at "Oudemia"[35] or elsewhere. And furthermore if you can spare me a likeness of your own phiz it will be most welcome. Remember me affectionately to Frank Seeley[36], and Brainerd & Tilden.[37]
Yours truly, E. H. Higley

Ezra Brainerd, n.d.
Photo Courtesy of Middlebury College Archives.

***

Leadership of the regiment and the brigade again changed that winter and dissension among officers of the 1st Vermont intensified. Colonel Charles Tompkins resigned on September 9th and returned to duties with the quartermaster department of the regular army. He later wrote that the regiment "was improperly officered," a situation made worse by the desertion of Lt. Colonel Kellogg in July, leaving Tompkins without the support of senior officers.[38] He was replaced by Edward B. Sawyer who remained in Vermont recuperating from injuries suffered during Banks' hasty retreat from the Shenandoah Valley in May.[39] Sawyer had successfully lobbied the state's governor for the position of colonel, receiving the promotion over another more senior officer and earning the resentment of many in the officer corps including Higley. On September 10th, General McClellan took John Buford as his chief of cavalry and Richard Butler Price, colonel of the 2nd Pennsylvania Cavalry, was assigned to replace him as commander of the brigade which now patrolled the lines of defense around the national capital. It would prove a poor replacement for the "talented Buford" according to one author.[40]

The shortage of serviceable horses in required numbers kept most of the regiment close to Washington. Price did manage a raid involving some troopers from the 1st Vermont under Lieutenant Colonel Addison Preston who led the regiment in Sawyer's absence. Their mission was to interdict part of the supply trains of Lee's army as it moved back into Virginia. A clash with the 6th Virginia Cavalry near Ashby's Gap on September 26th cost them the life of Dr. Selah

Colonel Edward B. Sawyer.
Photo courtesy of
Francis C. Guber Collection.

25

Perkins, Captain of Company H, a fellow resident of Higley's hometown of Castleton, along with Preston who received a painful wound in the skirmish.[41] Author Robert O'Neill suggests that this may have been Price's only engagement with the enemy in the war, being "content to cede control of the fight to his subordinates." Yet, over the next ten months, O'Neill wrote, Price sat in judgment of junior officers "who had either failed in combat or who were perceived to have failed." One of those in the spring of 1863 would be Edwin Higley.[42]

With Preston and Sawyer on leave in Vermont, the regiment was without any field officers and the regiment's former commander Colonel Tompkins complained of the "the abuses within the regiment" to Quartermaster General Montgomery Meigs who issued his own scathing assessment of the situation. An investigation ordered by General Banks found no official reason for Sawyer's prolonged leave of absence and criticized Sawyer's lack of military capability. A final report to Secretary of War Edwin Stanton recommended Sawyer be mustered out of the service, an action taken on October 27th, in part, "for inefficiency and neglect of the welfare of his regiment while a major thereof."[43]

Quartermaster General Montgomery Meigs. Library of Congress, LC-DIG-cwpbh-03111.

However, Sawyer rejoined the regiment in October and exercised his right of appeal once discharged.

In the interim, some officers and men of the 1st Vermont were openly and publicaly critical of Sawyer, including Lieutenant Higley and fellow college friend, Sergeant-Major Henry Smith. Smith wrote to the *Middlebury Register* disparaging Sawyer for taking a horse from the regiment without authorization. Sawyer successfully mounted a defense supported by other regimental officers, and was reinstated on December 20, 1862. One of his first actions was to strip Company K's Henry Smith of his stripes, busting him to private. On January 8, 1863, Higley added his name to the list of Sawyer's detractors, which included Major William Collins who had been passed over for promotion, accusing Sawyer of embezzling money from recruits and conduct unbecoming an officer. A subsequent investigation by Captain Wesley Merritt noted the two opposing camps within the regiment—a "lamentable want of good feeling, among the officers of the regiment," but found extenuating circumstances for Sawyer's actions, leaving this political insider in command. The fallout from the dispute would be followed by the resignations of several 1st Vermont officers who stood against Sawyer. Although Higley did not resign his commission, he confided to Noble in January 1863, that he and others are the "objects of Col Sawyers enmity," and whenever he is obliged to meet the Colonel, "the contact will be unpleasant."[44]

Higley mentions the arrival of new mounts for the regiment in the following letter, something gravely needed and a hopeful omen that the mundaneness of camp might soon be over. Rebuilding the regiment took place in winter quarters around Fort Scott guarding the approach to the Long Bridge spanning the Potomac. One author wrote that they "amounted to a cavalry unit in name only." The weeks of seemingly continuous patrol had sapped the strength and vitality of both troopers and their mounts. The stress on these horses was great from the beginning as Higley noted on May 22, 1862 in a letter to Noble. "My horse 'Brains' so far as I can learn is rather sorry that he enlisted. The hard fare which he has seen since he came to Dixie has greatly diminished his flesh."[45]

Cavalry orderly with horse, October 1862.
Library of Congress, LC-DIG-cwpb-01143.

Available horses healthy enough for service fell by over two-thirds. Higley placed the number at 125. Private Albert Sawyer wrote home that the regiment could do nothing "til we get our horses . . . the ones that are here have a hard life of it." By the time Higley wrote the following letter, Lt. Colonel Preston and the assistant quartermaster had acquired fresh Vermont Morgans during their stay in the Green Mountain state.[46] The first of them were on their way by rail. The Morgans were a "quintessentially American breed developed in Vermont," according to scholar Allen Ward, with "remarkable physical and mental capacities."[47]

Higley's thoughts are again of home, fraternity and his friendship with Noble. Following Higley's letter of November 1st, Lincoln removed George McClellan from command of the Army of the Potomac; a decision which Higley clearly disagreed with, although he surmised that Noble must be "gladdened" by the action. McClellan had the sentiments of the men in the field who appreciated his "bump of caution" which saved soldiers' lives but did little to seriously threaten the rebellion. McClellan's misjudgment at Antietam Creek, Maryland and his lethargy in pursuing a retreating Lee, haunted Lincoln.

1ˢᵗ Vermont Cavalry
November 20 1862

My dear friend Noble,

The perusal of
your welcome letter recalls to my mind a thought or fancy which used to
trouble me some – long ago – namely that I was too roughly and clumsily
constructed to chord with your finer perception and keener sensibilities.
I am reminded of this, I say, for when I stretched out my hand to greet
you, I find that my awkward fist came near knocking you down! But,
the blow was unintentional: for most assuredly when I hailed you as
the only brother left, I did not mean that the fraternal feeling was any
weaker toward you than it ever had been to others. Surely when two
orphan brothers are left alone in the world, and they look in each others'
face, clasp hands and say "it's only you and I now" surely they are not
less dear to one another than when the happy group gathered around the
family fireside. Since I wrote you we here have been grieved, and you I
presume gladdened by the removal of McClellan. Strange what varies
and diverse eyes men equally honest and earnest look through! I can
imagine what Mr. and Mrs. Denison⁴⁸ think of this subject.

I thank you heartily for the poem. It is no new thing for the
finest word-picture to be sketched by one unacquainted with the scene
described. And what little of battle smoke I have seen helps me not to
criticize but to appreciate its worth. If you are willing to trust any more
of these brain-children of yours to my unpoetic gaze they will be gladly
welcomed.

Perhaps it is well that you should cease to expect the return of
your soldier friend since so much of danger and hardship intervenes
before that return could be affected. But I am not disappointed at
the prolongation of the war. There is more at stake now than our
Revolutionary sires fought for. And why may we not expect as long a
struggle? God is not going to let us patch up any quickly broken peace,
until the truths and necessities of Human Freedom are so burnt into the

hearts of our people that centuries will not effect them. Thank God that I am here, for "Three years or d<u>uring</u> the w<u>a</u>r," and not a d<u>ra</u>ft frightened, b<u>oun</u>ty-bo<u>ug</u>ht, nine-months man!

Our new horses are beginning to arrive. We gladly hail them as an omen of action. I am tired of lying here in camp in this crippled condition. All our men who have horses – (some 125) are out "mit Siegel"[49] on 'the front.' Lt. Williamson is with them. Smith – the Sergeant Major is here. I saw Sturtevant[50] the other day, also Heslunes, Prindle[51] and several others.

It must be near time for Public Debate.[52] Will the Quintette Club[53] sing this year as it did last?

Surely Apollo and Mars are very nearly allied, as all we singers are now among the belligerents save Thomas.

The thought of your prospective teaching calls to mind my own maiden attempt at theater, down in Seeleys district. Since then I believe one of my scholars has died – Anne Goodrich. I saw her last fall at public debate and she kindly wished me a safe return from the war, little thinking that the "lethal stroke" would find her first.

I mean to take a trip to Mount Vernon in a few days. Some of our Regiment has been there. It is only about six miles distant.

Please don't address me as "Adjutant" if you write again, but 2nd Lt. Co. K. I am not Adjt. of the Regiment only acting in that capacity.[54] Also our Army Corps is the 3rd Heintzelmans' instead of the 2nd as you directed before.[55] Remember me to Seely[56] and the rest.

Truly yours,
E. H. Higley

Their assignment to the defense of Washington also kept the 1st Vermont away from the carnage of Ambrose Burnside's ill-planned assaults against entrenched Confederates at Marye's Heights outside Fredericksburg on December 13th; a crippling blow. Higley's thoughts mirrored the sinking morale of frustrated men after nearly two years of bloody war. "I feel too sad at our mournful defeat at Fredericksburg to ask any haunting questions about the magic doings of our new general," he wrote on December 18th, five days after Burnside's disaster. "I only feel more deeply the folly of our government in casting from it in the hour of need, the strongest arm and coolest brain which it had [McClellan]. But the great citizen soldiers who know so much up on the hill top have made up their minds and told Pres. Lincoln so that if the army would only move along and quit this awful system of getting ready and watching for opportunities that we could finish up the war, take Richmond, and do everything else in a few weeks. Hence the President said 'go over' hence we have got a terrible thrashing. But now the army of the Potomac instead of resting safe and sound will lie over with five thousand poor fellows sleeping in the bloody trenches, 5000 or more crowded with shattered limbs and wounded bodies into the hospitals all over the land and 5000 widows and orphans weeping at home. This is not a very bright result of 'On to Richmond.'" Higley closes the passage however, with some stoic sarcasm: "The central attraction of our table," he muses, "was that essence . . . emblem and educator of southern character and tactics, the possum."[57]

NOTES:

[1] Stephen Sears, *Landscape Turned Red: The Battle of Antietam* (New Haven, CT: Popular Library, 1983), 23.

[2] James McPherson, *Ordeal by Fire, the Civil War, Volume II* (New York: McGraw-Hill, 2001), 257-258.

[3] Gary Schreckengost, "Front Royal, Key to the Valley," *America's Civil War,* (January 2000), 26.

[4] See Collea, *The 1st Vermont Cavalry*, 37-39. Author Robert O'Neill argues that the regiment's first combat was a brief skirmish against Turner Ashby's rebel cavalry near Columbia Furnace on April 8th. See: O'Neill, *Chasing Jeb Stuart and John Mosby,* 138.

[5] Transcriptions of Higley Correspondence, April 18, 1862.

[6] Transcriptions of Higley Correspondence, April 23, 1862.

[7] Benedict, *Vermont in the Civil War*, 551-552.

[8] Transcriptions of Higley Correspondence, May 3, 1862.

[9] **Charles Henry Tompkins** (1830-1915) was a graduate of West Point. He was born in September 1830 at Fortress Monroe, at the tip of the Virginia peninsula where McClellan now staged his army for its push toward Richmond. As a lieutenant with the 2nd U.S. Cavalry he was the recipient of the Medal of Honor

for a charge against the enemy at Fairfax Court House on June 1, 1861; possibly the first engagement of the Civil War after the firing on Ft. Sumter. He is later promoted brevet brigadier general. See: Horace K. Ide and Elliott W. Hoffman (ed.), *History of the First Vermont Volunteers in the War of the Great Rebellion* (Baltimore: Butternut and Blue, 2000), 306.

[10] Shelby Foote, *The Civil War, A Narrative: Fort Sumter to Perryville* (New York: Vantage Books, 1986), 431-435. James McPherson, *Ordeal by Fire, Volume II* (New York: Alfred A. Knopf, 1982), 239-242.

[11] Transcriptions of Higley Correspondence, May 26, 1862.

[12] Benedict, *Vermont in the Civil War*, Volume II, 559.

[13] McPherson, *Ordeal by Fire, vol. II*, 240.

[14] Collea, *The 1st Vermont Cavalry*, 79.

[15] Transcriptions of Higley Correspondence, June 26, 1862; See also: the account of Jed P. Clark of Company B in Ide, *History of the First Vermont Volunteers*, 45-46.

[16] Transcriptions of Higley Correspondence about June 26, 1862.

[17] Ibid.

[18] Foote, *The Civil War…Fort Sumter to Perryville*, 528.

[19] Collea, *The 1st Vermont Cavalry*, 82-84. Benedict, *Vermont in the Civil War*, 570-571.

[20] Ibid., Collea, 89.

[21] Transcriptions of Higley Correspondence, August 10, 1862. Higley was a member of the Delta Upsilon fraternity.

[22] James McPherson, *Battle Cry of Freedom, The Civil War Era* (New York: Oxford University Press, 1988), 526-527.

[23] Benedict, *Vermont in the Civil War*, Volume II, 574.

[24] Transcriptions of Higley Correspondence, September 26, 1862.

[25] Letter, Higley to Noble, October 22, 1863, Evans Collection, Riverside Metropolitan Museum. Full transcription in this work.

[26] Benedict, *Vermont in the Civil War*, Volume II, 574.

[27] See: *Vermont History: Proceedings of the Vermont Historical Society For The Years, 1915-1916* (Vermont Historical Society, 1918), 112. Also, Middlebury History Online at http://middhistory.middlebury.edu/edwin-hall-higley-professor-of-greek-and-german/

[28] **John Rollin Converse** (1842-1864) was a law student at Middlebury College graduating in September 1862. He enlisted in Company I of the 14th Vermont Infantry as a private but rose to the rank of a Second Lieutenant. Mustered out in July 1863 he joined Company H of the 17th Vermont Infantry in May 1864. G.G. Benedict wrote that Converse "showed especial aptitude as a soldier; fought with noticeable coolness and courage at Gettysburg and was promoted to be second lieutenant in that regiment. He was killed early in the action on July 30,

1864 where his regiment was involved in the assault dubbed the Battle of the Crater before Petersburg, Virginia. He was buried within the enemy's lines. See: Benedict, *Vermont in the Civil War*, 519.

[29] **Chi Psi Fraternity** was founded in 1841. The chapter at Middlebury College started in 1843 but has been inactive since 1994. Their mission was "to create and maintain an enduring society which encourages the sharing of traditions and values, respect for oneself and others, and responsibility to the university and community." See: *The Chi Psi Story*, Bill Hattendorf, (ed.), (Nashville, TN: Chi Psi Central Office, 2005) and http://www.chipsi.org/?XYaMissionValues.

[30] **Ezra Brainerd** (1844-1924) entered Middlebury College in 1860 and was a tutor there from 1864 to 1866 after graduating. He attended Andover Theological Seminary in 1868 and was a professor of Rhetoric and English Literature at Middlebury from 1868-1880 and Physics and Applied Mathematics 1880-1886. He became president of Middlebury College serving from 1886 until 1908. Member of the Chi Psi Fraternity. See: *Catalogue of the Officers and Students of Middlebury College*, 218.

[31] Union General **John Pope** (1822-1892) had seen some success in the trans-Mississippi theater of the war capturing an island crucial to Union navigation of the northern part of the river. The 40-year-old Pope was a graduate of West Point (1842) and rose in rank during the Mexican American War. He worked as a surveyor on the transcontinental railroad in the 1850s. His appointment in June 1862 as head of the Army of Virginia infuriated Charles Fremont who had more seniority and precipitated Fremont's resignation from the army. Following his defeat at Bull Run, Pope was reassigned to Minnesota to put down an uprising by the Santee Sioux in August 1862. See: John H. Eicher, and David Eicher, *Civil War High Commands*. (Stanford, CA: Stanford University Press, 2001), 433-434; Foote, *The Civil War, A Narrative*, 528.

[32] Union Major General **George Brinton McClellan** (1826-1885). Due to his reticence to pursue Robert E. Lee after the Battle of Antietam on September 17, 1862, a frustrated Lincoln removed McClellan as commander of the Army of the Potomac on November 7th. See: McPherson, *Ordeal by Fire, vol. II*, 298-301.

[33] Union Major General **Nathaniel Banks** (1816-1894) was a "self-made man of forty-six" who had made his name in business and politics in Massachusetts where he had been elected governor three times. He went on to become Speaker of the Federal House of Representatives and president of the Illinois Central Railroad. Historian Shelby Foote wrote that "he was determined to do as well in his new career, which might bring him the largest rewards of all." See Foote, *The Civil War: Fort Sumter to Perryville*, 427. The rumors of Banks' Texas expedition had already circulated. Banks had been informed about his reassignment at the War Department on October 20, 1862. There was growing pressure on Lincoln to secure large areas of Texas especially the ports and facilitate the export of cotton again to the diminished mills of the northeast. There was also growing concern about assistance by the French imperial government in Mexico which was already providing a means for a flow of materials to and from the Confederacy. The 1st Vermont Cavalry was not part of the expedition. *The New York Times*

reported that the Banks' expedition set sail on December 4, 1862 from New York. See: Raymond H. Banks, *King of Louisiana, 1862-1865, and Other Government Work: a Biography of Major General Nathaniel Prentice Banks, Speaker of the U. S. House of Representatives*, (Las Vegas, Nevada: Privately Printed, 2005), 497-498. Also, *New York Times*, December 6, 1862.

[34] A mile long span across the Potomac River which connected Washington, D.C. to northern Virginia. A vital supply link for Union troops and as a secured point for the defense of the capital. See: Kenneth J. Winkle, *Lincoln's Citadel: The Civil War in Washington, D.C.*, (New York: W.W. Norton & Company, Inc., 2013).

[35] May be the Greek term for "not one" and may refer to an informal literary society at Middlebury College, however the editor of this work has been unable to confirm this.

[36] **Frank Hiram Seeley** born in 1839, graduated from Middlebury in 1863 and was ordained a Presbyterian minister in 1866 after attending the Auburn Theological Seminary. He was a minister at Richfield Springs, New York and Delhi, New York until 1912. *Catalogue of the Officers and Students of Middlebury College*, 214.

[37] **William Calvin Tilden** (1844-1905) graduated from Middlebury College in 1864 and entered Georgetown University as a medical student in 1864 graduating in 1867. He worked for the Agricultural Department in Washington, D.C. as an assistant chemist until 1871 also becoming an Assistant Professor of Chemistry at Georgetown and later at Howard and Wesleyan University. He died in Washington, D.C. on August 3, 1905. *Catalogue of the Officers and Students of Middlebury College*, 220.

[38] O'Neill, *Chasing Jeb Stuart and John Mosby*, 138. Kellogg had returned to Vermont before resigning his commission. Major John Bartlett resigned in April 1862 and Major William Collins was wounded during Banks' retreat from the Shenandoah Valley.

[39] Benedict, *Vermont in the Civil War*, 575; Collea, *The 1st Vermont Cavalry*, 73.

[40] Price was a 54-year-old shipping merchant from Philadelphia who formed the Pennsylvania regiment at the same time the 1st Vermont was organized. See: Robert F. O'Neill, *Chasing Jeb Stuart and John Mosby*, 8, 138.

[41] **Dr. Selah Perkins** (1829-1862) graduated Union College and Castleton Medical School. Quoting one of Perkins' friends, Benedict wrote " He was a man of much more than average ability, and superior culture, of elevated character, with earnest feelings, quick and tender sympathies and genial disposition. He entered into the war with enthusiasm and uniformly discharged his duties as an officer with fidelity and zeal." See: Benedict, *Vermont in the Civil War*, 579.

[42] Robert F. O'Neill, *Chasing Jeb Stuart and John Mosby*, 10.

[43] Hoffman in Ide, *History of the First Vermont Volunteers*, 64-67; Benedict, *Vermont in the Civil War, 579*. See also, O'Neill, *Chasing Jeb Stuart and John Mosby*, 138.

[44] Hoffman in Ide, *History of the First Vermont Volunteers*, 72-75; Letter, Higley to Noble, Evans Collection, January 3, 1863 in this work.

[45] Transcriptions of Higley Correspondence, May 22, 1862.

[46] The number of serviceable animals rose to 552 by January 1, 1863 and to 668 by January 24th. See: Collea, *The 1st Vermont Cavalry*, 93-94. Preston would not return to the regiment for months but used the time to secure 900 horses for Vermont's cavalry. See Hoffman in Ide, *History of the First Vermont Volunteers*, 64-65.The Morgans which the Vermonters rode had a glowing reputation. Charles Tompkins, later colonel of the 1st Vermont, called them "decidedly the best I had seen." George Benedict noted the interest of Louis Napoleon who desired them for his imperial stables. See Tompkins, "With the Vermont Cavalry, 1861-2, *The Vermonter, The State Magazine*, Vol. XVII, no. 4, April 1912, 505; and Benedict, *Vermont in the Civil War, 534. See:* Transcriptions of Higley Correspondence, Middlebury College Archives, May 22, 1862.

[47] Transcriptions of Higley Correspondence, May 22, 1862. Morgans were named for their breeder, Justin Morgan of Randolph, Vermont. Allen Ward wrote that they became the foundation of the "American Saddle Horse, American Trotting Horse, and the Tennessee Walking Horse. " Stallions were shipped across the U.S. in the nineteenth century, and when bred with western mustangs produced quarter horses valued for their endurance by cowboys of the plains. See: Allen M. Ward, "Edwin Hall Higley, An American Classicist," 80.

[48] **Edward Higley Denison** (1817-1866) and his wife Sarah were residents of Middlebury, Vermont according to the 1860 census. Edward was the first cousin of Edwin Higley's father Hervey. Edward Denison died two years after this letter was written in 1864. See: Mary Coffin Johnson, *The Higleys And Their Ancestry*, 265.

[49] Union Major General **Franz Sigel** (1824-1902) who was in command of the Army of the Potomac's XI Corps (heavily comprised of German immigrants) at the time the letter was written. Siegel was born in Germany and received his military training there before resigning to lead revolutionary forces in 1848. With the Prussian victory, Siegel fled the country finally settling in the U.S. In 1857 he taught at the German American Institute in St. Louis. With the start of the war, he served under Nathaniel Lyons in the Missouri theater fighting in the battles of Wilson's Creek (August 1861) and Pea Ridge (March 1862). Shortly thereafter he was transferred to the eastern theater of operations. Many German immigrants were attracted to serve under a German general but most had little command of the English language. This gave rise to their response when asked about their unit, that "I fights mit Siegel." This was popularized in song, *I Goes to Fight Mit Siegel*, written by William Keel. Higley is referring to two companies under Captain Josiah Hall who were assigned to Siegel at Winchester, to conduct reconnaissance . See: Benedict, *Vermont in the Civil War*, 568.

[50] Likely **Ethan Allen Sturtevant** (1839-1878) who graduated from Middlebury College in 1863 and studied law at the University of Michigan until 1865. Practiced law in Manchester and East Saginaw, Michigan and later Middlebury (1870-1878). He died in Middlebury, Vermont June 10, 1878. He was a member of the Chi Psi fraternity. See: *Catalogue of the Officers and Students of Middlebury College*, 215.

[51] **Harrison Prindle** (1839-1901) attended Middlebury College from 1859 to 1861 but did not graduate. He joined the 14th Vermont Volunteer Infantry becoming Adjutant of the regiment. After his discharge, he sold insurance and studied law and was admitted to the bar in 1864. He died in San Francisco, California on March 31, 1901. See: *Catalogue of the Officers and Students of Middlebury College*, 217.

[52] It is probable that Higley is referring to irregular debates sponsored by the **Philomathesian Society** of Middlebury College, a debate society begun in the early 19th century and incorporated in 1822. Ralph Waldo Emerson spoke there on three occasions. According to one school publication, the society's "annual public debate in the autumn filled the chapel to its capacity…" The Society would be later supplanted by introduction of fraternities but was reported to be still flourishing in 1863. See: *The Undergraduate*, vol. IV, no. 2 (Nov. 1878), 26 and vol. XVIII, no. 5 (Feb. 1893), 69 and the *Middlebury News Letter*, vol. XIV, no. 1 (Sept. 1939), 7.

[53] The **Mendelssohn Quintette Club** was a popular chamber ensemble in the latter half of the 19th century based in Boston. They toured throughout New England and eastern states. Joseph Mussulman wrote that the popularity of Felix Mendelssohn "gained momentum sharply after 1848, when more German musicians, some of whom had been Mendelssohn's pupils, emigrated to America…" See: Joseph A. Mussulman, "Mendelssohnism in America", *The Musical Quarterly*, Vol. 53, No. 3 (July, 1967), p.336 and Thomas Ryan, *Recollections of an Old Musician*. (NY: E.P. Dutton & Company, 1899).

[54] "Though scarcely emerged from boyhood, he [Higley] was inspired with the enthusiasm attending the early outbreak of the war for the Union, and in 1861 he enlisted in Co. K, 1st Vt. cavalry. During his service he was detailed as adjutant and as regimental commissary and in the latter part of 1863 acted as brigade ordnance office on the staff of Gen. G. A. Custer." See: Jacob G. Ullery, compiler, *Men of Vermont: An Illustrated Biographical History of Vermonters and Sons of Vermont*, Part III (Brattleboro, VT: Transcript Publishing Company, 1894), 83. As quoted on http://vermontcivilwar.org/get.php?input=2954

[55] **Samuel Heintzelman** (1805-1880). The Vermont cavalry had been in the 2nd Corps of the Army of Virginia until October 12, 1862, when the 1st Vermont was reassigned to the Defenses of Washington under the command of General Samuel Heintzelmann who commanded III Corps which had seen action on the peninsula with McClellan. Richard Butler Price took command of the cavalry brigade. Washington's defenses would later be consolidated under XXII Corps on February 2, 1863.

[56] **Frank Hiram Seeley.** See Higley to Noble, November 1, 1862, fn 35.

[57] Transcriptions of Higley Correspondence, December 18, 1862.

Chapter Three: 1863

The boredom of winter camp set in along with the sharp winter winds of 1862. Higley complained on December 9th, that his duties consisted of visiting pickets at various times of night and day to ensure that they were "awake and attentive to their duties. Meanwhile I have nothing to do in the military line." The inactivity would be used, he wrote, to acquaint himself with the area. "I intend to spend some of this leisure time in cultivating the acquaintance of various personnages in the vicinity, some of whom I am informed possess pianos."[1] The following letter on January 3, 1863 notes the success of his search.

Sherman home at Ash Grove.
Structure was rebuilt following a disastrous fire in 1960 from existing drawings and plans of the original home. Photo taken by the author.

On New Year's Eve in 1862 the family of James Sherman welcomed a very grateful Edwin Higley, now a 2nd lieutenant with the 1st Vermont, into their spacious home. Sherman was a 67-year-old farmer in 1863, living in Fairfax County, Virginia near the village of Lewinsville. In 1851 he purchased 500 acres called Ash Grove from the estate of Henry Fairfax, descendant of the colonial family for which the county was named. He moved his family there from Cayuga County, New York where he had been a sometime teacher as well as a Justice of the Peace and Commissioner of Deeds. Besides his wife Fidelia, two of his eight children still lived at home: 18-year-old Franklin and 25-year-old Caroline. The family was outspokenly for the Union, something that gained them the enmity of their more secessionist neighbors and the bands of Confederates who raided through the area just south of the Potomac across from Washington, D.C.

Higley remembered the evening fondly, recording the episode in a letter to Noble. He obviously feels the desire for the wintry traditions and warmth of home in Vermont. However, at the Sherman farm, he found a way to transcend or perhaps supplant the war outside with the "glorious times" he experienced. He had good food in a warm home and spent the night "in a fine parlor with a fine piano and a fine young woman" who belonged to the piano. Higley seems smitten by Caroline Sherman, describing her as "bold and dashing without being forward or too familiar." Caroline also rode well and could shoot his Colt revolver better than he could.[2]

The two surviving outbuildings at the Sherman home at Ash Grove were built in the late 18th century. Photo taken by the author.

My dear friend Noble,

'New Years' is always difficult
to appreciate I believe, but for me it is to-day a greater stretch than ever.
There is no snow, fleecy and feathery or crisp and sparkling, no keen edge
to the atmosphere, no fur robes or jingling bells, none of these wintry
appearances which always precede, accompanying, and give character to
the New Years _debut_ at home. We have instead a bright, warm sun and
smooth, dry roads; a pleasant Autumnal day. Then too the customary,
necessary and ou_ght_-_to-be_-profitable review of the past years scenes and
incidents, present to my mind something so diverse and discordant from
and with anything which has filled my previous annual page in my
unwritten diary, that on the whole eigh_teen_ six_ty_ th_ree_ is very hard to
write. New Years day however brought me one home-like pleasure which
I little expected — viz; a good dinner and a fea_ther_ b_ed_. Yea, verily, for
the first time for thirteen months, I eat a huge dinner of chicken, rabbit
etc — spent the evening in a fine parlor with a fine piano and a fine young
lady, & finis, undressed myself in a civilized ma_nner_ a_nd_ rolled into
a re_al_, ge_nuine_ do_wny_, fea_ther_ b_ed_! The most novel sensation caused
by this proceeding was the peculiar effect of the pillows – so different
from the sticks, stones, saddles and coats, which have formed my caput-
al[3] support for the last year. It seemed as though my head was sinking
back through the down, and it seemed possible that it might get stuck
somewhere between my shoulder blades and prove difficult of extrication.

I know you will
appreciate me when
I tell you that
"The ivory face of the waiting keys,"
beamed out upon me
like an old friend, and that a more intimate acquaintance was productive
of much pleasure. But you know my memory was always bad, and of
course I have no music here, hence my performances are productive of
but little satisfaction in others. I found however an old "Opera Chorus
Book," the same which we sometime used in Mid. and, revived some of

my remembrances of its pages.

The people here are Union, most of them; they have suffered a great deal from Secesh rule, and they are very cordial in their kindness to us. The young lady who "<u>belongs to</u>," the piano aforesaid, is decidedly interesting of herself. Very bold and dashing without being forward or too familiar; rides a horse well, and can shoot my Colts revolver better than I can myself. When you remember that my quarters are <u>all the time</u> in a house, at that I find a welcome at several such houses as I have referred to, you will understand that I am personally enjoying myself.

Affairs in our regiment as you perhaps know, are very unpleasant. Col Sawyer was dishonorably dismissed from the service some time since, by the Sec. of War for inefficiency; he has at last succeeded by very vigorous wire pulling in replacing his foot in the Regimental stirrup. There are some of us who still agree with Sec. Stanton in regard to his character. Hence we are now the necessary objects of Col Sawyers enmity. The Sergt. Major of the Regt. our class mate Smith was reduced to the ranks a few days since. So long as we remain out here, I shall be happy, but whenever I am obliged to meet the Col the contact will be unpleasant.[4]

Gen. Stuart[5] caused some excitement in our vicinity during his recent raid. He did not molest our detachment, but the pickets from our Regt adjoining us had a collision with him, one night, and lost several men. Lt. Cummings was wounded and taken prisoner. He was from Dartmouth Coll.[6]

My political and patriotic feelings are at so low an ebb just now that I will not expand them. I rejoice in the Presidents proclamation.

A letter from home just received is overflowing with Christmas rejoicings and gatherings.

I hope you much pleasure and success in your pedagogical proceedings, let me hear from you soon if you have the time and inclination.

Yours Truly
E. H. Higley

Higley mentions that the Sherman family had suffered a great deal from "Secesh" rule. James Sherman's son-in-law James W. Green provides details concerning this suffering in his deposition in 1874 as he sought compensation for his losses during the war by Union forces who used his home, and stripped his fields and buildings of foodstuffs and livestock. His home was only a half mile from his father-in-law, James Sherman, where one of his horses, an "iron grey" was commandeered by Union forces. Green told commissioners that he spent about half the war in the safety of Washington, D.C. or at Falls Church under the protection of Union troops in order to stay out of the way of Confederate raiders, particularly the men of John Mosby.[7] Green and Sherman successfully avoided the rebels until November 18, 1863, almost a year after Higley's visit, when they were taken prisoner by Mosby's rangers. As they were being led to rebel headquarters, Green took the initiative and risk, spurring his horse into the black cloak of night. Although pursued, he made it within Union lines. Sherman was reportedly later abandoned by his captors perhaps through the intervention of a friend of his daughter Fidelia Green, who was a Confederate sympathizer. He may have contracted pneumonia due to his capture and died April, 16 1865, a week after Lee's surrender at Appomattox Courthouse.[8]

Franklin Sherman joined the 10th Michigan Cavalry in July 1863 and rose to the rank of Captain. He married Caroline Alvord of Massachusetts who had come south to teach at a Freedman's school next to Ash Grove. Franklin acquired control of Ash Grove upon his father's death. He reportedly became a sheriff and member of the Board of Supervisors and today has an elementary school named for him in Fairfax County.

Caroline Sherman, the object of Higley's attraction, was living with her brother in 1870 and working as a clerk. There is no evidence that this bold and dashing woman ever married and is still clerking in 1880, this time for the War Department. By 1900 she is in a home for incurables in Washington, D.C. which took in people who were chronically ill, "could not be cared for at home or simply had no place to go." She died at the hospital December 4, 1907. Her brother died eight years later.[9]

***

By March 11th, Higley and his men had moved 12 miles northwest to the "disagreeable," "muddy" and dangerous hamlet of Dranesville, Virginia which occupied Higley's contempt in two communications to Noble; one shown in full on page 45. "Drainsville [sic] is a mean, lonesome place so far off that we can't get anything to eat for ourselves and our horses," complained Higley, "so we have been sharpening up our memory and our teeth by living on hard crackers and giving our poor horses a taste of starvation."[10]   Sergeant Henry E. Smith of Company E was anxious in January 1863 of Dranesville's exposed position, writing his mother that, "the rebels are most every night shooting at our pickets at Dranesville, they have wounded three and captured five." Rebel commander John Mosby considered the outpost easy prey. "They are so isolated from the rest of the command," he wrote, "that nothing would be easier than their capture."[11]

Men of the 1st Vermont Cavalry were posted at picket stations from the southeast at Mt. Vernon set against the Potomac River through Annandale and Dranesville in the northwest. They were sentinels against any threat to Washington but the duty varied from numbing monotony to sudden eruptions of violence. Responsibilities included picket duty, patrolling and scouting with patrolling the least dangerous, according to one writer. Troopers checked on pickets and looked for evidence of rebel activity but patrols were generally short lived and kept men closer to larger Federal encampments. Scouting, wrote Joseph Collea, presented the greatest risk precisely because of the distance from Union defenses. Threat of attack was great in the area around Dranesville; it was "alive with clandestine enemy activity," wrote Collea.[12]

Mosby was the newest lethal threat to the safety and security of the area. The "Gray Ghost" and his quick striking rangers plagued Union outposts and pickets throughout 1863. That area of northern Virginia comprised of Loudoun, Fairfax, Prince William and Fauquier counties became known as "Mosby's Confederacy." Initially on the staff of Confederate cavalry commander J.E.B. Stuart, Mosby asked and received permission in early January 1863 for an independent regiment of rebel horsemen to harass the Union lines and create havoc behind them. Confederate troops, particularly cavalry, probed for weaknesses in the defenses of the Army of the Potomac, now commanded by Joseph Hooker. With Hooker's elevation to the army's head, cavalry units were again reorganized, this time into one corps, under the command of Brigadier General George Stoneman.[13]

Rebel cavalry under General Fitzhugh Lee crossed the Rappahannock River at Kelly's Ford on February 24th and surprised pickets of the 3rd and 16th Pennsylvania cavalries near Hartwood Church. Efforts to pursue Lee taxed available manpower encamped near Washington which forced cavalry commanders to rely less on pickets and more on patrols to guard transportation corridors.[14] Higley writes of a patrol on March 2, 1863 which went badly for the Vermonters when Captain Franklin Huntoon and several other men were apprehended.

Colonel John Mosby, ca. 1862.
Library of Congress, LC-DIG-cwpbh-00633.

Union horsemen were in the area near the strongly secessionist community of Aldie, independently trying to locate Mosby's raiders. Aldie was thirteen miles from Dranesville on the road which led west through the Blue Ridge at Ashby's Gap to Front Royal. Vermont troopers under Captains Huntoon and John Woodward reached Aldie around noon, running into stragglers of the 18th Pennsylvania, who mistakenly reported the town free of the enemy but were unaware that Mosby and men were entering from the northwest, opposite from the Vermont riders. Mosby surprised the relaxed and now dismounted Yankees capturing Captain Huntoon and a number of men. In the confused action, Captain Woodward was severely wounded.[15]

The capture a week later of Brigadier General Edwin Stoughton by rebel partisans cost him his reputation and eventually his career. Before sunrise on March 9, 1863 Mosby and his men, some reportedly dressed in Federal uniforms, silently entered the township of Fairfax Courthouse easily overpowering the few Yankee guards. Moving to the home of Dr. William Gunnell, they posed as couriers from the 5th New York Cavalry to gain entrance and made their way to General Stoughton's bedroom where he slept off the party of the evening before. Seized by the rebels, Stoughton allegedly demanded to know who the intruders were, bellowing, "Do you know who I am, Sir"? Mosby is reported to have said, "did you ever hear of Mosby?" to which Stoughton replied, "yes, have you caught him? No," Mosby answered, "but he has caught you." Exchanged two months later, the nomination of Stoughton for brigadier general was withdrawn by the Senate and he left the army. The raid is considered by many to be Mosby's most famous.[16] However, it would be an attack six days later which altered Higley's military career and threatened his deep sense of integrity.

General Edwin Henry Stoughton, ca. 1865. Library of Congress, LC-DIG-cwpb-06346.

44

My Dear Friend Noble,

  A week since I left Anandale [sic] where I had been cosily-sojourning for nearly two months. At the time of our leaving we received notice of the disaster which befell a scouting party of ours, by which we lost Capt. Frank Huntoon[17] and eighteen men prisoners. And soon after we heard of the audacious & successful capture of Gen. Stoughton[18] and staff. Well, amidst the confusion of changing our quarters, and the excitement attendant upon the relation and discussion of these two disheartening and uncalled for losses, it has <u>gone from me</u> whether I answered your letter before leaving Anandale [sic] or whether I am still your debtor. I have a distinct remembrance of sending resolves and intentions to do so, but I am not at all sure whether said purposes produced any tangible or <u>sendable</u> result. My impression however is, that t<u>hey</u> <u>did</u> n<u>ot</u>: and at all events your letters are too great a treat, to risk the non-reception of another, even tho' it be at the cost of burdening you with a double ration of my own.

  I thank you for the photograph. We ought to be too good friends by this time to indulge in compliments: so I will simply say that I am pleased to see or to think that I see a more healthy glow upon that countenance than formerly.

  This Drainsville [sic] is not the most agreeable place in the universe. It is extremely muddy; is as far removed from the rest of the world that it is extremely difficult to get supplies, hence we have to live on hard bread again: Is without deserted houses, hence we have to dispense with the dignity of a roof, which we have been enjoying all winter, and come back to the more soldierly but less comfortable protection of a canvas covering. I am living in a stockaded wedge tent: that is; a pen built up of logs and "chinked in" with mud to the height of three or four feet, and then a tent spread over it. My domicile is nine feet square, and the furniture thereof consists of two shelves and a stove. One of the shelves is a wide one on which we (two of us) sleep, and the other a narrow one, is a table.

  Thurs. morn; A good old woman has just allowed me to pay her thirty five cents for a dozen of eggs which my Ethiopian attendant[19] is industriously preparing for breakfast - hence I have a prospective good meal.

I do sometimes whistle that retrospective melody "The Gal I left behind me,"[20] although I put the noun generally in the plural number. But, if you find anyone, or ones in your rambles through the "mountains round about Jerusalem"[21] who remembers an absent soldier I conjure you to whisper sweet things to her for him. I had a letter from Willie Tilden not long since which I will answer soon. I suppose Junior exhibition is approaching.[22] How I should love to be there! "Sed nom-"[23] Please tell me how college and class affairs go on; how Brainerd and Tilden behave, how "Oudemia" flourishes, etc. If you see Mr. Denisons people please remember me to them, also to Seeley and all the kind folks in and around his home.

Yours Truly,
E. H. Higley

I prize very highly the little poem which you sent to me sometime since. If such things continued occasionally to flow from your pen and you would sometimes send me one, in print or otherwise, it would be gratefully received.

***

Rebel activity had reportedly quieted following the embarrassing capture of General Stoughton. Major William Wells of the 1st Vermont, wrote to a friend that "our pickets have not been molested for some time, all is quiet at the front." A new watch post was established five miles south of Dranesville, along the Loudoun and Hampshire Railroad at Herndon Station. Units from the 1st Vermont and other regiments at Dranesville were under the command of Major Charles F. Taggart of the 2nd Pennsylvania Cavalry. Early

Lieutenant Perley Cheney ca. 1865.
Photo courtesy of
Francis C. Guber Collection.

on March 17th, St. Patrick's Day, Wells, accompanied by Captain Robert Schofield and Lieutenant Perley Cheney, rode to Herndon Station to investigate charges of plundering by Union troops; the visit coincidentally coming on the heels of plans by Mosby to strike the general area.[24]

At Herndon, at around 1 p.m., the officers accepted a dinner invitation from Union sympathizer Nat Hanna and his wife, Kitty. They were joined by Lieutenant Alexander Watson, who was in charge of the Herndon pickets. Watson's men were casually breaking camp at the sawmill, adjacent

Major William Wells.
Photo courtesy of
Francis C. Guber Collection.

to the Hanna home, preparing for their return to Dranesville. Kitty Hanna sent word to a nearby aunt for additional pies for her unanticipated guests, as the officers nonchalantly gathered around the Hanna table, spread with "milk, honey and all sorts of delicacies."[25] Five miles to the north, Higley, at roughly 1 p.m., was leaving Dranesville with 50 men, moving toward Herndon to relieve Watson's pickets just as Mosby and his raiders emerged from the woods northwest of town and began riding slowly down the road toward the train depot and mill which were the center of Herndon.[26] Even though the Union men at the sawmill viewed Mosby's approaching riders, no alarm was raised. They believed the Confederates, dressed in blue Union overcoats, were the relief they expected. When Mosby's men suddenly charged, it was too late for the Yankees. While most sought refuge in the upper reaches of the mill, in the confusion seven Federals managed to escape. Mosby's threat to fire the building soon resulted in the surrender of those in the barricaded mill.[27]

Herndon Station as it appeared in 1905.
Photo courtesy of the Herndon Historical Society.

Through the Hanna kitchen window, Kitty spotted, "a squad of grays," heading for the house. "The rebel yell was no louder than my scream, 'the Southerns!' as they came tearin' down the hill, . . . an' then the bullets jes' rained on our house," she later remembered. Wells and the other Union officers sprang from the table, strapping on their sabers, giving Kitty Hanna the idea they were going to fight it out then and there. "Gentlemen, go outside, or I'll be murdered in my own house," she screamed. Watson and Cheney apparently reacting to her pleas, immediately ran onto the porch, pistols blazing, only to be quickly subdued. Wells and Schofield scrambled into the home's attic hiding in the pitch darkness. Mosby's men entered the home and began to search. A rebel's random shot into the lightless garret, "had a magical effect," Mosby later wrote. "There was a stir and a crash, and instantly a human being was seen descending through the ceiling. He fell on the floor right among the men." Amidst the lime dust and mortar they found Major Wells, none the worse despite his short flight. Mosby wrote that the incident was a warm source of amusement for his men who then promptly devoured the table's foodstuffs meant for the now captive Union officers.[28]

Two miles outside of town, Higley had posted a ten-man picket at the Thornton's Mills' crossroads and was moving steadily toward Herndon when one of Watson's escaped troopers barreled onto the column at full gallop announcing the station had been taken and all captured. Higley dispatched a rider to Dranesville to report to Major Taggart and began with all haste toward Herndon. Conditions and circumstances, however, worked against Higley from the start.

Kitty Hanna later in life.
Photo courtesy of the
Herndon Historical Society.

Many of the problems facing the cavalry outposts defending Washington were beyond Higley's control. Regimental infighting, particularly dissension among officers, low morale, exhausted horses and over-extended defensive lines worked to create an atmosphere which was ripe for exploitation by shrewd marauders such as John Mosby. Higley was forced to draw his relief party from twelve different companies, many of them raw recruits and strangers to him. Most of the horses available were in a depleted condition, having lived on half rations or gone for days without hay or grain, a fact later corroborated by testimony of Major Josiah Hall who said that the horses of the 1st Vermont were in very poor condition.[29] The precariousness of outlaying patrols leading to the constant Union losses was addressed in writing the previous February by Major Wells, now among the captured. His direct

Major Josiah Hall.
Photo courtesy of Francis C. Guber Collection.

appeal to Major General Samuel Heintzelman had ended up on Major Taggart's desk increasing tension among the officers and particularly, resentment for those in the 1st Vermont Cavalry as noted by Major Hall.[30] "There was some ill-feeling existing between Major Taggart 2nd Penn. Cavalry and the officers of the 1st Vermont Cavalry. The distribution of supplies for the men and horses was not equal . . . ," he later wrote.[31]

The attempt by Higley for an orderly but rapid advance of his column of troopers immediately began to unravel. Men on tired mounts, struggling through the deep mud of the roadway, began dropping out of line on their own as discipline disappeared. "Some of the men straggled far in the rear apparently unable to urge their horses through the mud," Higley later reported. "Some actually fell out to water their horses or dismounted to adjust their blankets." Higley slowed the advance and rode along the line attempting to restore order while reforming and hurrying the stragglers. Three or four men, part of the "old guard" who were not part of Higley's normal command, "pressed out of the ranks and hurried on excitedly" breaking out in advance of the column without Higley's knowledge or consent.[32]

At Herndon, Higley verified initial accounts of the raid and hearing that the Confederates may be a half mile ahead, pressed his men forward but again reported that the straggling and

Northern Virginia in 1863.
Map Illustrated by Robin Hanks.

51

disorder became unbearable. Halting the column once more, he "emphatically" ordered his men to keep up and be prepared to fight. Moving on, they were intercepted by one of the "old guard" who had earlier broken from the ranks, riding hard upon the column yelling, "here they are." Higley and his men then emerged into an open meadow and saw the last of the rebels roughly a half-mile ahead across a creek, entering into the forest. "I dashed across the meadow at all speed, but they were soon out of sight over a descending piece of ground," Higley said. By the time he reached that point, the Confederates were nowhere to be seen. What Higley did not know was that Mosby had formed a rear guard of 30 men which waited ahead in the dense growth ready to attack any Federal pursuers. After conferring with his non-coms, and fearing that he exceeded his specific orders to picket and secure Herndon Station, Higley decided to return to the depot, set out his videttes and await new orders.[33]

Higley and his men remained on post at Herndon for twenty-four hours before returning to Dranesville. Nearly a week later on March 24, 1863, Major Taggart filed a report with brigade commander Richard Butler Price without first questioning Higley or the other men involved. In the report he castigated Higley for his failure to rescue the captives at Herndon. "Had Second Lieut. Edwin H. Higley, Company K, 1st Vermont Cavalry, who had started with the relief for the post, consisting of 40 men, together with 10 of the old guard, who joined him, performed his duty, the whole party could and would have been taken," Taggart wrote. It is the only mention of the affair found in the Official Records of the Rebellion. Corporal Daniel Warren wrote in his testimony on the incident that the accusations against Higley originated with two or three soldiers, "who did not belong to his command but who had volunteered to join in the pursuit and having strong and active horses dashed on in advance of the column coming in sight of the retreating foe before it was possible for the rest of the party to be aware of their proximity." Higley later noted that even upon his return to the Union post at Dranesville, Major Taggart never informed him of the charges levied against him. Price accepted the Major's report without question which one historian links to the close relationship between the two men.[34]

On April 1st, Higley was again part of a rescue operation following a botched attempt to intercept Mosby and his men later dubbed the "April Fool's Day disaster." The partisans had encamped at the farm of Thomas Miskel on the night of March 31st outside of Dranesville, after finding that the Federals had pulled back from that outpost. Word reached Taggart's command at Freedom Hill, near Vienna, Virginia that Mosby was in Dranesville and 148 Union troopers, again from various commands, were assembled under Captains Henry Flint and George Bean.[35] In the frigid early hours of April 1st, the Federals divided their force at Dranesville and followed the hoof prints of the rebels through heavy snow to the Miskel farm where the two units of cavalrymen approached the farm house and barn at different intervals. They appeared to have Mosby cornered. Forewarned, however, Mosby and his men used the farm's complex of gates and high fencing to their favor. Before waiting for support from Captain Bean, Flint mistakenly charged his men into the waiting volley of rebel pistol bullets. Taking to their saddles and using their sabers and revolvers, the mounted rebels sent the other Yankees into wild flight. Higley wrote Noble that while Mosby was found, they "found him in ambush and waiting for them and were so severely handled by him that less than forty of our men are left of the

Captain Henry Flint.
Photo courtesy of Francis C. Guber Collection.

53

party that went out." Struck six times, Flint was killed immediately, Lieutenant Josiah Grout was severely wounded and Lieutenant Charles Woodbury died from a head wound while trying to rally his men. Historians offer different numbers of the overall Union loss but upwards of 85 men were killed, wounded or taken captive and 95 horses were seized by the Southerners. Mosby lost four men, only one of those killed. With the additional indignity of Miskel's farm, Taggart was immediately transferred to the staff of Major General Julius Stahel who became cavalry division commander in March 1863.[36]

Lieutenant Josiah Grout.
Photo courtesy of Francis C. Guber Collection.

By April 2nd, Higley had relocated south of Dranesville, to Union Church near Vienna,—the move part of a recommendation by Taggart in his report to Price. Union defensive lines were pulled back east of a strong watercourse barrier called Difficult Run. This was fulfilling essentially the same suggestion made by Wells and other officers the previous February which earned the ire of Taggart. Ironically, on that same day Higley penned a note to Noble about the misfortune at Miskel's farm, General in Chief of the Armies Henry Halleck was approving Higley's dismissal from the army for cowardice. Secretary of War Edwin Stanton signed the order the following day. Special Order 158 officially removing Higley from the army was issued April 6, 1863.[37]

Secretary of War Edwin Stanton, ca. 1860.
Library of Congress, LC-DIG-cwpbh-00958.

Higley's April 2nd letter to Noble is the last communication that is known between the two men until August 1863, as Higley likely returned to Vermont to mount his defense against the odious charges directed against him. Within a few days, Higley rallied support among Vermont legislators and academia. An April 15th letter from Congressman E.P. Walton appealed to Secretary Stanton for a review of the case. Petitions of support on April 22nd and 23rd from a who's who of Middlebury College also had the support of Middlebury alumnus, U.S. Senator Soloman Foot. Assertions by brigade commander Colonel Richard Price that he had personally consulted with Colonel Sawyer, Majors Hall and Collins and several line officers who "without exception" had condemned Higley, were refuted in letter after letter from those same men to a military commission assigned to review the case. Sawyer procured affidavits from officers taken prisoner that day which countered Price's allegations that as Higley and his men came into sight of the fleeing rebels, the prisoners beckoned for aid which Higley refused.

In July 1863, the military commission, headed by Brigadier General James Ricketts, found that the original report accusing

Higley was made up of incorrect information and that "there is no evidence to show that the accused did not act with courage and zeal in his endeavors to overtake the enemy and rescue the captives." Higley was restored to his command on July 8th. Words such as courageous and zealous were common adjectives in statements supporting Higley. Former regimental adjutant, Edgar Pitkin, in his testimony, wrote that he could never believe any accusations of cowardice unless he saw it with his own eyes. Having seen Higley in combat on several occasions, Pitkin wrote that Higley "was always noticed for his coolness and bravery in every instance in his proper place. . . . I do not believe he is capable of fear."[38]

While it appears that the motives of Taggart's actions should have been questioned, and the absolute statements of Colonel Price challenged, military etiquette took precedence. Indeed, Major General Heintzelman wrote that he had been unable to get a "satisfactory report" of the incident. Despite the general feeling that Taggart had a disdain for officers of the 1st Vermont, Colonel Sawyer wrote that he imputed nothing to the officer who made the report although he added that the facts as charged, "appear so differently from what I had understood them to be that it does not seem the same case." Incredibly, while supporting Higley's restoration to service, Sawyer puts some blame on Higley for not defending himself more aggressively when first accused. "Candor

General James Ricketts.
Library of Congress, LC-DIG-cwpb-04627.

56

compels me to say that had the Lieutenant been less reserved and modest when these accusations were made against him, circulated and the facts as reported in Col. Price's report generally believed, and had he have made a representation of the facts as they now appear to some of his Commanding Officers he would never have been dismissed." A fairly indifferent statement given that Higley was only made aware of Taggart's allegations after reports were filed and his dismissal had been ordered. It appears that Higley's first chance to offer a defense was to the commission empaneled to hear his case.[39]

Higley's sense of outrage was certainly evident in a February 1864 letter to Senator Foot. Higley sought the legislator's aid in securing back pay for those months following his dismissal. It was not so much the lost wages, he wrote, but the loss to his honor that was so personally damaging. "Had I been dismissed for drunkenness, or fraud my restoration might have been due, partially, to promises of reformation, or representations of good conduct in other respects," Higley wrote. "But cowardice cannot be repented of. Once dismissed for so black a charge, it must be refuted and proven utterly untrue, before restoration can be effected." Given the humiliation which the charges represented to Higley, it seems very likely that, had Higley been aware of the charges, a vehement defense would have immediately been forthcoming.[40] As for his eventual reinstatement, Higley criticized the "season of delay" represented by the bureaucratic and time consuming loop of generals and lower ranks who only moved the paperwork along for two months without initiating any investigation; a cycle only broken by Foot's urging for a hearing by Rickett's commission.

Higley told Senator Foot that he was unable to rejoin his regiment until after the Battle of Gettysburg but maintained that he was with the unit in their last harassment of Lee's army at Hagerstown and Falling Waters before Lee re-crossed the Potomac River on July 14th. Stationed at Warrenton by July 31st, Company K, along with three other Vermont companies, were detached from the regiment and assigned to escort duty at the headquarters

57

of VI Army Corps.[41] However, Higley, along with Captain William Cummings and Lieutenant Eben Grant, had returned to Vermont nearly a week earlier where they remained until late September 1863. Higley was temporarily re-assigned to Company M of the 1st Vermont which suffered from an officer shortage, along with Middlebury classmate Lieutenant John Williamson. The officers were sent to procure new recruits for the regiment at Camp Holbrook in

Vermont Senator Soloman Foot, ca. 1860. Library of Congress, LC-DIG-cwpbh-02088.

Brattleboro, Vermont—a main center for new enlisted men and draftees. Army records show that the men reported for duty on July 23, 1863 at the Draft Rendevouz in Brattleboro from where Higley penned the next letter roughly a month later.[42]

The first two paragraphs of the following letter, offer an insight, if cryptic, into the relationship between Noble and Higley. While we do not have a record of what Noble expressed in his communication, Higley's reference to "John & Phineas" does offer some clues. Higley is likely referring to a popular Victorian novel of the era, *John Halifax, Gentleman*. The rise from poverty to prominence that is Halifax's story is inter-twined with that of his employer's disabled son, Phineas, who develops a deep love for the heroic John. It is a platonic adoration in a period where romantic affection, especially among the more literate, was expressed absent any sexual overtones.

My dear Noble,

Your letter was refreshing nectar midst the turbid water of this camp life I assure you. I can't speak my thanks as I feel them for the words, fresh and warm from your heart – which you sent. And yet I am half a mind to feel hurt at the termin_us_ thereto. I thought we talked things around to a "John & Phineas" platform from which we were safe from any such dangers as that.[43]

"Dash my + hearts mine by;" have I shown any disposition to do as? No, my dear boy, I must respectfully decline any such procedure. Even if I should find,-- which I never shall – the better flavored liquid to which you refer, my Yankee principles of economy revolt against the waste. You mustn't expect anyone who has been treated to so much dross and drizzle as I have been, to exhaust at a draught a wh_ole_ foun_tain_ of the clarified article, but I will drink as much as I can hold, and keep, coming again for more.

I am a good deal disappointed that this present writing finds me still at Brattleboro instead of on the homeward train-- But I could not get away. I shall try to do so on Monday, but it may be later.

A letter from my sister to-day is adorous of pic-nics, boat- rides and all sorts of tantalizing visions. Thomas is there.

Perhaps to-day you are watching the _great deep._ You must let me hear the melody which ocean plays upon your heart strings.

I had some expectation of coming down to Boston this week and surprising you. A party went from camp in charge of some conscripts. But I didn't happen to be one. We shall probably be stationed at Boston for a short time before we leave for Dixie-. So you can be preparing a guide-book of the most note-worthy lions against our meeting.

I shall probably come back to Brattleboro on "Monday week" and will stop at 'Leland House'[44] then or some other time with pleasure. Perhaps I can get away from here and stay a day with you before you go back to Midd. and then accompany you thither. At any rate I shall be sure to see you before I do Dixie.

Thine Ever,
E. H. Higley

Records show that Higley and the others were released from Brattleboro to return to their regiment on September 25, 1863, the same day Higley notes a stay in Springfield, Massachusetts, a stop on the rail line leading to Washington, D.C. He is in the nation's capital again four days later.[45]

Maggie Mitchell.
Wikimedia; taken from John Clapp and Edwin Edgett,
Players of the Present, 1899.

George Meade had followed Lee's army south as it pulled back into central Virginia settling behind lines at the Rappahannock River. The army moved farther south to the Rapidan following a probe by Union cavalry in September holding basically the same ground held by John Pope before Second Bull Run in August 1862. Part of the 1st Vermont had been at Waylands Mills, ten miles south of Culpeper, for about a week where Higley joined them by October 5th. Their brigade commander now was George Armstrong Custer after the regiment's transfer in late August. The stark camp accommodations Higley describes point to the continual movement of the regiment, maneuvering for a better position versus the enemy. Higley informs Noble of the enjoyable visits to the theater and concerts while in New York City and Washington. His fervor for actresses such as the bewitching

Maggie Mitchell is tempered by his subdued enthusiasm for the performance of great stage actor Edwin Booth, "which was satisfactory." Abraham Lincoln was also an admirer of Mitchell and is known to have seen Booth in Hamlet in March 1864.

Edwin Booth.
Library of Congress, LC-DIG-cwpbh-02679.

One highlight of the following letter, however, is certainly Higley's word picture of soldiers during mail call who surround the lone rider (an angel visit), "as the priceless treasures of the gray saddle-bag are poured out and assorted before them." His description of the "elated steps" of the joyous recipients and the "disappointed faces" of the empty-handed, expressively offer poignant images of lonely, weary men, hungry for some vestige of home.

Camp near Waylands Mills Va
Oct 5th 1863

My dear Noble,

  I am pretty much in the old harness again, and perhaps better able than ever to understand roughing it in the field, and living at home. I got initiated so gradually at first that I hardly appreciated the contrasts – both pleasant and disagreeable – which the two species of existence present to me now. There is an exhilarating sense of the wildness around us, which comes to me now with a keener relish than before. And there is alas a vivid realization of the lack of table furniture and the paucity of household appurtenances in general, which is decidedly amusing at least. I find the regiment in camp for a few days, ten miles south of Culpeper C.H. on the Rapidan, amid the scenes of our last years exploits under the great Generalissimo John Pope.

  I say we are "in camp," which is a figure of speech, for there are but three tents in the Regiment, and they are occupied by the Col and the Majors. The rest of us are sleeping under rubber blankets, bits of canvas or anything which we can have the good fortune to possess. Williamson is the lucky owner of a fly, (I believe you know what that is) and I am the lucky sharer of it with him. Hence you can gain the best idea of our house by remembering the "front porch" of my Brattleboro residence, and subtracting the residue of the residence therefrom. Then, for plates, we have a canteen split intwo which furnishes us with two very good plates. We have but one fork, and but one spoon: but are blessed with two knives. We comfort ourselves by the observation that the variety of things to eat, corresponds with that with which we eat, and hence contrive to extract some strength and a good deal of fun there from. We are I suppose somewhat in the sunny south yet it is rather chilly o'nights. Kilpatrick,[46] you see, is at the front, as he always is, and hence for the present, we are without baggage trains sutlers and various other little conveniences which cluster about the grand armée which slumbers in our rear. I am uncomfortably idle just now. The company are all with the Captain at Hd'Qurs' 6th Corps: and I have been assigned to no other duty, but am simply hanging on. I stopped for a day with the company before coming here, and thus made a visit with Edgerton, and Crane.[47] Proctor has gone to hospital, very sick, it is feared dangerously so.[48] I saw Newton,[49] who was of the class before us, and heard of Wilbur,[50] but did not go near him.

I find my horse in pretty good condition, also my aide de-camp, my ebony imp, my confidential advisor.

Your letter came to camp on the same day with myself. We stayed in New York over Sabbath. Saturday Eve I heard Edwin Booth in Hamlet,[51] which was satisfactory. Also the grand organ at Trinity Church which I heard on Sabbath morning. In the afternoon Saturday I went out to Central Park which, fully equaled my expectations. Dodworth's band played there; some exquisite thing, among which a March – No 40, from Schubert, which I particularly enjoyed.[52] I passed a very pleasant evening with Mrs. Akers. She has been very sick, for four weeks, and had not yet recommenced her work: but she was as kind and interesting as ever, and yet intensely sad. Did I show you her little poem "Empty-handed"? Ask Em for it, if I did not, and if you should like to see it.[53]

I heard Maggie Mitchell at the Theater in Washington, and was bewitched as everyone is. O, if you could but hear her in Fanchon![54] And if I could but be there to enjoy your admiration of her!

My boy, yesterday, as I was lying here on the blankets, I took out my memorandum book and the first thing that met my eye was a sheet of paper on which were written some verses; beginning – "Go!" I had used that book a dozen times and never seen them; but it seems that I was to wait until down here in the crowded solitude of camp, on Sunday, two weeks from that last Sunday, before they came to me. I was at first seriously inclined to believe that you had crept in unawares,– I had just been out on parade – and endowed my pocket without my knowledge. And after vainly searching for some explanation further, I returned and adopted my first fancy for my last belief; which I still hold in firmest faith: namely that on that calm Sabbath afternoon you were right here with me, nestling against my breast! May I stand fast in the faith? But you needn't answer me.

Next time I will tell you, I hope, something about "Counterparts."[55] I hope to write you often, but you must have charity and not go "taking hints", if I am not always regular. Remember that life here is in some respects very different from camp at Brattleboro;- that before I finish this letter, we may be ordered off on a raid, or a retreat; that probably before I write again the remnants of this army will be on *there[sic] way to Washington; that writing materials are sometimes separated from us for weeks; that mails are sometimes with-held for a week or two, etc, etc. On the other hand I wish I could make you see what angels vi<u>sit</u>s the mail-bags make us. I was particularly impressed by seeing the mail come in last night.*

Fancy the hush of twilight sending its solemn benediction through the grand, vast forest under which our Regiment rests; the men are silent, mainly invisible, or clustered in still groups around the camp-fires, which just begin to sparkle: the horses are quietly munching their evening meal; adding by their somber figures, as they are scattered here and there among the trees, to the prevailing idea of m<u>otion</u>less repose. All at once the light click of a horses hoof is heard, and the familiar form of the Regimental mail carrier is seen, as his steed trots leisurely into camp, and halts before the Adjutants quarters. The loudest alarm notes of the bugle could not go more quickly through the camp than those light hoof beats upon the forest carpet. Instantaneously from all parts of the woods the sun-browned and dusty figures of the war-worn troopers are seen flocking together around that solitary horseman. A ring is made; a blanket spread upon the turf, and the anxious faces peer eagerly on as the priceless treasures of the gray saddle-bag are poured out and assorted before them. It is soon over, and they scatter back; some, with disappointed faces; in the deepening darkness, to their fragile shelters; others with elated steps to devour the kind words of "Father", "Mother", "Sweet-heart", or "Friend" by the flickering light of the blazing fire.

Tomorrow we have a grand division review by General Pleasonton.[56] But you surely cannot charge me with brevity to day—

Deus vobiscum,[57]
Ever yours
E. H. Higley

***

Higley's prophetic comment about a possible surprise departure and the difficulties of correspondence proved true, when on October 8th, the regiment began several days of maneuvering against a flanking movement by Lee to the west, around the Union right wing; a tactic used against Pope a year before. As Lee crossed the Rapidan, Meade began withdrawing his forces north, back across the Rappahannock so as to not be wedged in between the two river systems. On October 11th, Higley and Company M at Culpeper, under command of Lieutenant Colonel Addison Preston, were deployed with other skirmishers to the rear of Custer's brigade which remained hotly engaged with the enemy. Confederates entering from the southwest pushed the Yankees through the town as Custer and Judson Kilpatrick began their march to the Rappahannock. Reaching Brandy Station, six miles to Culpeper's northeast, Kilpatrick realized that rebel forces had assembled on both flanks and in front, blocking their forward progress; they were surrounded. Kilpatrick eagerly accepted Custer's plan of a frontal assault on the Confederates holding the ground ahead, which commenced as rival artillery batteries sent shells flying both directions.

Judson Kilpatrick.
National Archives photo no. 111-B-4163.

Custer reported that he ordered his men to draw their swords and "informed them that we were surrounded, and all we had to do was to open a way with our sabres." After giving three hearty cheers, "the band struck up the inspiring air, 'Yankee Doodle,' which excited the enthusiasm of the entire command to the highest pitch, and made each individual member feel as if he was a host in himself." Kilpatrick described Custer's 3,000 screaming troopers accompanied by 100 blaring bugles, charging the rebel cavalry whose ranks broke and scattered, allowing a corridor for the Yankees to connect with Buford's division.[58] Higley and the rear guard units emerged onto the open field after Custer's determined assault and quickly realized their predicament of possibly being cut off from the main Union force. Higley offers a vivid account of the "concentrated electricity" of their horses' flight across the contested plain into the relative safety of a tree line where they turned again upon the Confederate pursuers.

George Custer.
National Archives photo no. 200S-CA-10.

Custer's penchant for motivating his men with patriotic musical scores was witnessed by Higley the day before the encounter at Brandy Station. The regiment was assigned support of an artillery unit near Kilpatrick's headquarters along the Culpeper Road near James City. As reciprocal shelling began, Custer positioned his company of coronets alongside the batteries and had the boisterous chorus of brass augment the bombardment. Higley described the moment for Noble saying, "the effect under the circumstances was more peculiarly grand and impressive than anything which I have ever heard." Higley also remembers the "majestic strains of the "Star Spangled Banner" and the "Marsailaise,"[sic] as part of the band's odd repertoire that day.

Having escaped the threat of calamity on the field near Brandy Station where they "overdid all sorts of huge and terrible things," Higley and the 1st Vermont crossed the Rappahannock, marched north along the tracks of the Orange and Alexandria Railroad until roughly eleven o'clock that evening exhausted from 48 hours of constant fighting and movement. "We unsaddled our horses for the first time for four nights," wrote Higley. After a little hardtack and an hour of sleep they were startled awake by bugles exclaiming "Boots and saddles," rousting their "jaded selves and horses" and rode through the chilly night and morning for another 24 hours of picket duty back along the Rappahannock River east of Brandy Station at Kelly's Ford where they were joined by the 5th Michigan Cavalry. Higley shares, however, that troopers, even astride mounts in poor weather, could find ways to sleep.[59]

Departing from the failed tactics of Pope, Meade had pulled his forces north to the area of Manassas Junction. Staying ahead of the flanking Confederates, Meade waited for a chance to strike back at the advancing Lee which he got on October 14th at Bristoe Station, four miles from Manassas. An impetuous General A. P. Hill ordered a hasty attack against Union forces led by General G. K. Warren, providing a lopsided Federal victory. Confederate casualties were 1,900; 1,400 of those deaths including two brigade commanders. The Yankees had 50 killed.

As Higley recaps the events in mid-October in the following letter, he is in camp at Groveton, roughly eight miles southwest of Alexandria. In this October 22nd letter, Higley omits any reference

Kelly's Ford across the Rappahannock River, February 10, 1864.
Drawing by Edwin Forbes, Library of Congress, LC-DIG-ppmsca-20625.

to another engagement at Buckland Mills on October 19th, which did not end as favorably for the Union. However, on New Year's Eve, two months later, he does give some detail of the action, suspicious that Noble may have not heard the exact truth about the cavalry's involvement from fellow Vermonter Albert Crane, who served with the 6th Vermont Infantry. Higley's units of the 1st Vermont had rejoined the division on October 13th at Bealton Station.

The clash on the 19th was precipitated by Lee's retreat on October 17th back down the Orange and Alexandria Railroad. Rebel horsemen guarded Lee's flanks and provided a rear guard against Union cavalry. Stuart positioned himself on the south side of Broad Run defending the bridge at Buckland Mills west of Manassas when Custer's 2nd Brigade, including Higley and the 1st Vermont, made contact. Stuart's sudden withdrawal was meant to lure the Yankees into a trap whereby Confederates under Fitzhugh Lee would assault their flanks as Stuart turned and attacked the front columns. The plan succeeded due to the rash actions of an angry Kilpatrick who pushed the 1st Brigade to blindly pursue Stuart after Custer halted his men for food and rest. After five miles down the Warrenton Pike, the trap was sprung. The stampeding retreat of Kilpatrick and the 1st Brigade, left Custer's men in the rear to fend for themselves. Higley was likely with his friend and fellow officer, Lieutenant Williamson leading dismounted skirmishers for a time. Higley was critical of Sawyer for miserably mishandling the regiment although proud that the men withdrew in "perfect order." A source of irritation for Higley was having found safety, for the first time, by falling back within the lines of the infantry (including Crane's 6th Infantry). The Union retreat that day and the subsequent five-mile pursuit by rebels became known sarcastically as the "Buckland Races."[60]

The cavalry division played no part in Warren's victory at Bristoe Station on the 14th and instead waited on the killing fields of Bull Run. Higley's description of the eerie landscape in the following letter is as poetic as it is ghoulish; the white bones shimmering under a gloomy forest. Civilians and military authorities were completely unprepared for the numbers of dead produced at places such as Bull Run or Gettysburg. The bodies of those who fell may have had a few shovels of dirt thrown on them or were left unburied, but were often exposed to weather and scavenging animals which violated the corpses. Hollow-eyed skeletons of former brothers in arms, Higley noted, seemed to beckon the living to a similar fate—a "mighty strain," he said, on the men's courage.[61]

Unburied dead on the Bull Run battlefield, 1863.
Drawing by Edwin Forbes, Library of Congress, LC-USZ62-126956.

My dear Noble,

I am your debtor so much for your frequent and fragrant letters that its no use to attempt to make my obligation equalized. But I can and do promise that if this "cruel war" will allow me to do so I will be more prompt hereafter. Since I last wrote you we have performed the huge retrograde movement of which I hinted the probability. Then we were ten miles below Culpepper; now our Regiment is, for today, on the Bull Run battle-ground. And during the time intervening between then & now we have been in five fights and it has been one long march and tour of picket duty, for the rest of the time. Hence you may imagine that we have not had time for literary or epistolic operations. In fact we haven't even attended properly to our eating and sleeping. I sent a pencil scrawl home to let them know that I was alive, as soon as I could after the Culpepper fight; though I find that there was no necessity for so doing as the papers have given you no idea of the amount of fighting which has been done. The infantry have been kept out of danger, but it has been our work to keep a wall of steel round about their precious heads and it has been a fatigueing [sic] and sometimes perilous task. Riding day and night, through cross roads, forests, and swamps, in passing from one exposed point to another and exerting a sleepless vigilance all the time; dashing against the pursuing foe when in his eagerness he approached too near; never unsaddling and rarely feeding our poor, patient, <u>patriotic</u> horses, shivering, without blankets or tents awning the cutting frosts, or quailing beneath the beating of the rainstorms, - this is what the past two weeks have been filled with. We don't exactly understand what it all amounts to. We have fallen back almost to the Washington fortifications and then have again advanced to the Rappahannock, without either army making a trial of its strength. But we suppose it "all helps to put down the Rebellion." Perhaps the campaign is not yet over, but it looks like it. Yesterday the army advanced its Hd. Qus to Warrenton and last evening we were sent back here to picket the line of communications to the rear. It isnt likely that we shall be here many hours.

Oh, this is a terrible place! A year ago and more, we were here when the hot shell were bursting around us, and the shouts and crashing of the angry armies were filling the air. But then our blood was up to fever heat and it was with clenched hands, furrowed brows, and burning cheeks that we went back over Bull Run Creek. But now all that is gone. The air is heavy with stillness and nothing but the mournful wrecks of that day remain. Our Governor speaks in his message of "bones bleaching in the Southern sun," but I fancy with but little appreciation of the re<u>ality</u> of the phrase. But if you were here I could take you, in five minutes ride, to a sight which appeals to humanity every day. The poor fellows who fell here last year have never been buried save by few stones or a spade-full or two of earth thrown at them as they lay, which the winds and rains and turkey-buzzards have removed now. And so, the other day their white bones shimmered under the gloomy forest, for nearly a mile as we rode along: their bony fingers pointed at us; their hollow eyes stared at us: sometimes a fragment of the blue uniform clung around a skeleton limb; now and then a horse stumbled, and you looked down to find his hoof kicking against a struggling skull! Ah! I tell you, it was a mighty strain on a fellows courage to ride as we did through the fatal forest, expecting every moment to hear the rifle-crack of the opening fray sounding at the head of the column, while these ghastly, grinning skeletons of our brothers of a year ago, seemed welcoming us to their own grim state! And then to reflect, Hamlet-like, upon any individual remains – "This man had a m<u>o</u>ther- a c<u>hi</u>ld- a w<u>ife</u>"--O, the heart would cry out in bursting with agony, - My God! How long shall this murdering contest wage?

We had a right smart time when we left Culpeper. So far as I can learn, the papers have said nothing about it. I wont bore you with very much of an account thereof – in fact I couldnt do so: But it was somewhat after this wise. Our division was left until last in Culpeper to superintend the removal of stores, etc. and we were kept there until we were pretty much surrounded by the pugnacious chivalry and Kilpatrick had to put forth the most vigorous exertions to save his command from destruction. My own company is as I believe I told you on escort duty at Sedgewicks'[sic] Hd. Qurs.[62] and so of course were not in the fight. Williamson and myself however are in charge, at present, of Co. "M" which has no officers of its own with it. We were deployed as skirmishers in the rear of our column. At Brandy Station, which has been the scene of several cavalry fights, Kilpatrick found the rebel cavalry massed to receive him on his front and right while they were follow[ing] us, as they had been for two hours, closely in the rear. He at once collected his forces in two solid columns of regiments and by a series of desperate charges, *cleared out the force in his front, pushed on and formed a junction with Buford, and then turned upon the gray backs with his artillery which must have been destructive in their compact ranks. They however responded with similar spirit and the fight waxed hot. All this – before our companies of rear skirmishers had come up. When we did come out upon the open plain near Brandy Station; turning to fight the rascals in our rear at every step, the black, dense mass of rebels was on our right, and our own lines in front; each actively engaged with artillery. As soon as we came in view, a column of rebs started out, unseen by us, for the purpose of cutting off our party from our main force. They had reached about mid-way of the distance necessary to intercept us, before we saw them; occupied as we were with our assi<u>du</u>ous reti<u>nu</u>e in the rear. I first pointed them out to Lt. Col. Preston, who commanded our party. He gave one look and one word of command and laid the spurs to his horse. Then did I verily make a similar appeal to my little black mare, for an increase of retrograde velocity! Right handsomely did the little darling respond. And we dashed over the plain with something less than the speed of concentrated electricity. The air was hot with the seething shell from both our own and rebel guns, which however hissed harmlessly over our heads. We were just in time. We reached a corner of the woods just ahead of our eager foes and halting at once, poured into them with our pistols and carbines, first checking and finally driving them back to their friends, while we hastened on to our own. We lost three officers and several men from the Regt. during that fiery day. Among the former was Capt. Adams, a universal favorite with the Regiment for his bravery.[63] He was severely wounded in the engagement wherein Capt. Perkins was killed, and had but just recovered there from. It is feared that he is killed this time, although we hope no better. He, too, leaves a young wife. Why are they taken, and young fellows who could die as well as not left unharmed?*

Maj. Hall, brother of N. B. Hall who graduated some time since was taken prisoner recently also.[64] Well Ive made a long story of one fight so that I musn't [sic] say anything about the others. But stay I must tell you of a musical incident which accompanied the fight at James City on Saturday the 10th the day before we left Culpeper. This fight was for an hour or two an artillery duel between opposing parties, the hostile batteries being planted on two well-chosen hills about a mile from each other. Gen. Custer, who commands the Brigade has a cornet band of which he is very proud. At this time he drew them up in line, by the side of his guns, in full view of the chivalry opposite, and by whom they must have been distinctly heard. And as the guns opened they began to play. The effect under the circumstances was more peculiarly grand and impressive than anything which I have ever heard. As the majestic strains of the "Star Spangled Banner" and the "Marsailaise"[sic] rang out their proud defiance on the air, the guns would boom out one after another in a kind of terrible rhythm, sending their hot vengeance whistling and crashing toward the foe, as it seemed in grim illustration of the harmonious challenge.[65]

The other day we took a prisoner and brought him to the rear where the bands were playing "Star Spangled Banner" and the poor fellow burst into tears and sobbed out, like a child, "I want to go home!" All these things serve to keep in my mind what Chas. Auchester says that "Music is."[66]

As you may suppose I haven't progressed very much in "Counterparts." It rides in my saddle-bags however and I shall get to it if we ever stay long enough in one place to unsaddle.

Your last letter came yesterday. I am glad of the proposed educational concentrations but fear they will all end in smoke. I haven't seen the papers for so long that I don't know what you mean by "McClellans effort against Gov. Curtin." But that he should make an effort against him would not surprise me at all or in any way change my opinion of him. I never claimed that he was a Republican in politics. He has always been a Democrat. But that is in no way connected with the question of his military ability or integrity. We are all glad over the results of elections in Pennsylvania and Ohio.[67]
Would you let me see some more of "College Dreams" sometime?

I had a kind letter from Mrs. Akers yesterday, enclosing this poem of hers which you will appreciate better after you have seen Washington and seen the poor horses looking through the iron fence at the Capitol grounds. Her ever present kind-heartedness shines in it with its usual pathos. After you have read it, let Allie send it home to Emma[68] "if you please."

Now, my boy, Good bye
Yours Ever,
E H Higley

By October 24th, Higley was performing as the Brigade Ordnance Officer on Custer's staff and by the end of the month, Meade had moved his army slowly south again stationing along the northern shore of the Rappahannock River with their base around Fredericksburg, site of Burnside's disastrous assaults of a year earlier.

With the near continuous fighting for the regiment since his re-instatement, Higley hopes for rest for the "ragged and hungry men" and the "lean and lame horses." Noble's pragmatic embrace for "an indefinite continuance of the war" if necessary, finds approval with Higley who feared an earlier naïve assessment of "speedy doves and olive branches," by Noble. Higley, the veteran, disparages a seeming lack of commitment for victory even from honored professors such as Middlebury's Brainerd Kellogg, who had petitioned for Higley's re-instatement. Referring to Noble's physical frailties, Higley wonders why Noble's "glowing soul" could not inhabit an "iron-nerved 'strapling.'"[69]

> 1st *Vermont Cav*
> *Catletts Station Va.*
> *November 6 1863*

My dear Noble,
       Your ever punctual letter came along day before yesterday, making the second one received since I wrote you before. I wrote then from an old stone house on the Bull Run grounds; the Stone Hospital which was rendered famous at the first Bull Run.[70] We left there on the following morning and returned to Gainesville. We have seen no Rebels since, but have been in motion most of the time. While at Gainesville I was detailed as Brigade Ordnance Officer on Gen Custer's staff[1] a position which I filled for one week and started yesterday in accordance with an order from the War Dept. dispensing with Ordnance officers for Brigades, and transforming their duties and stores to Division

officers; an order whereat I greatly rejoice as it relieves me from a disagreeable duty. I have the most extreme disgust for all the domestic duties connected with the army: if I may so term the feeding, clothing, furnishing, equipping, repairing etc branches of service.

Kilpatrick made a reconnaissance to Falmouth from which he returned last evening. We are watching with some eagerness for the next move. We hardly expect to remain here for the winter. I think we shall soon fall back again and transfer our operations to Acquia Creek or the Peninsula. But this is only a conjecture among a thousand.

We are a good deal anxious in regard to impending operations, because _we_ _want_ _rest_. Our horses are lean and lame. Our men are ragged and hungry. And we need some quiet for a few weeks at least, in order to put us again in trim.

You "believe in an indefinite continuance of the war." Good. Not that such a continuance is good, but it [is] well to look our situation squarely in the face.

I will remember how when I made some such proposition to you, a year ago, that you said in reply "I will believe in speedy doves and olive branches." And I said to myself when I read it – "That's the kind of _veal_ the nine months men are raised on." I am glad to see this improvement in your creed.

What will they do about the three hundred thousand more? I tremble to think of it. Why dont somebody wake up? Why dont Prof. Kellogg[72] open both his eyes and his mouth and head a stampede of the whole college! Why don't whole-souled fellows in all our colleges and theological seminaries inaugurate a movement which should kindle again a wildfire of enthusiasm through the whole crust of society and send the regiments flocking down here as they did in months gone by! Why haven't some small-souled, weak-kneed, over-grown lubber got yo_ur b_od_y, or why hasn't some big-handed iron nerved "strapling" your glowing soul, or why isnt something fixed somehow so that this need; this double cry of country and of heart might be answered! God bless you my boy! Those are right glorious words with which you sent me. Your heart is sound. And after all I suppose that we may as well watch and wait, as fume and fret. "Hold fast and see the salvation of God!" says Honest Abe.

Well I have read "Counterparts." I will return it to you if I can *do so in any readable or tangible condition. I like it as much I think as you could wish. I found one thing in it which, as I wish to be candid in all things with you, I shall tell you I do not like. The chapter on "Odyle" I should most emphatically term with Bernard "psychological fiddlesticks!"*[73] *Surely it is not necessary, in order to evolve her heartsful theory, or to show how soul touches soul, or in any way to illustrate the inter-communings of spirits, to introduce that sensual, physical, animal effect which it is to me absurd and repugnant in the extreme? But in grand and (to me) hitherto unseen revelations of the depth and power of passion, in its unveiling, its probing the depths of the soul, and above all in the unanswerable force with which it asserts the oneness of all true and glorious life with true and eternal love – in there, it is rich; it is satisfying. I accept it as worthy of the authoress of "Charles Auchester," which is equivalent to placing it on the top shelf of my brain! I have read it all manner of places, and among varied scenes – on the march, in the saddle, sitting on fences; perched in trees; once I remember during a heavy rainstorm when I cuddled on the ground with my rubber coat around me and my head bowed down to my knees; but most and best when stretched at night on the blankets, in regal comfort, before a blasting fire, after a day of rest.*

I am now commencing "Barnaby Rudge."[74]

I have been reading in to-days paper a report of the great organ opening. A fine programme, wasn't it? The last that I had read there were a set of fogies trying to crowd Mendelssohn out. It was well enough to leave out Beethoven, and to put his statue over the instrument. He presides well over all music; but his truest mediums of interpretation are the piano forte and orchestra. This is a private opinion of my own.

I am glad you heard Mrs. Little. My only acquaintance with the "Stabat Mater"[75] *is through my own thrumming not from any hearing of it. I remember the Inflammatus [sic] however quite distinctly.*

The subject of re-enlisting and going home has been presented to the men and discussed in the regiment, but I think is now dying out. It is a fine offer for us and would be a saving thing for the country if all these veteran troops could be kept in the field next summer when there comes a crisis as there will. But we haven't any Col, to speak of, and our Regiment can do no such thing in harmony.

I venture to send you another of Mrs. Akers' poems which I found by chance in an old Magazine. I think it was written some time since; while her husband lived. The versification is unique and pleasing and I think it one of her very b<u>est</u>. A letter from home says that perhaps you may spend Thanksgiving there. I can assure you that it is a good place to spend Thanksgiving.

Perhaps I should apologize for these chips of paper. I didn't want to frighten you with a broad-side of foolscap and resorted to this awkward stratagem to avoid doing so.

Hard tack[76] is getting wormy, and we sigh for soft bread. If we remain here for several days we shall get it, but I think we'll not stay.

Good-night

E. H. Higley

Stone House Tavern at Bull Run, March 1862.
Library of Congress, LC-DIG-ppmsca-35124.

***

On November 7th a breakthrough was made at the vulnerable Kelly's Ford where two Confederate regiments were taken. Union troops also crossed the river upstream at the Rappahannock Station bridge; the combination forcing Lee to move his army south across the Rapidan River on November 10th. With the successful action by Union forces at Kelly's Ford on November 7th, the regiment crossed the Rappahannock on the 8th and moved into winter quarters near Stevensburg, Virginia eight miles east of Culpeper which they had abandoned only a month earlier. Fifteen days after his previous letter, Higley is safely ensconced in paperwork at the 1st Vermont's camp, having endured the soggy depredations of picket duty. His thoughts turn to literary nuances as found in *Counterparts* by Elizabeth Sheppard. Following on the recent discussion about John Halifax, Higley now considers the effect of manhood and religion embodied in the ideal of "muscular Christianity;" a concept popularized through the writings of Charles Kingsley, whereby physical vitality and Christian morality together produce a growing Victorian chivalric ethic.

Ammunition train of 3rd Division Cavalry Corps, Brandy Station, 1864
Library of Congress, LC-DIG-ppmsca-33254

Camp 1ˢᵗ Vermont Cavalry
Near Stevensburg Va. November 21ˢᵗ 1863
Saturday night

My dear Noble,

I suppose that you are writing me to-night, and I am sure that it is sweet that I should look toward you at the same time. Perhaps my letter may catch some of the same worth which suffuses the Saturday night message with which you have so regularly blessed me. I believe that I need not tell you how much they are worth to me. Perhaps it is not known to you how the fact of their regularity increases their intrinsic value. I always know "what to depend on." By Wednesday or, at least Thursday they have always reached me. Last Saturday I was down on the Rapidan. Williamson and myself had spread out our fly and were getting cosily settled for the night, when it began to rain. It so happened that we were in a low swamp, which soon became flooded, and our blankets swam; our contraband brought us a large door taken from an old house, near by (which we, being on picket had not thought proper to enter) But in a short time the door swam also, and our condition was decidedly too aqueous for comfort. At last, desperation drove us to the deserted house aforesaid, we; smothering any superfluous qualms of the military conscience by expressing the belief that the water would forcibly move us from our post before morning; hence a prudent removal to terra or domus firma⁷⁷ would save our valuable lives to the service. But it was all the while raining like – Virginia, and we were well drenched for the night, before our transfer was effected. Williamson was having a similar experience to-night perhaps. At least it is very rainy and he is down at Racoon[sic] Ford on picket whither the regiment went this morning. I am left in camp, and have no command, and as I wish to make out some returns required by the Ordinance Bureau to absolve myself from my accountability during my brief tour of staff duty to which I referred. Hence to-night I am under the fly which by the aid of sundry ponchos makes quite a protection.

Here is a letter from home saying that you will be there next week, so I will send this to you there. I presume you will hear something interesting from this army by the time this reaches you. Present indications point to a grand advance and soon; but of course we can tell nothing positively. Col. Sawyer has gone to Vermont, recruiting. Perhaps you may have the pleasure of seeing him.[78]

Williamson is reading ~~Charles~~ "Counterparts," and pleads to be allowed to finish it. I will send it if he can preserve it. I didn't intend to refer to any sexual influences or emotions in what I said about "Odyle;" And when you spoke of my being "disgusted" at the chapter, I half repented of having found any fault with the book at all. As a whole it is so exquisitely perfect that it is difficult to give it anything but admiration. I was clumsy enough always, but out here in the woods, where I never hear or see anything accurate or scholarly, I must be unsuccessfull [sic] in trying to express shades and distinctions of thought. But I object simply to the introduction of the mesmeric doctrine and to the doctrine when introduced. That one man, by the simple exertion of mental or spiritual force, can in any way effect or control anothers physical status or condition is to me absurd, and by sufficient extension can easily be rendered disgusting. I have a little extra feeling on this subject which, if you knew how it had intruded itself almost into our own family and wrought bitterness there in my earlier days you would understand. I think that we should agree perfectly on the "muscular Christianity" question which you touched upon.[79]

We have had soft bread here for several days. Hence we have not disturbed the inhabitants of our "hard-tack." A fellow can get a grim sort of satisfaction when eating worms, by reflecting that he is taking vengeance beforehand, upon them, for their future eating of him! Which reminds me of another original "goal" which came to me all at the other day, and which I will give you the benefit of – Query. What passage in Hamlet is most suited to Gen. Fremont's private readings? Ans. "O! my offence is rank!" – Dont think that I am becoming volatile when I add a new Axiom which we manufactured recently. – "He that eateth worms and knoweth it not; knoweth not that he eateth worms!"

I bequeath to you my share of the Thanksgiving dinner. Pay my most earnest devoirs-ous[sic] to the Chicken pie and all the bewitching appurtenances and appendages thereof which my beloved mother will serve out to you. Ah! well a day! why should I think of them. They are grace notes in lifes melody and have no place in this solid national harmony which I am strumming at.

Tell me what you hear from Brainerd. I see another book from

80

Mrs. Sheppard's pen advertised. Do you know of it? What do you
decide for the winter? At present and with our present prospects you
would be as inaccessible to me at Washington as in Vermont. But if we
should happen to be near the city; I should want you.

Good night
Yours ever E. H. Higley

***

Flush with the recent victories at Rappahannock Bridge
and Kelly's Ford, Meade decided to see if he could further
dislodge Lee by a quick strike across the Rapidan the day after
Thanksgiving. He relied on speed and a simultaneous dash of his
divisions across the Rapidan at the various fords to the enemy's
east. The Mine Run Campaign involved the 1st Vermont Cavalry
at crossings such as Morton's Ford on November 26th and later
Raccoon Ford. Rousted from slumber on the 26th, they awaited
orders at the ford while their dynamic brigade commander
Custer (temporarily heading the division) "electrified" his troops
with a vigorous speech atop a caisson attracting the attention
of defiant rebels across the river who responded with scattered
gunfire. Higley places the failure of the campaign, conducted
from November 26th to December 2nd, at the feet of the infantry
with some justification, but Lee also had the advantage of being
forewarned of Union preparations and although lacking the Union
troop numbers, had shifted his manpower accordingly. Higley's
contempt for the infantry is only matched by his disapproval of
Henry Halleck who operates as chief of the armies until he will be
relieved by Ulysses Grant in 1864.

Higley's next letter shows him caught in the soldier's paradox;
fighting again and again over the same ground, "as if nothing had
happened." He also despairs of the public attitude embodied in
a recent article by Horace Greeley, the erratic editor of the *New
York Tribune,* who questions whether Union generals are fulfilling
their duty. He finds the two-hour oratory by Edward Everett at

the dedication of the Gettysburg cemetery, "lame, watery, and miserably wanting in fire," when compared with the passionate declarations of clergyman, lecturer and abolitionist Henry Ward Beecher, who was touring England for the Union cause. Interestingly, he does not mention the short comments of the president at Gettysburg despite wide-spread newspaper coverage.

Henry Ward Beecher, ca. 1860.
Library of Congress, LC-DIG-cwpbh-03065.

Camp. 1ˢᵗ Vermont Cavalry
Near Stevensburg Va. Dec. 8 1863

My Dear Noble,

    Well, we are here again, just as if nothing had happened. A few files are missing, but we close down the line and forget them. Thanksgiving morning we broke camp at day-light and started southward; inflated to the full with the prospect of "_big_ Things," before us. We halted at the brink of the Rapidan right under the loaded bluffs on our other side. Here our whole division formed close column of regiments _En masse_ and Gen. Custer (now commanding the division) mounted a caisson and with his ringing voice electrified us with the cheering telegrams from Grant, and we gave them three cheers of exalting defiance, which brought the startled "rebs" to peering curiously over the battlements in crowds, and which induced them to return the compliment by straight way opening their guns upon us. We moved into a little more favorable position and spent the day in receiving and replying to their occasional shots. Next morning we charged across the ford, into their rifle pits,- taking fifty prisoners, skirmished through the day with Hills' Corps and recrossed the river at night. The following day we did the same thing over again – our regiment having the advance. Our duty, during the entire movement seems to have been to make a diversion at the upper fords, and wait for Meades thunder below. It was with no slight satisfaction, I assure you, that we thus, -comparatively- laid on our oars and waited for the infantry, whom, since Gettysburg, we have shielded from exposure,- guarded from danger,- fought and ridden round about, protecting their flanks,- covering their retreats,- making their way clear for their advances,- to step up and bear their part in the performance.

    And I presume that our disappointment was only equaled by your own, when we heard but little thunder, and gradually discovered that the grand advance was destined to be a fai_lu_re. Its not a disastrous one, however. And I dont blame Meade at all. Ha_lle_ck is the trouble with this army.[80] Beecher was right about "Apron-strings" last summer. Grant may thank God "for the Allegheny mountains." Every military man has seen the folly of trying to force a way to Richmond through these successive ranges of impassable barriers. But Halleck is a military m_ule_ and persists in dashing his armies against them, and then beheading the Generals who survive. If it hadn't been for Halleck, McClellan would

83

have been in Richmond, last summer, a year ago, and "sanguine people" might look for the end without the aid of so much imagination as is now necessary.

Apropos of that end, I can hardly tell you of what a sickening sensation it gives us fellows down here to read that article of Greeleys in a late Independent, in which he says that "if the Generals in the field do their duty next spring will see our banner waving over a restored Union."-[81] It's not that we are grumblers, or faint of heart: but it shows such a faint appreciation on the part of the people;- (for I suppose lots of them believe it) of the work we have to do, and we fear their exertions to meet it will be correspondingly feeble.   These nine days of motion have given us some terribly cold beds o'nights,- some drenching rains, and rather short rations. They were furthermore like a kind of relapse into the dark ages, by reason of the total absence of all mail, or other communication with the world during that time. When the connection again commenced your Thanksgiving, or rather Castleton letter reached me two days before the one written the previous Saturday at Midd. I am glad you found as much to enjoy at home, also that they enjoyed your presence there as much as you could possibly do, which they tell me is the fact. I rejoice much at some expressions, which I think I understand, in your last Midd letter. You have my hearty God- speed.

I sent a letter to Allie at Midd, which I think did not reach him. Will you look in the office for it and if there send it to him? The boy has done well – he will do better before he is through. His temperament is not of the sky-rocket kind.

I have not seen the Dec. Atlantic but will do so when I can.

I have been reading all of Beecher's late speeches both here and in England.[82] What a glorious thundercloud he is! How lame, watery, and miserably wanting in fire, seems Everetts Gettysburg oration beside him.[83] Did you read it? And do you remember how he compared the martyred heroes who sleep there, with the black hearted leaders and authors of this rebellion, and condescended to say that the former occupied a more desirable position then awaited the latter? I wonder if it is a necessity that a life of scholastic study and purely literary pursuits should give a man such absence of back-bone, faith, or fire, as he exhibits. -- But I ought not to raise the questions. You are a scholar--

Good bye, -- Yours ever,

E.H. Higley

***

Higley is encamped near Brandy Station with the headquarters of VI Corps and is again handling the paperwork of an ordnance officer. For the first time in his military career, he is also on the sick list with an inflamed ankle. He has learned of the death of General John Buford under whom his regiment served in the summer of 1862 as part of Pope's Army of Virginia. His praise for the cavalry commander is effusive but in line with General Buford's earned reputation. His December 16th death is believed due to typhoid.

> *Head Quarters Cav. Escort*
> *Sixth Army Corps*
> *December 20 1863*

My dear Noble,

I have been reading your two last letters of the 7th and the 14th; both of which were written without any word being received from me, and may I tell you that my heart throbbed with a grateful glow as I thought "his heart is surely warm for me, as his interest is not dried up by so long a silence." – Don't accuse me of being willfully remiss as an experiment on your fidelity! But really I mean, if our present prospective quiet continues and grows to be a fact, to endeavor to make some more exhibition of the gratitude which I feel for your punctual and priceless letters. I believe I never felt more self-convicted of meanness in my life, than when it was presented to my mind in your last, that you were paying for one of my letters with two of your own.

I have been visiting for a few days with my company, which is here in good Quarters. (the big "q" is right) I am also in a somewhat crippled condition;- A week ago a little pimple or boil made its appearance on my ankle, which I treated with dignified disregard – allowing my boot to chafe and gall it;- the water to wet it, and the cold to chill it, as if its existence were a myth. The consequence is that the thing has finally become sorely galled by its non-appreciation, has become inflamed with pain and anger and has finally become so swollen up with its retaliatory feelings that I am forced to exhibit nearly twice my *customary pedal dimensions, and like the "Ould Irish gentleman" – to relinquish the custom of wearing "leather on my toes."[84] And so I sit here in the very comfortable tent – warmed with a stove borrowed from a neighboring citizen; and make out returns to the Qur. Masters and Ordnance Bureaus for the Captain, and to-day, thinking of my non-biped or rather <u>biped-and-a-half</u> state I wonder if campaigning will also compel my intellect to hobble club-footed through life. – A train of thought to which your kind words are most cheeringly suited.*

I have never before been subjected (since I had the measles when three years old) to more than half- a day's deprivation of full physical health and activity, and these few days of disability have been not very contentedly endured, nor altogether free from gloomy thoughts, such as that this was a sort of preparatory discipline for the loss of a limb! etc.

Last night, along with your letter came the December Atlantic directed by Mrs. Akers graceful hand.[85]

There is some talk of our Regiment yet accepting the re-enlistment propositions and going home to recruit, but I have small hopes of its being brought about. Jo. Perkins has word of Mr. Dennisons serious illness. I trust it is not dangerous.

My friend "Frank,"[86] sent me a small photographic picture of Beatrice. So your room and my valise have some adornments in common.

Perhaps I have no need to tell you how gladly I have welcomed the poem which you sent me, or how rejoiced I am at the con<u>fiding</u> glimpses which you have lately occasionally given me of your impulses and intentions in regard to the future. I was glad to hear of Brainerd. He and I never got very near together, although we were growing so when I left college, and I fancy the boy has thought that society changes had produced a partial estrangement on my part. But although thus "standing afar off" I have ever felt the warmest appreciation of his strength and worth. If you write him assure him of my sympathy.

I have never been so saddened by the death of a stranger, as I have been by that of Gen. Buford.[87] I have already spoken of him to you I believe, but I have never, I am sure, expressed half of the admiration, the respect and enthusiasm which I and all of us have felt for him. He was our Brigade Commander during Pope's campaign of a year ago, and I was thus daily a personal observer of his doings and of himself. He was young, - when I first saw him I thought him boyish, in appearance. But a more intimate observation dispelled the impression; Calm, gentle, dignified, possessing the mildest, purest blue eye which I ever saw in man or woman; his _personél_ in repose was winning and attractive. But under fire he was sublime and glorious. His countenance was radiant, his eye flashing, yet he never lost that calm, confident smile which inspired his men ever with absolute trust in his ability. During the last six months activity he has commanded a rival division to our own (Kilpatrick's) And though our admiration has often been strong for our present commander yet Buford's old men have only loved him the more from the comparison. He had more than Kilpatricks electric rapidity of conception and action, and none of his heedlessness. Kilpatrick is always unsuccessful in a retreat. Buford could never be thrown by any catastrophe into disorder. Then, his patriotism was remarkable. A Kentuckian by birth, of a wealthy secession family, with all the personal interests urging him to the other side, with the bribery of ~~high~~ offers of high position, tempting him to the rebel cause, yet his high chivalric sense of honor decided him to leave home and friends and wealth and offered rank, rather than desert the flag whose breezes had nourished him, and for which his love had grown with his growth. He has not been honored according to his worth,- He was not a politician or a wire-puller hence he was not promoted. He was not a newspaper man like Kilpatrick, hence he was not known to the world. But those who served under him grieve that their bright glorious hero has gone, and that he has left a va_cuu_m in the army which n_o_ li_vin_g cava_l_ry officer is large enough to fill. You will understand, when I say this how I can be very glad that the rumors that our nominal leader Pleasonton, was to supercede Meade, have subsided.

It is getting on in the night – cold as winter – but I am warm. I wonder how Williamson fares down on the Rapidan on picket without a tent. Ugh! I am not quite so sorry about my foot after all!

Good night
Ever yours

E. H. Higley

On the last day of 1863, Higley has returned to the regimental camp finished, for now, with his administrative ordnance duties at Corps headquarters. Readying for the bleak winter days ahead, they've received permission to establish more permanent winter housing. Reflecting on this pause in the fratricide, Higley looks skyward and imagines the sleigh-bells of home and revels in the news that Noble has, as a surrogate, found Christmas in Castleton with Higley's loved ones. But always he comes back to the comfort given by his books, offering his critique of Elizabeth Sheppard's *Rumor* and its metaphorical representation of Beethoven. He encourages Noble's own "miscellaneous writing" and points with a youthful pride that it is '64 and they both "own a share in the word." The youthful survivor of two years of war then remarkably notes that in two short months he will be, "of age," by turning 21.

Edwin Hall Higley, ca. 1870.
Photo courtesy of Francis C. Guber Collection.

[While this letter is dated New Years Eve 1864, it is clear that it was composed during the evening of December 31, 1863 and perhaps the early hours of January 1, 1864. Higley was being held as a P.O.W. between June 1864 and March 1865. (ed.)]

Camp near Stevensburg Va.
New Years Eve 1864

My dear Noble,

Your welcome letter came with more than usual promptness, reaching me yesterday. I have just returned from my prolonged visit to the Sixth Corps and the cozy quarters there, and find that even the Cavalry have at last received permission to make themselves comfortable. All day yesterday and to-day we have been hard at work, endeavoring to do so, but our efforts have not yet reached completion. Let not anything of you save your spirit wander hither to-night! It seems to me almost impossible that these troopers have lived in the open air until now, with such good health and spirits.

To-night the air is cold and crisp; to look up at the clear winters sky one can almost imagine that he hears the music of the sleigh-bells,- but a glance at the ground with its ragged stucco-work of frozen mud, dispels the home-sickening illusions.

I was as much pleased as surprised to find you at Castleton. Your letter which reached me Christmas hardly gave me reason to suppose that you were there at "home." It is very pleasing to me to see that you find it pleasant there. I have had some good-natured epistolary sparring with my friend Frank on Church questions. She, you know, is a rigid Episcopalian, and recently flung at me the old Puritanic abhorrence of ke<u>epin</u>g Ch<u>rist</u>mas; and I am very glad that your report of our Christmas festivities will give me a weapon to strike back with. I have nothing to say of "Sunbeam." Her name accords well with her shining face, but for my further particulars I must refer you to Allie.

I received "Rumor" a few days in advance of your letter, and have commenced it with much interest. I find it hard to reconcile my idea of Beethoven with Redomont's contempt for the <u>pia</u>no. I suppose that I am somewhat sensitive upon the subject ~~of~~ it being my only and favorite instrument. But I am sure that <u>all</u> of Beethoven's piano music was <u>not</u> "spun from the refuse of his brain." To say nothing of his *Adelaide* – which R.S. Willis, I think, has said would alone place him highest among musicians,[88] and which contains fully as much in its warbling accompaniment as in its voice parts; there are some of his Sonatas written expressly for the Piano, in some of his later days,- the *Pathetique* for one – I think. I may be foolish to say this, out here in the woods, where I can get no confirmation of ~~this~~ what I say. But I have so strong an impression that I dare do so, and am willing to be corrected. I am sure as I think I said once before that Beethoven has left us hardly anything which is so well adapted to the organ as to the piano.

Be patient – Williamson has nearly finished "Counterparts," in more senses than one, and I will send what is left thereof. Please read what she says of Cecelia's *Airo de Ballet*, remembering her treatment of Chopin. I had a good talk with Crane a few days since. He confessed that he had been discussing the merits of cavalry with you. I regret that it was in his power to give an account of an affair which was not particularly to our credit. At Bucklands Mills, for the first time in my cavalry experience of two years, our division (which was moving in advance of the army, as usual, and making it safe for our infantry friends to follow in) was compelled by Kilpatrick's rashness to fall back inside of our infantry lines. And, as ill luck would have it, the Sixth Vermont were the supports of those lines. Our regiment, although miserably handled, (Col. Sawyer was in command) went off in perfect order. But some Michigan troops, which had been dismounted to fight on foot, and had been separated from ther horses, were obliged to mount at random and get back in considerable confusion. Now it is a well-known fact that to infantry and all uninitiated eyes a score of mounted men, moving at a gallop, appear a hu<u>n</u>dred; and hence these stragglers seemed to the gallant Sixth, as a multitude. Our division was followed only by a small squad of rebel cavalry to pick up stragglers, and these our friends easily repulsed, and supposed that there had driven back the whole horde who had routed us. I wanted you to have my own (ergo, the true) version of this affair. Don't think that Crane and I, or any of us have any personal feeling on the subject. Our antipathy is confined entirely to the two arms of the service in the abstract.

The pictures are most welcome. I hardly recognize the ambrotype. It is an excellent picture, but perhaps it is the plumpliness to which you allude. But the eyes, if you will let me say so, seem to

*have less eager burning and a more well-fed expression than I have
remembrance of. I presume that this is due to your having laid aside
work, and entered upon the "library-browsing" of which you spoke.*

*If our plans work well, by tomorrow night, we shall have some
conveniences for keeping you warm, and I need not tell you that if
any plan could be made to work by which you could act upon – the
suggestions of a visit which you have dropped of late, that nothing could
be more pleasing; unless perhaps I should except the ending of the war
and disbanding of the army. You must give me a taste now and then of
that "miscellaneous writing" which forms part of your daily programme.*

*This is '64. We own a share in the word, 'though it will never
mean to me all that it must ever be to you. This too is January – O dear!
I shall soon be of age! A happy New Year – a million of them to you!*

Goodnight

Ed

NOTES:

[1] Transcriptions of Higley Correspondence, December 9, 1862.

[2] Sherman family files, Fairfax County Historical Society. See also: Gary William Hanson, "Descendants of James Sherman," *The Sherman/Morgan Family Home Page*, (March 14, 2001). Web, 11/20/2103. http://familytreemaker.geneology. com/users/h/a/n/Gary-William-Hanson/GENE2-0002.html; Transcriptions of Higley Correspondence, January 7, 1863.

James Sherman purchased Ash Grove on June 20, 1851. According to the *Ash Grove Historic Site General Management Plan and Conceptual Development Plan*, Sherman's migration south paralleled that of many northerners of the time. The report says that Sherman was a "person of some prominence." See Historic Site General Management Plan, (April 2000), 3. Ash Grove today is a county park site. Higley was made a 2nd lieutenant on July 16, 1862.

[3] The word caput in Latin literally means head or top. This may be Higley's own slang for the Latin word capitula which refers to any head or head-like expansion.

[4] Colonel **Edward Bertrand Sawyer** (1828-1918), whom Higley had criticized and openly opposed, along with other of the regiment's officers. Sawyer studied law with his father and was admitted to the bar in 1849. He was a Vermont delegate to the convention which nominated Abraham Lincoln. His strong hatred of slavery drove him to volunteer in 1861. He assisted in forming Company D of the Fifth Vermont Volunteers and recruited for Company I of the 1st Vermont

Cavalry. Sawyer's command ability would again be called into question during the Dahlgren-Kilpatrick raid on Richmond in March of 1864 when he held brigade level responsibilities. He was transferred after the raid to administrative duties and finally pressured to resign his commission in April 1864, a move endorsed by Brigadier General Custer who believed it would be in the best interest of the service and "particularly for the regiment." See: Hoffman in Ide, *History of the First Vermont Volunteers,* fn 15, 334; Collea, *The 1ˢᵗ Vermont Cavalry in the Civil War,* 222; Benedict, *Vermont in the Civil War,* Volume II, 576.

[5] **James Ewell Brown "Jeb" Stuart** (1833-1864). Stuart was the very capable commander of Confederate cavalry during the war, known for his ability at reconnaissance. As a young officer, Stuart served in the west during the violence which plagued Kansas just prior to the Civil War. There he married the daughter of Lt. Colonel (later Union General) Philip St. George Cooke. Stuart would be mortally wounded at the battle of Yellow Tavern May 11, 1864 where Union Cavalry, including the 1ˢᵗ Vermont Cavalry, were engaged. See: Jeffry D. Wert, *Cavalryman of the Lost Cause: A Biography of J.E.B. Stuart* (New York: Simon & Schuster, 2008).

[6] **William G. Cummings** (1838-1918) was taken prisoner while on patrol on December 28, 1862. He was a 2ⁿᵈ lieutenant of Company D. He was paroled in May 1863 and would later rise to the rank of lieutenant colonel. See: Hoffman in Ide, *History of the First Vermont Volunteers,* 322, fn 1. Also: Collea, *The 1ˢᵗ Vermont Cavalry in the Civil War,* 112.

[7] **John Singleton Mosby** (1833-1916), nicknamed the "Gray Ghost," was 28 when the war broke out. He was raised on a farm near Charlottesville in Albermarle County, Virginia. Of slight build, and prone to illness, he became sensitive to others' comments about his physical ability, and was known not to suffer insults easily; a man "not to be trifled with," according to author Robert O'Neill. While at the University of Virginia, Mosby gained a reputation for confrontation and a quick temper. He joined a militia company, the Washington Mounted Rifles, in late 1860. Mosby is credited with discovering the vulnerability of McClellan's flank during the Peninsular Campaign in the spring of 1862 precipitating Stuart's famous "Ride Around McClellan," which secured both men's reputation. Detailed to the command of Thomas Jackson in the summer of 1862, Mosby was captured on July 20ᵗʰ by Judson Kilpatrick while waiting for a train to Gordonsville. He was exchanged after being imprisoned ten days in the Old Capitol Prison in Washington. He convinced J.E.B. Stuart, his commander, to let him form a partisan cavalry unit in the first days of 1863 as allowed under the Confederate Partisan Ranger Act of April 1862. At war's end, Mosby disbanded his partisan unit but never formally surrendered. Ironically, he became a Republican after the war supporting Ulysses Grant in his two presidential bids although he remained a consistent defender of his friend J.E.B. Stuart. He was appointed consul to Hong Kong and later worked for the Southern Pacific Railroad, and the General Land Office in Nebraska before becoming an assistant attorney for the U.S. Department of Justice. He died on May 30, 1916, twenty-five days after the death of Edwin Higley. See: Robert O'Neill, *Chasing Jeb Stuart and John Mosby,* 4, 52-55 and Teri Johnson, "MOSBY'S MAGIC," *America's*

Civil War, vol. 23, no. 6 (January 2011), 30-35. History Reference Center, EBSCOhost (accessed January 9, 2014), 35.

[8] See: "Fairfax County, Virginia," James W. Green, Deposition, Claim 18595, *U. S. Southern Claims Commission, Allowed Claims, 1871-1880,* December 20, 1875, 100-144.

[9] See: Edith Sprouse, *Fairfax County in 1860: A Collective Biography,* Historical Society of Fairfax County, 1996.

[10] Transcriptions of Higley correspondence, March 10, 1863.

[11] Henry E. Smith as quoted in O'Neill, *Chasing Jeb Stuart and John Mosby,* 64; Mosby quoted in O'Neill, 79. Henry E. Smith of Company E should not be confused with Henry Dwight Smith of Company K who was the classmate of Higley.

[12] Collea, *The 1st Vermont Cavalry in the Civil War,* 111, 113.

[13] General **George Stoneman** (1822-1894) was made a brigadier general of volunteers in August 1861 and was chief of cavalry for George McClellan during the 1862 Peninsular campaign. Born in Busti, New York in 1822, he commanded Fort Brown, Texas when the Civil War began. He refused orders by his superior, General David Twiggs, to surrender all Federal installations to the Confederacy. In 1864 he was in charge of cavalry for the Army of the Ohio. See: Columbia University, Press. "George Stoneman," *Columbia Electronic Encyclopedia, 6Th Edition* (September 2013): *History Reference Center,* EBSCOhost (accessed January 8, 2014).

[14] O'Neill, *Chasing Jeb Stuart and John Mosby,* 94, 100-101.

[15] Benedict, *Vermont in the Civil War,* Volume II, *582.* Captain **John Woodward** of Company M, will later be killed during desperate fighting near Hagerstown, Maryland on July 6th during Lee's retreat. Shortly before his death, he had received word that his betrothed had died of typhoid fever. George Benedict wrote that Woodward exposed himself more freely after that and "evidently welcomed a soldier's death." The 1862 graduate of the University of Vermont was buried next to his deceased fiancé in Cambridge, Vermont. See: Benedict, 606.

[16] O'Neill, *Chasing Jeb Stuart and John Mosby, 110-111;* Mosby biographer Virgil Carrington Jones as quoted in Johnson, "MOSBY'S MAGIC," 33.

[17] **Franklin T. Huntoon** (1841-1922) was born in Rutland County, Vermont in 1841. He joined Company H of the 1st Vermont Cavalry in October 1861 and was promoted to captain a year later. On March 2, 1863, Captains Huntoon and John Woodward and a detachment of 50 men, were surprised at Aldie, Virginia by the famous Confederate raider John Mosby. Both Huntoon and Woodward were taken prisoner. Huntoon was paroled by the end of the month and discharged from the regiment on March 25, 1863. The *Vermont Phoenix* newspaper reported on April 9, 1863 that General Heintzelman considered Huntoon unfit for an officer following the incident which occurred on February 26th at Aldie. One news account reports that he joined the U. S. Navy in July 1864 and remained in

the service until August 1865. Huntoon died in New York on April 9, 1922. See the *Rutland Daily Herald,* April 11, 1922 and James J. Williamson, *Mosby's Rangers* (New York: Ralph B. Kenyon, 1896), 31-32.

[18] In November 1862 **Edwin Stoughton** (1838-1868) was made Brigadier General of the 2nd Vermont Brigade. On a rainy March 8, 1863 Mosby and his men made it past Union pickets to Stoughton's headquarters at Fairfax Court House and took the General prisoner. The event ruined Stoughton's military career. Having not been officially confirmed as a Brigadier General, his nomination was withdrawn and he was not re-appointed after being exchanged two months later. He left the service and became an attorney in New York City. See G.G. Benedict, *Vermont in the Civil War,* Volume II, 426-430.

[19] Escaped slaves were often put to work by Union commanders. It was not uncommon for escaped blacks to be assigned as a servant to an officer in the field. The term Ethiopian was an oft- used euphemism for African Americans in the 19th century. W. Storrs Lee wrote that "one day in spare time he would be teaching his blackamoor aide de camp to read from a primer sent down from Vermont and invariably the lesson would bring back some Middlebury incident." See: Lee, *Father Went To College,* 141.

[20] Popular marching song during the Civil War. The original folk song is believed to be of Irish origin.

[21] A line from Psalms 125:2—"As the mountains are round about Jerusalem, so the Lord is round about his people, from this time forth and for evermore."

[22] A festive gathering at Middlebury College generally near the close of winter term in March. Activities included essays and displays of rhetoric along with musical performances and dancing.

[23] May be abbreviated from the Latin phrase Non nobis, non nobis, Domine Sed nomini, sed nomini tuo da gloriam; Not to us, not to us, O Lord, But to thy name give glory.

[24] O'Neill, *Chasing Jeb Stuart and John Mosby,* 118. Author Elliott Hoffman asserts that Taggart rode into camp drunk on March 17th, according to William Wells and that Wells left for Herndon, not wishing to confront the major. See: Elliott, "A Shot in the Dark, *Vermont History,* vol. 47, no. 4 (Fall 1979), 276.

[25] John Mosby as quoted in Charles V. Mauro, *Herndon: A Town and its History* (Charleston, SC: History Press, 2005), 53.

[26] "St. Patrick Day Herndon Raid Reenactment, March 17, 2013," Herndon Historical Society, Web, January 13, 2104, http://www.herdonhistoricalsociety. org/images/58. St_Patricks_Raid.pdf; O'Neill, *Chasing Jeb Stuart and John Mosby,* 119.

[27] Ibid., O'Neill.

[28] "St. Patrick Day Herndon Raid Reenactment;" Mosby as quoted in Mauro, 54. **Kitty Hanna** recalled that Mosby returned to Herndon two weeks after the incident and apologized to Mrs. Hanna for his men shooting in her home. Seeing a stack of newspapers, Mosby asked if he might have one to read, to which

Kitty responded no , he could not. The polite Mosby reportedly turned and walked away. Hanna's recollections were produced in *Reminiscences of an Oldest Inhabitant: (A Nineteenth Century Chronicle)*, published by the Herndon Historical Society in 1976.

[29] Edwin Higley Volunteer Service File, RG 94, Entry 496. Copies supplied to the editor by the Middlebury College Archives.

[30] Benedict, *Vermont in the Civil War*, Volume II, 581; Hoffman in Ide, *History of the First Vermont Volunteers*, 90-91.

[31] Edwin Higley Volunteer Service File, RG 94, Entry 496. The poor condition of the Vermonters' horses was supported by later testimony including that of Corporal **Daniel Warren** of Company H, who wrote that "our horses had received very poor fare at Drainesville as we often had to go three or four days in succession without grain. Hence there was a good deal of straggling and confusion as some of the horses could not keep up . . ."

[32] Ibid. The "Old Guard" referred to may be members of the 3rd U.S. Infantry, which is the oldest regiment in the American army. It saw combat during the Civil War and was often stationed near brigade or division headquarters. Today it serves as a presidential honor guard. See: http:// www.3rdusinfantrycompanyb.org/

[33] Ibid. The information concerning Mosby's rear guard preparations came from testimony by Lieutenant Alexander Watson, taken captive that day, who heard it from Mosby the day after the Herndon raid.

[34] Edwin Higley Volunteer Service File, RG 94, Entry 496; Report of Charles F. Taggart to Col. R. Butler Price, March 24, 1863, *The War of the Rebellion: A Compilation of Official Records of the Union and Confederate Armies, 128 volumes, Washington D.C., 1890-1901*, Series I, Volume XXV, Part I, page 65. Daniel Warren in Edwin Higley Volunteer Service File, RG 94, Entry 496. Robert O'Neill wrote that Taggart was a "very intimate personal friend of Price who believed Taggart to be '"a man of merit and sterling integrity.'" See: O'Neill, *Chasing Jeb Stuart and John Mosby*, page 281, fn24.

[35] O'Neill, *Chasing Jeb Stuart and John Mosby*, 141.

[36] O'Neill, *Chasing Jeb Stuart and John Mosby*, 142-144, 281, fn 24,; Benedict *Vermont in the Civil War*, Volume II, 585-587; Transcriptions of Higley correspondence, April 2, 1863. Taggart was killed in action on October 22, 1863.

[37] Transcriptions of Higley correspondence, April 2, 1863; Edwin Higley Volunteer Service File, RG 94, Entry 496.

[38] Edgar Pitkin in Higley Volunteer Service File, RG 94, Entry 496.

[39] Colonel Edward Sawyer in Higley Volunteer Service File, RG 94, Entry 496. Accounts of Higley's dismissal for cowardice began appearing in area newspapers by early April. The *Burlington Free Press* touted Higley's promotion under Colonel Tompkins for meritorious service. "He is apparently dismissed," wrote the paper, "on the recommendation of one Colonel [Taggart] for lack of the very same qualities which gave him prominence under another." The *Vermont*

Watchman and State Journal was "confident Lt. Higley was unfairly treated." See: *Burlington Free Press*, April 17, 1863, pg. 1; *Vermont Watchman and State Journal*, May 15, 1863, pg. 1.

[40] Higley to Senator Soloman Foot, February 10, 1864 in Higley Volunteer Service File, RG 94, Entry 496.

[41] Higley to Senator Soloman Foot; Benedict, *Vermont in the Civil War*, Volume II, 610. Since Higley received the paperwork authorizing him to rejoin his regiment on July 9th, he had time to participate in the 1st Vermont's re-occupation of Hagerstown, Maryland on July 12th. The regiment and other cavalry units were shadowing the retreating Confederates of Lee's army and harassing them when possible. Colonel Sawyer rejoined the regiment on the 10th and Colonel Othniel De Forest took command of the 1st Brigade on July 9. The 1st Vermont Cavalry reportedly did not participate in the skirmish at Falling Waters on July 14th, as cavalry under George Custer attacked Lee's rear guard at the Potomac River crossing. See: Collea, *The 1st Vermont Cavalry in the Civil War*, 193.

[42] See: National Archives and Records Administration (NARA); Washington D.C; *Returns from U.S. Military Posts, 1800-1916*; Microfilm Serial: M617; Microfilm Roll: 1497.

[43] It is highly probable that Higley is referring to a very popular Victorian novel of the day, *John Halifax, Gentleman* published in 1857 by Dinah Mulak (later Dinah Mulock Craik). The story follows the rise of John Halifax from poor orphan to self-made hero and gentleman. Temple University Professor Sarah Mitchell, wrote that Craik celebrated middle-class values such as "self-help, self-denial, and self-control." Part of Halifax's evolution is the trust imparted to him as a caretaker for the disabled son of his employer, Phineas Fletcher. Any flaws in Halifax's character are muted as he embodies "faith in continued progress," wrote Mitchell, displacing the idea that poverty was a disgrace. The purpose of the character of Phineas, Mitchell said, "is to admire John Halifax. He unabashedly loves his friend…" Dr. Richard Price of the University of London, Institute of English Studies, explores the relationship further, placing the affection between the two men in a Victorian context. "The author is quite explicit," he wrote, "that his [Phineas'] love for John 'surpasses the love of women.' It is all very innocent, of course, but the adjective 'homoerotic' still applies. . . . Mrs Craik was lucky to be writing in the pre-Freudian era, when the omission of sex was not seen as an evasion." See: Mitchell, "John Halifax, Gentleman: Epitome of an Age," *The Victorian Web*, Web. January 24, 2014, http://www.victorianweb. org/authors/craik/mitchell/3.html; and Price, Amazon Customer Review, Web, January 24, 2014, http://www.amazon.co.uk/review/RCVJMDCZF3YT5.

[44] Higley may be referring to one in the chain of hotels owned and operated by the Leland family in the 19th century.

[45] (NARA), *Returns from U.S. Military Posts, 1800-1916*; Transcriptions of Higley correspondence, September 23, 25, 1863.

[46] General **Judson Kilpatrick** (1836-1881). Kilpatrick, dubbed "Kil-Cavalry" by the men who served under him, was as reckless as he was ambitious. He

chronically sent his men into situations without judgment or knowledge of his enemy's strength. He graduated 17ᵗʰ in his class at West Point, exiting on May 6, 1861. Despite his irresponsibility in the field, he continued to advance, becoming a brigadier general in charge of the 3ʳᵈ Cavalry Division in late June, 1863. A blatant womanizer, he often kept prostitutes with him in camp and was imprisoned for three months in late 1862 and early 1863 for confiscating private property and selling it for personal profit. Considered by some as noble, aggressive and heroic, others derided Kilpatrick as a braggart without brains. Edward G. Longacre referred to Kilpatrick as "flamboyant, reckless, tempestuous, and even licentious." After the war he ran unsuccessfully for governor of New Jersey but political favors secured for him the post of ambassador to Chile where another scandalous sexual affair finally drew the enmity of new president Ulysses Grant, who removed him. Two further political attempts at the New Jersey governorship and Congress failed but President Garfield reappointed him to his former post in Chile where he died of Bright's disease on July 20, 1881. Biographer Samuel J. Martin wrote that "Kilpatrick built his career on boasts, lies, and imaginary victories," but was among the new breed of aggressive cavalry leaders. His poor performance, however, added Martin, "made him stand out in ridiculous contrast to [those] competent officers." Higley's brigade was in Kilpatrick's 3ʳᵈ cavalry division. See: Martin, "Kil-Cavalry," *Civil War Times Illustrated*, (February 2000), 23-30, 56-59; See: Longacre, "Judson Kilpatrick," *Civil War Times Illustrated*, vol. X, no. 1 (April 1971), 25.

[47] **Francis Monroe Edgerton** (1840-1907). He attended Middlebury College in 1860-1861 before enlisting where he was Adjutant of the 2ⁿᵈ Vermont Infantry of Volunteers. He later became a real estate agent. He died December 17, 1907. **Albert Abijah Crane** (1836-1864) attended Middlebury from 1859 to 1861 when he joined the 6ᵗʰ Vermont Volunteers as a 1ˢᵗ lieutenant. He was killed at the Battle of the Wilderness, May 5, 1864. *Catalogue of the Officers and Students of Middlebury College*, 216, 221.

[48] **William Henry Proctor** (born February 12, 1840) attended Castleton Seminary before going to Middlebury in 1859. He left in 1861 and joined Company E, Second United States Sharpshooters, later Company B, 6ᵗʰ, V.R.C. and 24ᵗʰ U.S.C.T., After the war he was a farmer and real estate agent and served in the Vermont legislature from 1890 to 1892. See: *Catalogue of the Officers and Students of Middlebury College*, 217.

[49] **Charles Gastine Newton**. From Rochester, Vermont he went to Middlebury in 1861 and 1862. He enlisted as a second lieutenant with the Tenth Vermont Volunteers and was killed at Cold Harbor, June 4, 1864. *Catalogue of the Officers and Students of Middlebury College*, 225.

[50] **Eugene Wilber** from Lawrence, New York. He was at Middlebury from 1860 to 1862 before becoming captain of Company H of the 166ᵗʰ New York Volunteers. He survived the war and practiced law in Saginaw, Michigan. *Catalogue of the Officers and Students of Middlebury College*, 222.

[51] **Edwin Thomas Booth** (1833-1893), born in Maryland, was the second son of the acting family and the older brother of Lincoln assassin John Wilkes Booth.

He was considered by some to be the greatest American actor and greatest Hamlet of the 19th century. He was performing Hamlet at the Winter Garden Theater in New York City in September 1863 when Higley passed through the city on his way to reinstatement with his regiment. Edwin Booth became co-manager of the Winter Garden in 1864. Between November 26, 1864 and March 22, 1865 Booth performed Hamlet on 100 consecutive nights becoming indelibly associated with the role. Booth mitigated the usual bombastic style of stage acting of the time typified by his talented but flawed, alcoholic father. Biographer Gene Smith wrote that Edwin Booth was "vibrant, poetic, spiritual, his lines delivered with flawless elocution . . ." When asked to compare himself with his father Booth responded, that "I think I am a little quieter." In an ironic twist, Booth is credited with saving the life of President Lincoln's son, Robert Todd Lincoln, prior to the assassination. In the rail station at Jersey City Booth witnessed a young man amid a large crowd on the platform buying a ticket when he lost his footing after shifting train cars startled the bustling throng and he fell between the platform and the rail car and was in danger of being crushed by a wheel. Booth snatched the man by the collar and pulled him to safety. The young Lincoln reportedly recognized the famous actor and thanked him by name. Booth disliked being recognized and hurried off. Booth learned the identity of the young man after a friend, Colonel Adam Badeau, wrote him. Badeau had heard the story from Robert Lincoln himself as both men served on the staff of General Ulysses Grant. See: "Edwin Booth," Encyclopedia Britannica, Web, http://www.britannica.com/EBchecked/topic/73702/Edwin-Booth; Gene Smith, *American Gothic: The Story of America's Legendary Theatrical Family* (New York: Simon and Schuster, 1992), 65, 103.

[52] The Dodworth band reigned over the American musical landscape from 1836 until 1891. The Dodworth family headed by **Harvey B. Dodworth** (1822-1891), were composers, instrument makers and dancers who regularly performed at concerts, political rallies, balls and social events. Harvey Dodworth supplied an estimated 500 musicians for the Union cause during the Civil War, designed the bell back coronet and was the first to introduce reed instruments to military bands. Harvey Dodworth died in Hoboken, New Jersey on January 24, 1891. His brother, Allen Dodworth, considered to be a "dancing master," died in Pasadena, California February 14, 1896. See: "Dodworth Saxhorn Band," Web, http://www. dodworth.org/; *New York Herald*, March 25, 1896, p. 12: *Grand Forks Daily Herald* [ND], January 25, 1891, p. 1.

[53] Poet and journalist of the period, **Elizabeth Ann Chase Akers** (1832-1911) was best known for her poem "Rock Me To Sleep, Mother" written around 1860 and popular during the Civil War. The poem begins: —"Backward, turn backward, O Time, in your flight, / And make me a child again, just for to-night!" She married Maine sculptor Benjamin Paul Akers in August 1860 but he died in 1861. In 1865 she married Elijah M. Allen. See: "Elizabeth Ann Chase Akers Allen," *Encyclopaedia Britannica*, Web, March 12, 2014, http://www.britannica.com/ EBchecked/topic/16165/Elizabeth-Anne-Chase-Akers-Allen.

[54] **Maggie Mitchell** (1832-1918) or Margaret Julia Mitchell was born in New York City in June 1832. She followed her half-sisters into acting first performing when

only 12. In 1861 she opened the work *Fanchon, The Cricket*, in New Orleans. It is based on a novel by George Sand entitled *La Petite Fadette*. Her performance, including an "entrancing shadow dance," created a sensation. She was performing this work at Ford's Theatre in Washington, when Higley saw her. Other admirers included Abraham Lincoln and Ralph Waldo Emerson. Mitchell retired from the stage in 1892. See: "Maggie Mitchell," *Encyclopedia Britannica*, Web, http://www.britannica.com/EBchecked/topic/385948/Maggie-Mitchell.

[55] *Counterparts or The Cross of Love*, was another romantic novel from Elizabeth Sara Sheppard, written when she was 17. George Upton described it as a "musico-philosophical romance" dedicated to the wife of British writer and politician Benjamin Disraeli. See: Upton's introduction to *Charles Auchester in Two Volumes, Vol. I* (Chicago: A.C. McClurg and Company, 1891), 5-9.

[56] Major General **Alfred Pleasonton** (1824-1897) was born in Washington D.C. in 1824 and graduated from West Point in 1844. He served as a lieutenant during the Mexican American war and later with the 2nd U.S. Dragoons (cavalry). He commanded a division of cavalry during the Peninsular campaign and Maryland campaign. In June 1863 he was given command of the Union cavalry corps whose division commanders were John Buford, David Gregg and Judson Kilpatrick. Custer's brigade, including the 1st Vermont, served under Kilpatrick beginning in August 1863. Custer was a favorite of Pleasonton. Pleasonton was replaced by Philip Sheridan in March 1864. He resigned from the service in 1868 and died in Washington, D.C. in February 1897. See: *American Civil War: The Definitive Encyclopedia and Document Collection*, Spencer C. Tucker, (ed.), (Santa Barbara, CA: Abc-Clio Incorporated, 2013), 1538-1539.

[57] Latin for God be with you.

[58] Benedict, *Vermont in the Civil War*, Volume II, 618-619.

[59] Transcriptions of Higley Correspondence, October 22, 1863; Benedict, *Vermont in the Civil War*, Volume II, 623.

[60] Foote, *The Civil War, A Narrative: Fredericksburg to Meridian*, (New York: Vantage Books, 1986), 790-796; Letter, Higley to Noble, Evans Collection, December 31, 1863 to January 1, 1864, (New Year's Eve) in this work.

[61] *Official Records of the Union and Confederate Armies*, Series I, Volume XXIX, Part I, pages 397-398; Higley to Noble, Evans Collection, November 6, 1863 in this work.

[62] Major General **John Sedgwick** (1813-1864) was an 1837 graduate of the United States Military Academy assigned as a lieutenant of artillery in the Mexican American War, emerging as a Major after two brevet promotions. He participated in the Seminole Wars and fought against Plains Indians prior to the Civil War. He was commissioned a lieutenant colonel with the war's onset and was given command of a brigade in February 1862 by George McClellan. Known as "Uncle John" by his men, his personal appearance, according to author Wilmer Jones, was unpretentious. "Sporting a full beard and curly hair, he was short but muscular, weighing over 200 pounds. He frequently wore plain clothes without an insignia of rank and was often mistaken for a common soldier." He was severely wounded during the battle of Antietam and did not rejoin the army

until December 22, 1862. He commanded VI Corps of the Army of the Potomac from Chancellorsville in May 1863 until his death by a sniper at the Battle of Spotsylvania May 9, 1864. See: Jones, *Generals in Blue and Gray*, Volume 1, (Mechanicsburg, PA: Stackpole Books, 2006), 215-228.

[63] **Charles Abraham Adams** (1837-1902) enlisted at the age of 17 and mustered into service on October 1, 1861 with the rank of 2nd lieutenant. He received the rank of 1st lieutenant on October 4, 1862 and was made captain of Company H on April 1, 1863, the same day as the skirmish at Miskel's Farm against John Mosby. Higley feared for Adams' life, when he and 13 other men were taken captive after being cut off from the rest of the regiment. Taken to a prison in Charlotte, North Carolina, he escaped March 1, 1865 (or February 16, according to Elliot Hoffman) and made his way to Union lines around Knoxville, Tennessee and was soon reunited with his regiment. He later received the brevet rank of major in November 1864 and finally lieutenant colonel. After the war he moved near Chillicothe, Missouri and developed a very successful dairy operation. According to a family genealogist, one of his customers was Fred Harvey whose restaurants dotted the Santa Fe railroad line. He met Harvey in a confederate prison. See: Linda M.F. Welch, *Families of Cavendish and the Black River Valley of Windsor County, Vermont, Vol. 3* (Cavendish, VT: Cavendish Historical Society, 1998) as used at http://vermontcivilwar.org/units/ca/adams.php; Benedict, *Vermont in the Civil War*, Volume II, 622; Hoffman in Ide, *History of the First Vermont Volunteers*, n. 11, 330.

[64] Major **Josiah Hall** (1835-1912), born in Westminster, Vermont February 5, 1835. He enlisted as captain of Company H of the 1st Vermont Cavalry on October 17, 1861. He was promoted to major of the regiment October 4, 1862 when Addison Preston was made lieutenant colonel. He would spend time in several Confederate prisons before being paroled on August 3, 1864. He became lieutenant colonel of the regiment on November 19, 1864 and colonel of the regiment May 23, 1865, roughly a month before his discharge from the service. He died a farmer in California March 15, 1912. See: Web, http://www.findagrave.com/cgi-bin/fg.cgi?page=gr&GRid=9747201. Hall, weak from an illness, left the field with the assistance of an orderly. He was captured while trying to relocate and rejoin the regiment. Josiah was the older brother of Nathan Hall who had graduated from Middlebury College in 1861. See: *Catalogue of the Officers and Students of Middlebury College*, 204.

[65] Regimental bands played an important part in the Civil War, not only entertaining troops, providing inspiration or keeping up morale, but supplying a steady cadence for marching troops. Most consisted of brass and percussion instruments. Custer was fond of using his musicians during combat. In 1867, while in command of the 7th Cavalry he adopted a traditional Irish tune Garryowen written for a quickstep dance. The band and that song led the charge on November 27, 1868 as Custer's men attacked the Cheyenne camp of Black Kettle on the Washita.

[66] While it is impossible to know exactly which part of the Sheppard novel Higley is referring to, two passages seem to fit the moment at hand: "Music is, and is eternal. We cannot add one moment to its eternity, nor by our inaptitude

diminish the proper glory of our art." Also, "You all forget that music is the highest gift that God bestows, and its faculty the greatest blessing." See: Elizabeth Sheppard, *Charles Auchester, in Two Volumes, Volume I* (Chicago: A.C. McClurg and Company, 1891), 18, 273.

[67] Following McClellan's decision not to pursue Lee after the battle of Antietam on September 17, 1862, several Union governors met in Altoona, Pennsylvania at the urging of that state's governor, Andrew Curtain. During the meeting, Curtain, a staunch Lincoln ally, and his peers, endorsed the president's emancipation plans and called for the removal of McClellan as head of the Army of the Potomac. In the aftermath McClellan endorsed anti-war Democrat Judge George Woodward who opposed Curtain's re-election in 1863--McClellan regarding it "as called for by the interests of the nation." Curtain won a substantial victory on October 13, 1863. See: *The Daily Intelligencer* [Wheeling, West Virginia], October 20, 1863. In Ohio, Clement Vallandigham, perhaps the most well- known Copperhead leader of the anti-war movement, lost by 100,000 votes in his bid for governor conducted from his exile in Canada.

[68] Higley younger brother Alfred and older sister Emma.

[69] Family friend E.W. Dennison notes that Calvin Noble "was hampered always by a feeble physical frame." See: *Riverside Press and Horticulturist*, July 30, 1885, pg. 4.

[70] Built in 1848, the building was initially the home of the family of Henry P. Matthew. The safety of its stone walls and availability of nearby water made it a perfect site for a field hospital and it was used that way in both battles at Bull Run, in July 1861 and August 1862. It was primarily used by Confederate forces on both occasions. The names of two wounded troopers from the 5th New York Infantry can still be seen in an upstairs room where they were carved. See: "Stone House," *National Park Service*, Web, http://www.nps.gov/resources/place. htm?id=71.

[71] Brigadier General **George Armstrong Custer** (1839-1876) graduated last in his class at West Point in 1861. He was elevated to the rank of captain while on the staff of George McClellan. With reorganization of the Union cavalry following the battle of Chancellorsville in May 1863, Custer was promoted to brigadier general and given command of the Michigan brigade which in August 1863 would include the 1st Vermont Cavalry as well. Vermonters welcomed the change to Custer's command, since it meant more mounted charges and fewer dismounted skirmishes. Known as the "boy general," since he was only 23 when given his general's star, Custer was known for his daring on the battlefield which endeared him to his men as well as for his showy and unorthodox attire. Jeffry Wert noted that, "he wore a uniform of black velveteen, with gold lace that extended from his wrist to his elbow, a wide-collared blue sailor shirt with silver stars sewn on and a red necktie around his throat." Custer's storied Civil War career would be tarnished by the mistakes he made on June 25, 1876 when attacking a camp of Lakota and Cheyenne at the Little Big Horn; mistakes which cost Custer and 268 troopers their lives. See: Wert, "Custer: Boy Wonder Under Arms, Reality and Myth Still Collide on the Battlefields of Virginia and

Pennsylvania," *Civil War Times*, vol. XLV, no. 2, (March/April 2006), 24-25, 28.

[72] **Professor Brainerd Kellogg** (1834-1920): Kellogg graduated from Middlebury College in 1858 where he would be a professor of Rhetoric and English Literature (1868-1880). He then taught at the Polytechnic Institute of Brooklyn where he was Dean of the Faculty from 1899-1907. He was a long-time trustee of Middlebury College (1885-1920). See: Middlebury History Online, http://middhistory.middlebury.edu/brainerd-kellogg-middlebury-college-trustee/.

[73] Characters in *Counterparts*, another romantic novel by Elizabeth Sara Sheppard. Mabel Parker Clarke Hamilton wrote that "*Counterparts*, in its absorption with spiritual contradictions, anticipated a coming fashion, a proceeding as fatal to contemporary fame as falling behind the times." See: Hamilton, *The Lantern* (Bryn Mawr College, 1897), 17.

[74] The initial attempt by Charles Dickens to write a historical novel. Published in 1841, the story is "a case of mistaken identity[;] Barnaby Rudge, the intellectually disabled son of a murderer, is arrested as a leader of a mob of anti-Catholic rioters. Although he is subsequently jailed and sentenced to death, he is pardoned at the scaffold," according to *Encyclopedia Britannica*.

[75] **Stabat Mater:** A medieval Latin hymn on the suffering of the Virgin Mary at the Crucifixion. Generally accepted that the term refers to a 13th-century Catholic hymn to Mary, whose authorship is attributed to either Franciscan Jacopone da Todi or Innocent III. However, Higley is undoubtedly referring to the work produced by Gioachino Rossini, based on the traditional hymn, for chorus and soloists. It contained twenty, three-line verses in ten movements. The eighth movement for soprano and chorus was called the Inflamatus.

[76] Hardtack: A hard cracker or biscuit carried by most soldiers during the Civil War. Made simply of flour, water and salt, it was inexpensive and could be carried for indefinite periods with no threat of spoilage, if kept dry. Due to its hardened consistency, soldiers generally soaked the biscuit in coffee or perhaps cooking grease before consuming.

[77] Latin for solid house.

[78] Sawyer reportedly left that same day along with a man from each company significantly reducing the regimental strength. A year-end report had 623 men and officers on the roster with only 400 available for service, the rest on detached duty. See: Benedict, *Vermont in the Civil War*, Volume II, 626.

[79] The concept of **"muscular Christianity"** became popularized in the mid-19th century. It was the idea or ideal that sport and Christian morality or religion-- physical fitness and manliness-- mutually worked together. The work of former minister, critic and writer **Charles Kingsley** (1819-1875) is largely given credit for promoting these concepts and the phrase although Kingsley reportedly disavowed the connection. The idea fit nicely with Victorians' preoccupation with health and physical vitality. It has some roots in the chivalric traditions of the Middle Ages. R. J. Park wrote that the ideal stressed, "the gentle and perfect knight, loyal to both his king and his God, bound to defend the weak and put down evil; a man who lived in this world and in the enjoyment of wedded life."

See: Park, "The Contribution of Charles Kingsley to the Concept of Muscular Christianity," N.A.S.S.H. Proceedings, University of Maryland, (May 1978), 17-18.

[80] General **Henry Wager Halleck** (1815-1872) graduated from West Point in 1839 and entered the Corps of Engineers and served in California during the Mexican American War. In 1853 he left the army and became a lawyer in California. Appointed a major general in August 1861, he replaced John Fremont in the Department of Missouri in March 1862. Capable as an organizer, his reputation was enhanced by western victories under Ulysses Grant and others. He returned to Washington, D.C. after successfully seizing Corinth, Mississippi and was made General in Chief of the Armies. He was criticized for his indecisive actions and said to favor his demotion to Chief of Staff under Grant in March 1864. He held the command of the Division of the South following the war until his death in 1872. See: "Henry Wager Halleck," *Columbia Electronic Encyclopedia, 6Th Edition* (September 2013): *History Reference Center*, EBSCOhost (accessed January 8, 2014).

[81] **Horace Greeley** (1811-1872) was publisher of the *New York Tribune* which he founded in 1841, making the paper one of the leading newspapers in the country. Considered a member of the radical Republicans, he was often critical of Lincoln's caution in attacking the institution of slavery. He did not support Lincoln's re-election bid in 1864 and by that time had promoted a peace policy which called for negotiations with the South and northern Copperheads. He ran on the presidential ticket of the Liberal Republican Party in 1872. His defeat at the polls, the loss of editorial control of his paper and the death of his wife a few days before the end of the campaign, unbalanced his mind and he died insane on November 29th, 1872. See: *The Columbia Encyclopedia, Second Edition, Volume II* (New York: Columbia University Press, 1958), 816.

[82] **Henry Ward Beecher** (1813-1887) was the fiery, liberal Congregationalist minister and a vehement proponent of abolitionism. He raised funds for the cause of keeping Kansas a free state in the 1850s, sending shipments of Sharpe's rifles to the violent territory which became known as "Beecher's Bibles." The brother of Harriet Beecher Stowe who wrote *Uncle Tom's Cabin*, he journeyed to England in 1863 lecturing against the Confederacy and building support for the Union cause in that important country. The *St. Cloud Democrat* (Minnesota) newspaper called him a preacher without counterpart and a man without precedent. See: *The Columbia Encyclopedia, Second Edition, Volume I*, 174; *St. Cloud Democrat*, December 17, 1863.

[83] **Edward Everett** (1794-1865) was perhaps the most well-known and respected orator of his day. A former president of Harvard, U.S. Senator and Secretary of State, he could "hold mass audiences in thrall," according to Garry Wills. Everett, who was a vice-presidential candidate on the Union ticket in 1860, was also a professor of Greek and praised as the father of Greek revival in the United States. Many felt him the Pericles of America referring to the famed Greek master and he was lauded by Transcendentalists such as Ralph Waldo Emerson. Everett was the keynote speaker on November 19, 1863 at the dedication of the Gettysburg cemetery giving a two hour address prior to President Lincoln's "few appropriate remarks." Later when asking the president for a copy of his

dedication, he said, "I should be glad if I could flatter myself that I came as near to the central idea of the occasion, in two hours, as you did in two minutes." See: Garry Wills, *Lincoln at Gettysburg: The Words That Remade America* (New York, N.Y.: Simon & Schuster, 1992), 24; David Herbert Donald, *Lincoln*, (New York, N.Y.: Simon & Schuster, 1995), 464-465; Paul Revere Frothingham, *Edward Everett, Orator and Statesman* (Boston: Houghton Mifflin, 1925), 92.

[84] The expression "Leather on my toes," can be found in an 1871 work, *Comic Lindley Murray, or the Grammar of Grammars* (Dublin: A Murray and Company, 1871), 56. This was an anonymous parody of work written by Lindley Murray, a grammarian in the early 19th century who produced books on English grammar. Murray (1745-1826) was an author of school textbooks and the largest selling author in the world in the first half of the 19th century. His 1799 publication *The English Reader* was a best seller in the United States running through 256 editions. Abraham Lincoln called this Reader, "the best schoolbook ever put into the hands of an American youth." It is likely that Noble and Higley would have, at some time, used the primer in their school work growing up. The expression and reference to the "Ould Irish gentleman" are probable excerpts from Lindley's books. See: Charles Monaghan, "Lindley Murray and the Enlightenment," *Paradigm*, no. 19 (May 1996), Web, February 4, 2014, http://faculty.education. illinois.edu/westbury/paradigm/monaghan2.html.

[85] Mrs. Akers had published a new poem in the magazine called, "In An Attic." Its last two stanzas are:

> So all who walk steep ways, in grief and night
> Where every step is full of toil and pain
> May see, when they have gained the sharpest height,
> It has not been in vain:
>
> Since they have left behind the noise and heat,--
> And, though their eyes drop tears, their sight is clear;
> The air is purer, and the breeze is sweet,
> And the blue heaven more near.

See: Mrs. Paul Akers, *The Atlantic Monthly*, vol. 12, issue 73, (December 1863), 768.

[86] "Frank" is the nickname Higley has for Noble's older sister Frances Emeline Noble who married Foster Elliott Swift in 1859. See: Boltwood, *History and Genealogy of the Family of Thomas Noble of Westfield, Massachusetts*, 156.

[87] General **John Buford** (1826-1863) graduated from the U.S. Military Academy in 1838. One of his closest friends at the time was upperclassman George Stoneman who commanded the cavalry corps in which Buford would serve as a division leader in 1863. According to historian Edward Longacre, Buford did not get along with Stoneman's roommate, "a dour ascetic from western Virginia, Thomas Jonathan Jackson," later known as "Stonewall." As a young lieutenant he saw service in the west against the Lakota and Indians of the southern plains and spent time in Kansas during that territory's bloody days of the 1850s. He was an assistant inspector general attached to the defenses of Washington, until July 1862 when made a brigadier general in Pope's Army of Virginia

which included the 1ˢᵗ Vermont. He was made chief of cavalry under George McClellan at Antietam and was a corps commander under Meade at Gettysburg and provided valuable assistance to Meade during his October 1863 retrograde movement (Bristoe Campaign) to escape Lee encircling him. He is best known as the commander of dismounted Union cavalry which engaged Confederate troops on the morning of July 1, 1863 at Gettysburg, starting the war's bloodiest conflict. The delaying tactics employed by Buford gave time for Union infantry reinforcements to secure the high ground south of the town which was critical to the Union victory there. Higley's earnest tribute to Buford was in reaction to his untimely death. He became ill in December 1863 probably with typhoid and died December 16, 1863 in Washington. See: Edward G. Longacre, *General John Buford: A Military Biography* (Cambridge, MA: De Capo Press, 2003), 20-50; J. David Petruzzi, "John Buford by the book," *America's Civil War* (July 2005), 24-27; O'Neill, *Chasing Jeb Stuart and John Mosby,* 138.

[88] In Sheppard's novel *Rumor,* published in 1858, Beethoven is portrayed through the character **Rodomant,** cast as the hero of the work, who "has been placed into a love-versus-duty subplot of post-1848 imperial proportions," according to author Matthew Guerrieri. "But all the familiar traits are there—the irascibility, the iconoclasm, even, in the end, the deafness. In great, heavy skeins of Victorian purple, Sheppard winds her tale to a climax replete with an insane asylum, a thwarted engagement, and a heroic carrier-pigeon." **Richard Storrs Willis** was a co-editor of the publication *The New York Musical World* first printed in September of 1852. Willis was a composer in addition to providing many of the magazine's musical reviews. In 1858 his collection of church music titled *Willis' Service Music* appeared in the periodical. See: Guerrieri, "5 Books Inspired by Beethoven's Fifth," Web, January 27, 2014, http://publishersweekly.com/pw/by-topic/ industry-news/tip-sheet/article/54755-5-books-inspired-by-beethoven-s-fifth.html and David A. Day, The New York Musical World, New York, 1852-1860. (Repertoire international de la presse musicale), (Retrospective Index of Musical Periodicals, 1993), ix, http://www.ripm.org/pdf/introductions/ NYMintroEnglish.pdf.

Chapter Four: 1864

Higley is still near Stevensburg, Virginia providing duties of administrative staff as a commissary officer for II Corps of the Army of the Potomac. His friend and fellow officer John Williamson —"glorious Jack"— has gone home on a 15 day furlough. Higley somewhat tersely corrects Noble on his interpretation of the army's special orders incentivizing the re-enlistment of veteran soldiers with a bounty and leave time. It required three quarters of a company to participate for the group and an officer to receive the time away from the battlefield which Higley's company lacked. Otherwise Higley sings the praises of English writer, poet and critic Charles Kingsley and his piano instructor, German-born George Mietzke, who had a great influence on the "growing" musician— the "sad, rippling, foamy tones" of the former mingling with the Teutonic enthusiasm of the latter.

General Judson Kilpatrick with staff and ladies at his headquarters at Stevensburg, Virginia, March 1864. Library of Congress, LC-DIG-cwpb-03721.

Camp 1ˢᵗ Vermont Cavalry
January 12, 1864

My dear Noble

Williamson has just left for the north on a fifteen days leave of absence and left me alone in my glory or rather in my shanty. Dear, honest, faithful, impulsive, stubborn, unflinching glorious old Jack! Thick-headed, in appearance, and (in some things) in reality.-- Yet underneath his blunt exterior, lie finer jewels of feeling, than are possessed by many an empty polish. His patriotism is _perfect_. The duty-path is to him very plain and straight. — The National life is attacked:-- every son of the nation must defend it. — this is his brief summing of the question, and his life conforms, and ever will, to that conclusion.-- This is his first doffing of the harness since he entered the service. You will see him, I hope, before he comes back. If you want to amuse yourself with the cavalry-prejudice, ask him his opinion of the _infantry_ service.

Now I have a mind to deal you a scolding for the presuming manner in which you speak of the probabilities of _my coming home_. If I had discussed _McClellan_ with you, you would have been familiar with some of my philippics¹ against _newspapers_. But I thought that certainly you would not presume to put their statements before _mine_. But here I tell you that we are not coming home, and you prove to me out of the _Burlington Times_ that _we are_! How dare you, sir?

For the facts;--the order allows or rather allowed a regiment to go home if _three fourths_ of its strength would re-enlist. Of course none can enlist save the old original men. Now it happens that the _old men_ do not compose three fourths of our regiment, augmented as we were a year ago by two new companies and over three hundred recruits.²

Hence we cannot go as a regiment without special permission which can not be obtained. About one hundred and fifty have enlisted and will soon go home with some officers. Our company has furnished but eight veterans — not enough to take an officer with them. I suppose you know that persons holding commissions are not _enlisted_ men and can not re-enlist. I was mustered into service for three years from date of *my commission—July 16, 1862.*

     *You ask me a question about the "Sands O; Dee" to which I
cannot give you a very "straight forward" answer. To answer it at
all, I should have to acquaint you with a little heart-history of my
own,--a history as full of shy sensibilities and stunted petty hopes
that I hardly understand it myself, and never tried to make anyone
else do so. I should have to tell you how when fifteen years old and
when I was (musically) growing the fastest—fed by Mietzke's German
enthusiasm and practicing daily on Juliet's piano—I first met with those
weird words of Kingsleys' and how their sad, rippling foamy tones,
mingled with the strains of overtures and symphonies, then sounding
continually in my brain by day and night,--and how half impulsively
and half involuntarily, I gave to the song a musical utterance.[3] There
I was so pleased with the conception of the song—was so sure that it
was really an artistic expression of the spirit of the ballad, that I feared
lest I had borrowed it from the music which I was hearing, instead of
having produced it from my own fancies. So I sang it cautiously to
a few persons asking them if they had ever heard it before, of course
making no claim to its ownership on my part. I found that no one had
heard it before,--that Juliet and another friend said approving words of
it,--and then late with boyish pride I wrote it out and sent to a second-
rate city periodical which furnished regularly a few strains of original
music. Then I waited for two long weeks to see it rejected as worthless.
I presume you never saw anything of your own in the list of "rejected
manuscripts," so you can hardly understand how crushed I was at this
result of my boyish hope, or how I made deep vows never again to think
of , sing, or hum the spurned melody. But this wouldn't end the matter.
Juliet had heard it,--fancied it—called it her song, and so urged me to
sing it to her and a few others whose sympathy I was sure of, never
revealing its origin, but concealing it by all sorts of wicked deceptions,
until at last, I believe, they assumed that it was mine without my
consent. I sometimes used it as a kind of feeler, to ascertain (as I fancied)
the depth or tone of peoples characters,--reasoning that if any persons
liked my song, they would probably like me. So when you asked me to
sing, --yearning as I was to find something wherewith to reach you—I
sang this,--not without some timid fears and vague hopes. When you*

gave it some words of praise, it would have been most errant vanity for me to have claimed it there. Afterwards, when our confidence was more perfected, I should have told you had the time or the talk ever suggested it. —There! my dear boy,--if you would, in the future, avoid a similar rigamarole of egotistic reminiscences,--beware how you ask me such questions!

With this I return your "Counterparts" or what is left thereof.

I have got further on in Rumor, and am ready to retract what I said last, about Rodomonts affected contempt for the instrument, on which, next to the orchestra he displayed his greatest power of creation.

I have been unable to obtain the Harpers which had the organ-picture.

They write me from home sad news of Mr. Denison.

I am still on duty as Commissary though somewhat afflicted after the manner of Job. But I try to imitate the old fellow in character as well as condition.

I had a pleasing letter from Tilden a few days since, who doesn't like his situation very well.

Good-bye

"Fondly thine own"
E. H. Higley

Did I ever send you these lines of Mrs. Aker's? "Frank" says they were written for me.

***

109

Some of the new recruits for the regiment have arrived even as some of the veterans who did not re-enlist leave for home.[4] Higley's new duties now include reciting or directing the recitation by particularly non-commissioned officers, of tactics and army regulations, becoming a sort of "regimental school master," he wrote. The mundane of army requisites and the mud which inundates the camp, give way to his wonder of the novel *Rumor* by Elizabeth Sheppard whose chief character Rodomant is her metaphorical Beethoven—"a glorious willful rugged human with whom we are often indignant." Hearing that Noble will attend a concert of the famous pianist Louis Moreau Gottschalk accompanied by violinist Carlo Patti, the brother of opera star Adalina Patti, has Higley wishing for "wings like a dove."[5]

Louis Moreau Gottschalk, ca. 1860.
Library of Congress, LC-DIG-cwpbh-02956.

Camp 1st Vermont Cavalry
Near Stevensburg Va   January 18, 1864
Monday Evening

My dear Noble

I took up pen to write you an hour ago but was interrupted by the advent into our camp of one hundred and fourteen recruits;--tired hungry and muddy from their equestrian journey from Washington here. I believe enough men are enlisted to fill our regiment. This morning we bade farewell to our Veterans, as they started on their home-ward way. There is but one among them from Middlebury—W.F. Johnson. He, although a cipher[6] so far has personal worth of character, has been a daring and generally faithful soldier, and could tell you many interesting incidents, should you see him.

This coming and going of men has made it a busy, and a heavy rainstorm has rendered it a rather unpleasant day. Mud! Mud! Is now everywhere the cry which greets our ears, and also the reality which splashes in our faces.

I have finished "Rumor," and at Emma's earnest request will send it to her. True enough, "Miss Shephard,[sic] her mark" is upon it and yet how entirely different in many respects from her other books. In the two books which we have read she has given us the phenomena of fictious-novels,- remarkable for the absorbing fascination which clings to them, and yet devoid of that almost inevitable ingredient,- the novelists Villain. But in "Rumor" she seems to have taken a new pen and indulges, as you have noticed, in several hits at sundry of our friends, and also introduces the Villain in various forms and shades, such as Helen Jordan, Porphyro, Rosnelo, and Geraldi. In the latter we have the Villain's absolute—as she says "given up entirely to self" one who would have "made old races take their stand on facts of Satan's influence from the Lord-demon direct." I am somewhat provoked at the heroic death which she finally allows him. My repugnance to him as a character is increased by the mild handling which Miss Shephard gives him all along, in spite of his devilish doings. I wonder if that is really the subtle touch of the master-creative power, which, in order to make an odious character stand out in more detestable colors, touches it gently, as it were, drapes it with a gentle surroundings? I have sometimes thought so. Or is it due to Miss Shephards (as I think) too great tendency to overlook the necessity of an everlasting, though subdued E*vil*, in her exaltation of the E*verlasting* L*ove*?

The l*ove* cannot be too much exalted;-neither do I desire that the Evil shall be constantly harped on and reverted to, but any con*tradiction* of the f*act* my Calvinistic blood jumps at. I was struck with the perceptible difference between her treatment of Rodomant and Serraphael. The former she ad*mired*;-the latter she a*dored*. Rodomant is a m*an*, a glorious willful rugged h*uman* with whom we are often indignant, and out of patience.

But no tint or taint of earthly vesture is allowed to mar or mingle with Serraphaels celestial raiment. Her treatment of Chopin I can no more understand than that of Mrs. Browning. I can readily see how Beethoven, with his strong, vigorous, healthy brain could dislike a musician of so different a cast as Chopin;-just as naturally as Chopin with his shy, sensitive, restive, nature, should be unable to tolerate the bold harmonies of Beethoven,- should feel them jarring upon his restless longings, and unattained hopes. But how Miss Shephard, who should consider not their different temp*era*ments simply, but their individual contributions Toward Art,-should refuse to allow them both a leg*itim*ate albeit distinct niche, in Arts grand temple, I cannot understand.

But I have "rumored" enough I dare say. Do you know that I have been favored with the reading of "College Dreams"?

I see that Gottschalk and young Patti, the violinist (brother of the divine Adalina) are to be in Washington tomorrow evening. "O! for wings like a dove!"[7]

Now that we are surely, and for myself rather leisurely settled the longing for music is getting strong. I have just room enough for a piano in my shanty and am half tempted to make a raid on the inhabitants of this dreary region and forcibly seize one.

We are improving the time (according to order from Hd. Ques.) by having recitations in tactics and Army Regulations-twice a week. The officers all recite to the Lt. Col. Commanding-so you see I am not wholly bereft of study .

Goodnight
Yours,
E. H. Higley

***

Higley received "papers" and "primers" from Noble, which according to one writer were to be used to teach "his blackamoor aide de camp to read." But it is certainly the un-bridled affection for Higley's brigade commander, George Armstrong Custer which springs from the next letter.[8] The "boy general" has captured the enthusiasm of the young lieutenant like none since his esteemed John Buford. Higley was even invited to attend Custer's upcoming nuptials, among others we presume, but, of course could not, although he assisted with sending a gift. Interestingly, initial thoughts that Custer's flamboyant dress signified perhaps their new leader's "effeminacy" were soon quashed by his "irrepressible gallantry" as Custer lived up to his daring reputation as an officer who led from the front. Life at headquarters permitted Higley a close personal glimpse of the renowned Custer even sharing cider with the tee-totaler and his staff.

Contraband youth Nathan Jones, taken at Camp Metcalf, Virginia, ca. 1865. Library of Congress, LC-DIG-ppmsca-11192.

113

My dear Noble

How fare you, you shivering tantalizer, from the frozen region of the North? I write you from the "sunny south,"-now a bright golden reality, and no misnomer.

Such days as this and its predecessors for a week have been, soft and sunny without any glare or snow blindness,-mild and breezy without any bluster,-are the best antidote for your tempting touches of winter enjoyments. And then the moonshine-your crisp, sparkling article is no such stuff as ours,-mellow-soothing, wooing in its glowing richness. Mud alone mars the beauty of the clime, and that is rapidly disappearing. But ah! me!—the brightest land, you know, may be a golden vacuum.

We have diverted somewhat from the ordinary camp routine by the prospective marriage of Gen. Custer who commands our Brigade. Have you ever heard of him? He has a character and person as much adapted to create enthusiasm as any officer with whom I have ever been thrown in contact—Young,--a "boy-general"-he left West Point just before the breaking out of the war with the reputation of being the best swordsman and horseman there in it. He was assigned to the corps of Topographical Engineers—(the highest honor) and served on the staff of several Generals—McClellan for one-by whom he was promoted to a Captaincy for his conspicuous gallantry. His appearance suggested to us effeminacy, for though tall and compact,-his frame was slight and he wore his hair in long, flowing, curling locks down to his shoulders and that hair was moreover of a sunny golden hue. In his style of dress and equipage he carries dash and brilliancy to the highest degree, yet avoiding a tawdry or tinseled appearance.—He wears generally a suit of rich black velvet—the jacket made with a wide flowing collar, upon whose either fold shines a glittering star, and gold lace adorns the whole equipment. Contrasting with this showy presentment, is his perfectly simple and unassuming manner;-and will according with it- his unequalled, irrepressible gallantry-himself actually and really leading every charge-present in every assault.—All of which tends to make the young general *a favorite in the Brigade, although in judgement and skill in handling troops others may be his superior.*

He sent us an invitation to his wedding ceremony at Munro[sic] Michigan on the 10th of February next. As the exigencies of the service dont admit of our leaving the front at present we have made arrangements to send our regards in the shape of a present to the bride.[9] The other evening we all were invited to the general's head quarters, where he treated us to cider (he uses nothing stronger),-told us many pleasant anecdotes of officers-rebel and loyal; with whom he had been acquainted. In parting with us he said — "Gentlemen, I am going to the Department of the West to get either a new <u>command</u> or a new <u>commander</u>, I have not yet ascertained which!" I have had a glimpse at a piano, and next Saturday night shall have another. It's a good instrument, but is in a house used as the Head Quarters of the Division Quartermaster, so that a crowd of shoulder-strapped gentry will be in the room smoking, and drinking punches while I play. — So that I shan't get up a very high inspiration. I know few things more oppressive than to see the "ivory face of the waiting keys" wooing one to the grandest heights and depths of Tone and yet be restrained by an uncongenial atmosphere, from anything more than a trifling, dallying performance.

A grand review of the Division filled up day before yesterday. Some thirty or forty ladies were present, and half a dozen generals. Colonel Sawyer as yet appeareth not,--but recruits are plenty enough. Williamson will be back this week. I shant be surprised if you are disappointed in him, after my apostrophizing in my last. But the gold is there nevertheless, albeit the surroundings are very rough. Those "will-poems"-have helped me. — thank you; from my heart.

I will say more next time
Good bye
E.H. Higley

***

General Gouverneur Kemble Warren.
Library of Congress,
LC-DIG-cwpb-05647.

Still on duty with II Corps, Higley recounts the irritation of being shaken from his rest in the middle of the night to outfit his regiment and gives a blow by blow explanation of the required bureaucratic slogging to accomplish the task which nearly brought him to the point of profanity. After recouping his lost sleep, his boredom is such that he decides to follow the column of Major General G. K. Warren, whom he described that day as "looking gay and full of fight." Warren's demeanor aroused Higley's interest enough to join the troops and witness the action at Morton's Ford. The "demonstration" at the Rapidan River crossing, the day before Higley wrote the following letter, was an attempt to pressure the defenses of Richmond after Lee's shifting of several thousand men to North Carolina. The II Corps crossed at Morton's Ford and after some early success was pushed back across the river by the early hours of February 7th. Warren is reported as leaving the field due to illness early on February 6th presumably a short time after Higley spied the general in such vigorous health. Warren returned and assumed command of the engagement by three that afternoon.[10]

Higley's discussion of the importance of the Sabbath is noteworthy given the pious upbringing of this New Englander. His dread as a youth of the stoic day of "gloom and restraint" is now imbued with the artist's sensibilities and a wider definition of God's love—"shining out from everything . . ." The Sabbath is to be observed, wrote Higley, but free from sanctimony. Whatever is "true" and "beautiful" is a service to God, he argued, whether it be Shakespeare or Soloman or a spiritual liberty found in music, art or nature.

Camp 1st Vermont Cavalry
February 7 1864

My dear Noble

*This letter has been delayed somewhat by the recent-and
I may say present-activity of men and matters here. Night before last
I was aroused from my peaceful slumbers a little after midnight by an
order to issue three days rations to the regiment immediately.*

*I was profoundly sleepy and in the hazy condition of half awakened
consciousness this order seemed stunningly absurd. I can laugh now at
the lethargic logic through which I labored. — My duty being simply to
victual the regiment, I never keep any stores on hand, but draw and issue
at stated periods what is required by the number of men then present in
camp. How they,-thought I — can I issue three days rations tonight? I
have no rations. But at last the conviction forced itself upon me that I
must get them; and this presented so active a necessity that I arose and
awakened to a sense of the situation. To get them, I must arouse the
commissary-sergeant, arouse the teamsters and the mules, arouse the
Adjutant, make out the necessary form for a provision return, get the
number of men, get the signatures of the Regimental commander and of
Brigade-commander – (a mile distant) find the way to the Subsistence
depot of the Brigade- see the proper allowance weighed and measured
and loaded into the wagons and brought back to the regiment, all in
the darkest of night and deepest of mud. Not a very immense thing to
do - yet requiring considerable patience, patriotism and piety to perform
it without some profanity. – (Said more for the sake of minding my
"ps" than any "qs") All this betokened something. And here comes
the detestable part of the position which I now occupy - concerning
which I believe I have before given you my opinion. For after doing the
aforementioned duty I laid down to finish my sleep; while the regiment -
the fighting part thereof - went forth with the division and Kilpatrick and
the rations which I had given them!*

*After I had slept my fill and had arisen the infantry of the 2nd Corps
began to march past the door of our shanty and finally with them rode*

their little commander, Gen. Warren,[11] looking so gay and full of fight, that it aroused my enthusiasm and curiosity to see what he intended to do. And so I rode down with them to the Rapidan and saw the operations of yesterday; saw the soldiers charge across the river at Morton ford (where _we_ charged at the time of the former crossing)-- saw and heard the shells which the rebels threw at them- saw the prisoners taken and the wounded brought off, and the other proceedings of which you will have heard before this will reach you. I came up at night leaving the 2nd Corps across-where they may still be for anything I know. Our division returned to-day, having been down to the lower fords and taken a few prisoners, and slept in the rain, but achieving nothing of importance. It is rumored that a grand movement of the army may take place soon,--but we dont anticipate it.

Two hours later. The infantry are all coming back and everything will probably relapse again to quiet. It was interesting to see the infantry fight as I have been heretofore too much engaged myself to notice them particularly. Williamson is back and has been out with the regiment. He says that the moral standard of the Northern community has _declined_. What do you think of that? He has seen a good deal of Wilbur with whom and whose apostacy [sic] he is thoroughly disgusted?[12]

The or_gan_ arrived and has been duly "stuck up" in our shanty.

I am so much pleased with what you said about the doc_trinal_ question which you touched upon in your last that I am going to ask you another:--namely what do you t_hin_k of S_und_ay? Today is Sunday and the question is certainly in place, if ever. The exigencies of the service have of cou_rse_ de_moral_ized me considerably out_ward_ly and perhaps inwardly upon this subject, but it was always something of a bugbear to me. Dont take what I may say as mental con_vic_tions but rather as tendencies. When I was small, and Sunday was always a day of gloom and restraint, dreaded on its approach,-en_dur_ed on its arrival,--and gladly bade farewell,-and people used to say that Heaven was an Et_ern_al Sab_bath_, I—in common, I suppose, with every boy— used to hope that it might be many, many years before I should be called to go there. And all through the succeeding years the question of the truest observance, has been often cogitated upon, and I have finally formed tendencies, at least, somewhat antagonistical[sic] to the Shorter Catechism. Of course the Sabbath is to be observed. It is one of the few forms by which Christians manifest to the world and to God their obedience to his will. And hence, the observance outwardly, by public worship, songs, hymns, and words of praise is ever necessary. But our early instructions enjoined that we should – apart from this – in our private acts and inner most thoughts exclude the world and worldly things and confine them to contemplations similar to those suggested by the public service. Now although it is certainly fit that every Sabbath should witness a private and personal review of individual progress and responsibility,- yet it seems to me that an attempt to confine the range of one's thoughts exclusively to a theological, doctrinal, or religious channel – besides being an absurd impossibility, – would have, if successful- a narrowing and contracting effect upon a soul, instead of expanding and enlarging it. A man should have his heart so full of God's love that he will see it shining out from everything around him. And so standing free in the liberty of the gospel he should take at will the whole world of Nature of Thought and of Sound and make it all increase his worship. So that it is not by avoiding and excluding the world – that we keep holy the day (the monks tried that) but by using and ennobling it. So I deem the received notions about "Sunday reading" as erroneous. Whatever is good and high and beautiful and true whether it by Shakespeare or Solomon is at his service. The same is true – peculiarly – in respect to Music and Art, and man's wanderings and communings[sic] with the woods and the flowers. Above all, the day should be bright and joyous, a sort of oft-returning Christmas,- free from frivolity but equally so, from sanctimony and gloom. I wish you would talk to me a little about this matter and tell me if I am heretical.

I heard from Prentiss[13] a day or two since, by way of our former Adjutant – Pitkin – who is boarding with his father.

Col. Sawyer is with us again. He is commanding Brigade during General Custer's absence.

My recitations progress passably. My class is quite large, and generally intelligent. If they don't pay attention to the lessons charges for disobedience of orders, and reduction to the ranks would follow.

The wife of one of our Captains arrived in camp last evening.
There are a large number of ladies throughout the army.

Goodbye
Thine Ever
E.H. Higley

***

The day prior to the next letter Edwin Higley turned 21 years of age. It was also the day for a grand review on behalf of corps commander Alfred Pleasonton; the celebratory trappings certainly adding to Higley's personal milestone. Rumors are already circulating that Kilpatrick may be making a move to the Virginia peninsula—the first hints of what will be the controversial raid on Richmond by Kilpatrick and Colonel Ulric Dahlgren in just a few days.

Otherwise Higley muses on great artists of the stage including Gottschalk, and another Lincoln favorite, Felicita von Vestvali, whose popularity was not diminished by her open homosexuality and the rare woman whose theatrical performances of Hamlet were accepted.

George Custer and General Alfred Pleasonton on horseback, April 1863
at Falmouth, Virginia. Library of Congress, LC-DIG-cwpb-04041.

My dear Noble

We had yesterday the grandest review of the season—a review of the 1st and 2nd divisions of Cavalry by the corps commander,-Gen. Pleasonton. It was so grand a sight,-fluttering pennons,-[14] prancing horses,- flashing sabers,-glittering buttons and shoulder-straps,-all the cannon bristling, -all the music and bugles sounding and all the vast plain resounding, quaking under the mighty head; and besides and beyond all,-a brilliant array of feminine beauty,- that I wished from my heart, my dear fellow that you could be there. Parades of ceremony are the only things in which we get the _beautiful_ in this business. A review such as we had yesterday is ideal hero-worship re_alized_ or perhaps I should say emblematised.[sic] —The commanding General is the _Chieftain_ – _the hero_. And the whole parade is ostensibly to do him honor. So when he appears along the line, with his brilliant retinue,-all the banners droop,-ten thousand sabers flash and fall, "Hail to the Chief" — bursts from the bands, -the bugles blare the "flourish," and all in reverent ho_m_age to the hero of the day.

Had I not been required and employed, by the proceedings of yesterday I should have written you then,-For you know yesterday was the 15th,-_my birthday_. The boundary line between youth and manhood is past,-let no one call me _boy_ again! Alas! When I was a boy, and used to look forward to _majority_, in the far distance, how much higher in thought and attainment I expected to be on its arrival, than I now find myself! I don't say this so much disconsolately or regretfully as re_flectively_. It is possible that a maturity which my bluff hearty brother by your side does not need, I may gain in this rough collision with men and things.

I went to ch_u_rch twice last Sunday. There has been erected under the auspices of the Christian Commission a canvas chapel for our Brigade, which makes quite a comfortable little place for worship. Kilpatrick too has been erecting a division "Hall"—as he calls it—which it is intended to use for theatrical and generally didactic purposes. It is quite tastefully trimmed with ~~satin~~ silk muslin[15] in stripes-red, white, and blue and the stage is adorned with much care. Here we had preaching on Sabbath P.M.

121

On the right of the pro-*tempore*[16] *pulpit was a rough but well-done fresco full length figure of Kilpatrick-standing in full dress and characteristic posture,-"a la slouch;" on the left of the reverend gentleman was a not over-dressed figure of the Goddess of Liberty. But we had a very good sermon nevertheless. I had another good letter from Mrs. Akers a little since. How I wish you could know her. – She sent me another little snatch of poetry which I enclose and would like again. Did you notice the allusion to Italy in her "Snow?" It is a frequent occurrence in her writings and her talk. Indeed in almost all of her quiet, glad poems, of recent date something of Italy occurs. It was there that she spent her happy days—full of golden joy they must have been. (more glad because of sad ones which had preceeded them)—while her husband lived. I never heard Gottschalks "Dying Poet" of which you speak. But from two full evenings of his playing, and a little private dallying with his compositions – I think you would not find in it all which you would seek. Gottschalk is the greatest artist whom I ever heard. But he is a part of Nature, – not human nature. He attains almost to perfection in rendering the ripplings of winds and waters, the rustling of leaves, the weird whisperings of the night, the flashing of fire and lightning, and in witching "Coquetries," "Fantasies" and appeals to voluptuous passion. But he rarely attempts and (to my mind) never succeeds in expressions the royal wealth of love, of any dealings with the world of soul. He is a larger way like Moore of Burlington,[17] – full of grace and elegance and beauty, and of course not devoid of feeling, and yet somehow not satisfactory in bottom. I have never heard anyone who fed me so much as Mietzke, and he lacked tenderness and delicacy. I have never heard Thalberg or Wallace,[18] the latter of whom I fancy is our truest pianist.*

The wind is howling fiercely to-night, and has been all day shaking and straining our canvas covering, and giving us some few apprehension ~~that~~ lest it tear the old weather-beaten thing to shreds.

A squad of shivering recruits arrived to-night. "Poor fellows!" says my cynical little African imp. — "they came out for money, – Let em shake!"

I have been rather hoping to be able to go to Washington before the winter is over, but presume I must give it up. The theatrical season has been quite a brilliant one there. Mrs. Akers speaking of Vestvali,[19] who has been attracting attention there and elsewhere says although "I am not apt to be carried away by burnt cork, carmine and the glare of footlights,--I do not hesitate to say that I think her a grand woman, possessed of more force and power than generally falls to the lot of even distinguished women."

There is a rumor, which we don't believe, that Kilpatrick with this division will go to the Peninsula to Butler.

Our Generals are all away just now. — Col. Sawyer is commanding the Division temporarily.

I must get this into to-night's mail. With the first benediction of my new m*an*hood (pray God it may be real as well as nominal)

I am yours

E.H. Higley

Sheet music featuring Felicita Vestvali. Library of Congress. Music Division. Microfilm M 3106 M1.A12I vol. 75 Case Class.

***

Higley describes the hurried but thorough preparations for the famous raid on Richmond. The stated goal was to liberate Union prisoners from the city's pestilential Libby and Belle Island lockups. Papers allegedly found on the body of the dead Dahlgren will raise the specter of much more—a plot to kidnap or kill Jefferson Davis and his cabinet. Sedgwick's VI Corps was to create a diversion along the Rapidan permitting Kilpatrick and his nearly four thousand riders to slip behind enemy lines unnoticed twenty miles downstream. In a new twist, cavalryman Higley will not be with his regiment but has been assigned to Battery C of the 3rd U.S. Artillery since many of their re-enlisting veterans have traveled home for furlough, leaving the unit shorthanded. He humorously points to the gaps in his training with artillery telling Noble that the only command he really knows is, "Fire!" Perhaps his greatest disappointment due to the latest military action, however, is being forced to miss Karl Anschütz perform Faust in Washington.[20]

General John Sedgwick, ca. 1862.
Library of Congress, LC-DIG-cwpb-06381.

My dear boy

I cant write you what I wish, nor as much, this afternoon because things are getting "somewhat mixed" as we say, and there is a prospect of speedy movement of some kind. I wont be divulging state secrets (for by the time this reaches you it will be no more a secret), that we move to-night at dusk, and anticipate something huge. The Sixth Corps went toward Culpeper yesterday and all the other cavalry have gone somewhere, so that something of importance is going to happen. I wouldn't write you until it was all over only that I have waited too long now and it may be a week before we are quiet again. And then too it may all be only a sham, and you will smile as you read this over my dampened anticipations. But I believe you have generally found me pretty "konservitiv," and not over-sanguine, on army movements heretofore. This is one of the intoxicating, bewildering and yet fascinating parts of "the business." Nothing is known, definite, or positive; – but everything vague, ominous and portentous. Rations of hard tack coffee and sugar accumulate to the disparagement of rations of fresh beef, soft bread, potatoes and other vegetables. Ordinance [sic] officers are examining and replenishing amounts of cartridges . – Servicable horses are picked out and assigned to serviceable men. – Saddles and other accoutrements are examined, repaired and renewed. – Recruits are sent (with ludicrously forlorn and fortified faces) to grind their sabers. Instructions are given for but one blanket and overcoat to be worn or carried, – And yet no one in the Regiment has the least idea in what direction or with what intent anything is proposed to be done.

I am not pleased at the part I am to fill in the performance, but it is much better than being left behind. The battery men Attached to the division have recently re-enlisted as Veterans, and now half of their men and two of their officers are absent on furloughs and leaves. Hence there [sic] places are filled from the cavalry, and I am one of the officers detailed. Artillery service is glorious (compared with infantry), and good by its own merits. But I am utterly ignorant of its every detail, – dont know an order in its tactics (except "Fire!") and couldn't execute an item of its manual. Imagine me, there on "ye fiery feylde"[sic] "standing by the guns."—"Un-hitch that thing behind there!"- "Head it round the other way!" "Shoot her off!" etc will be my intelligible instructions. However, being nothing but a Second Lut,[sic]-I trust that no particular responsibility will fall upon me. We are visited this morning by quite a number of citizen dignitaries from Vermont. Arriving there are his Excellency Gov. Smith, Mr. Holbrook Jr.[21] and also I notice Dwight Smith's amiable correspondent—Mr. E.S. Dana of the patent office who married one of those big Squires' damsels from New Haven with whom I used to go to school at Castleton Sem[inary].[22]

I am very grateful for the account which you give of your Ripton [Vermont] experience and the rest which I needn't refer to now. You are not mistaken in the inference which you give that such intelligence is somewhat interesting to me.

I was glad to hear that Kent was coming down here, but am afraid that he will have trouble in getting into the regiment as it is now nominally full.[23]

I am sure you will like this little poem of Mrs. Akers. As you have noticed heretofore, she seems inclined to think that my little friend <u>Frank</u> fills a somewhat different <u>niche</u> from what I have yet discovered her in.

Tomorrow Carl Ansehults'[sic] German Opera commences at Washington with "Faust."[24] If it hadn't been for the prospective move I had proposed an attempt to hear it. With Congress, Civilization, The Opera and Mrs. Akers for an incentive I should have made a violent effort to go.

Well my dear fellow,--here's goodby 'till next time. I know you wont fret or worry because we are in motion, but will just go along and see that everything is all right.　　Goodbye

<u>Ed.</u>

***

In his March 17th letter Higley provides an interesting and detailed account of the failed but audacious Union raid on Richmond. A small detachment of 500 men under Colonel Dahlgren, including companies G and K (Higley's regular company) of the 1st Vermont Cavalry, crossed the Rapidan River late on February 28th and proceeded to Spotsylvania where they turned west intending to cross the James River near Goochland so as to enter the rebel capital from the southwest. Higley's contingent of artillery remained

Evarts B. Kent of the 6th Vermont Infantry.
Photo courtesy of Francis C. Guber Collection.

with Kilpatrick's column on a more direct path to Richmond that followed around an hour after Dahlgren. Slipping across the Rapidan in the early hours of February 29th, by roughly noon on March 1st, they were at the gates of Richmond. Kilpatrick believed the old men and boys of the Confederate home guard no match for his troops but his error was realized when the Yankees came under well aimed and prolific cannon fire for which Higley and his men provided counter action against the rebel emplacements.

Dahlgren, meanwhile, relied on the guidance of a young Negro, Martin Robinson, from a nearby plantation, to locate a ford across the James. As the sun rose on March 1st, Dahlgren was

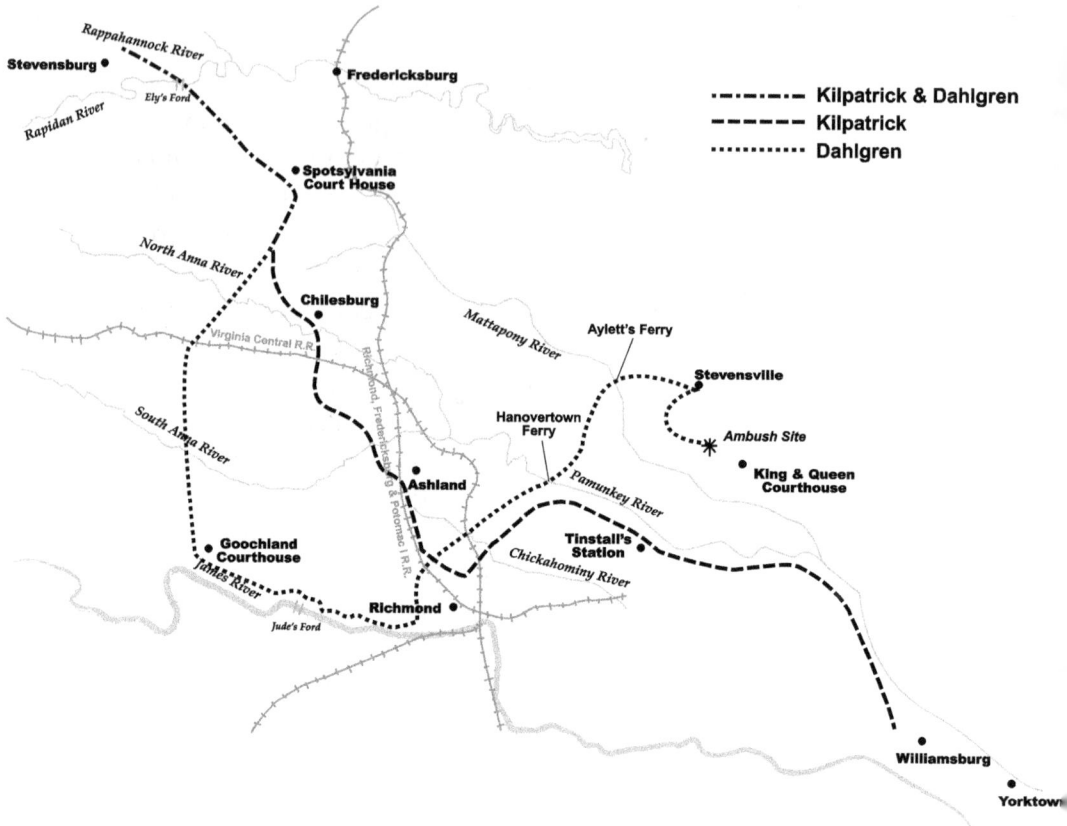

Raid on Richmond by Judson Kilpatrick and Ulric Dahlgren, March 1864.
Map Illustrated by Robin Hanks.

led to Jude's Ford where two days of rain had swollen the river making the crossing impassable. Angry and frustrated over the delay in his critical timetable and despite pleas of innocence, he left Robinson hanging by the neck from a nearby tree limb as he spurred his men forward to look for an available crossing. Sniped at by rebel militia, his fatigued men and horses pelted by a hard rain and sleet, part of his command became lost in the confusion the night of March 2nd. Realizing the original mission was now an impossibility, he began to retrace his initial movements back to the northeast to rejoin Kilpatrick. Nearing the King and Queen Courthouse Dahlgren's men were attacked by militia supported by regulars of Fitzhugh Lee waiting in ambush. Struck by four bullets, some reported the young colonel dead before he fell from his mount. Most of his men were either killed or captured, many ending up in the same prisons they had hoped to liberate. Roughly 250 troopers would eventually make their way back to Kilpatrick who had withdrawn from Richmond's outskirts stifled by enemy resistance and the imagined arrival of reinforcements to the city. Kilpatrick and his men found safety by moving east down the peninsula to Union lines near Yorktown on March 4th. Of the 340 overall casualties, 71 men were from the 1st Vermont Cavalry and Higley notes that 20 came from Company K who were with Jack Williamson although the lieutenant made it back safely.[25]

Higley and his battery are given credit for sending the first Federal artillery shells into the enemy seat of government and Higley on March 2nd, does note that they were "throwing shells into the city."[26] However, Higley, in the following letter, clarifies and adds greater detail to his duties on March 1st. With 170 incendiary shells and the buildings of Richmond only two miles from Union lines, he was apparently ordered to concentrate on the immediate fortifications and trenches which had unexpectedly stymied Kilpatrick. "We could have set the whole city in flames," he tells Noble. "But . . . we did not fire a shot at women and children."

While on the peninsula, Higley caught up with two Vermonters and fellow Middlebury alums, Henry Herbert and Sylvester Partridge. He and Partridge toured the scarred landmarks of the area around Yorktown and Williamsburg dating from Washington's victory in the country's previous rebellion to McClellan's more recent 1862 campaign. There is also hopeful anticipation for the arrival of the "successful Western element" of Ulysses Grant as general in chief. Appointed to the command in November 1863 he had met with Meade at his Brandy Station headquarters just a week before the following letter.

General George Meade, ca. 1862.
Library of Congress, LC-DIG-cwpb-05008.

Stevensburg Va. Mar. 17 1864

My dear fellow

   I ought to write you three letters in one to-night instead
of which I fear I shall hardly construct a respectable writ. I can hardly
tell you how gladly I read your letters on my return to camp, or how
emphatically I rebuked my Ebony attendant because I feared he had lost
one of them—which I afterward found in the Adjutant's desk,—Well—
the raid is over and I am back from my experience in the doubly new field
of the regular and the artillery service, and have dosed myself with some
sound and protracted slumber. The regiment has not yet returned,-is
still at Alexandria or on the march from there hither. This transporting
troops by water is rather slow work, and we came with the battery on the
first boat from Yorktown.

I am very glad that your anticipations did not reach to the capture of the rebel city, so that you were spared the disappointment which many felt who had appreciated the desir<u>a</u>bility of such a result rather than the difficulty of obtaining it. But few of those who accompanied Kilpatrick anticipated entering Richmond; -I dont think he did himself;-but he is of just such a dashing reckless character that he would purpose[sic] to go as near as possible, and in if <u>he</u> <u>could</u>. There is an attempt being made in some military circles to injure Kilpatrick on the ground of his pretended failure;-overlooking the fact that no other cavalry movement of the war has approached it in daring impudence, or has inflicted so heavy a loss upon the enemy with so little loss to ourselves. —It has shown them, as Williamson says, "that its not safe for those Secesh nabobs to keep <u>blood</u> <u>horses</u>[27] even though they are within a few miles of Richmond!" That it struck an unlimited amount of terror into the hearts of the dwellers in the city can be seen by the howling anathemas which, on their recovery, are their only means of vengeance. [The whole experience was exciting, fatiguing and dangerous beyond anything I have known before. —Most exciting that first Sunday night when we galloped in the hazy gloom through the lines of Lees army,-- holding our breath as we looked with frequent, anxious glances at his large camp-fires so near us—exciting too when in the bright sunshine of Tuesday afternoon our column marched up the broad road to Richmond; saw the guide-boards "To Richmond five miles"---"four miles"—"three miles,"—and then rode up through the strong barriers of the first line of defences [sic]—and still everything moving quietly quickly, and in order and <u>not</u> <u>a</u> <u>shot</u> <u>fired</u>! Then it was that for a few moments the rumor that the city was evacuated spread and seemed credible. But a little further investigation showed us how every one of the few forces were kept back to man the strong works in the city's immediate front. Then we knew that we had reached our limit. The rebels opened upon us with thirty-two pounders. Four of our little three-inch pieces replied. And compliments were exchanged for two hours probably effecting no injury to either side. Our guns were within less than two miles of the city, and had the one hundred and seventy fire shell been thrown at <u>it</u> instead of the works in front, we could have set the whole city in flames. But in spite of the barbarity attributed to the raiders by rebel termagants[28] –frightened by our coming and maddened at our escape,-we did not fire a shot at women

131

and children.

*This too was the fatiguing part of the trip. For from the first
Sunday eve at 7 o'clock we neither slumbered nor hardly slackened our
gallop until we stopped before Richmond on Tuesday at 8 oclock. And
from there on, till we met Butlers pickets there was but little decrease in
the matter of perpetual motion, although some in velocity. Some men
from Gregg's command who were detailed for the expedition say we were
eighty-two hours in the saddle without rest, – but then they exaggerate.*

*It was most dangerous and disagreeable when, on that same
Tuesday night, we groped around in the swampy forests near Richmond,-
-encountering foes at every turn, hearing shell thunder and whiz around
us, wandering through intricate and crooked paths, all in the blackest
darkness, and amid a howling storm of sleet and snow. I use the word
dangerous as applicable to the whole command. Individually and
comparatively I was at no time in any danger. And the skill, or fortune
or Providence which brought so large a command through, with so little
fighting and peril and loss was and is, a marvel to me.*

*This cannot be said of Williamsons command which was with Col.
Dahlgren. They saw fighting and trouble enough. Poor recruits!
Twenty from our company were killed or captured near Richmond. It
may be well for Kent that we hadn't room for him. If the war lasts ten
years the infantry will never have time to get up into such a scrape as
that.*

*I had a brief visit with Capt. Henry Herbert[29] 6th US. Col'd. Troops. He
was kind and cordial of course; – was very comfortably situated there,
and much pleased with the service which he is in. He went off with
his brigade to Portsmouth and back and I saw but little of him. I had
more of a visit with Partridge[30] who is stationed there and has lots of
leisure. With him I rode over McClellans' old works and Cornwallis and
Magruders[31] — saw the house in which Cornwallis signed the articles of
surrender, – and talked over all sorts of past present and future matters
with a great deal of pleasure. Partridge is a fine, whole-souled fellow who
has a genuine healthy ring to him, upon whom army life has had no evil
influence. I was much pleased to meet with an intelligent loyal fellow —*

fully up to the times, who had been through the Peninsular campaign and who thinks somewhat as I do about McClellans military character. — He is First Lieutenant in the _Signal Corps_.

I am interested and pleased at all which you tell of the Society proceedings.

We are glad of the prospective coming of Grant to this army. Not because there is any mistrust of _Mead_ [sic] but because the infusion of so much hitherto successful Western element is a good omen to begin the campaign with. How soon said campaign may begin we know not. We are under marching orders now, but don't apprehend an immediate move. I have received a letter to-night since I began this from one of our recruits in Richmond prison, who reports of our missing men as with him and well. I was yesterday blessed with another letter from Mrs. Akers. Letter is hardly a fit word, 'twas a whole _visitation_. I wish I could send you one of her bountiful messages — they contain so much — so full an insight into her character — lonely, — sad, --and bright and earnest. Perhaps I will if I can find room. I fear it will be banner work for you to write one tomorrow night —no letter from me for three weeks, – but we don't make raids often.

Good-night
Yours ever
E.H. Higley

***

Kilpatrick and his division returned to northern Virginia by steamship. Higley records that he was in Annapolis, Maryland on March 6th and in Alexandria five days later. As the previous letter showed, Higley was back in camp near Stevensburg by March 17th and again with the staff of II Corps which on March 24th was placed under the command of Major General Winfield Scott Hancock replacing G. K. Warren. For the next two weeks the regiment was again riding picket along the Rapidan River. With the last remnants of winter lashing at his tent, Higley settles into reading works by English novelist and social critic Charles Reade and a tattered copy of George Sand's *Consuelo*. Colonel Sawyer again has command of the brigade following an accident by Custer who is now attended by his new wife. Music, of course, occupies Higley's time with a lucky, if mistaken, re-routing of sheet music to his address and the willing participation of fellow soldier/vocalists who render works by Mendelssohn and Beethoven "quite well." Music was also part of the ill-fated Richmond raid, with Higley noting that Kilpatrick instructed his band to play national airs for the entrenched secessionists with all possible furor even as the eruptions of shell fire punctuated the serenade.

English novelist and dramatist Charles Reade.
Britannica Online for Kids, Web. 6 June 2104.
http://kids.britannica.com/comptons/art-57589.

134

My dear Noble,

The rain is driving furiously against my canvas covering tonight and I am not altogether free from apprehension lest the wind may exhaust the patience with which the old weather-worn and tattered fly has been clinging to our domicile all winter, and thus unroof us entirely. Although seldom spoken of, it is not one of the least of the drawbacks upon a residence in these moving houses,- this eternal flapping and snapping and whipping and jerking of the walls and roof of your abode, – a continual worry to your nervous nature, trifling in itself but amounting to considerable in a whole winter's wind. Early in the week we had a snow-storm, six or eight inches, which has melted into rains and we are again in the wind.

Gen. Grant is actually with us at last. We are pleased at his coming and hope for his previous success. There is some danger however lest he may not find a hearty co-operation among all his Generals in which case he cannot succeed anymore than did Burnside. Thank Heaven that Halleck is laid up to dry, at last!

I have been reading considerably since the raid. Have read Charles Reade's "Hard Cash."[32] It is quite a pleasing, healthy book, I think. As a work of art, it is somewhat strained and affected. For instance where he makes the beautiful and fascinating Miss Julia talk bad grammar, as she does all along – so as to be more true to nature! I am now reading – you musn't tell – a dingy volume which says (or said, before it was torn off) on its fly-leaf "Consuelo, By George Sand."[33] A very wonderful, and in some respects charming work, although there is much that one wouldnt care to read.

Williamson has been appointed Provost Marshal of the Division[34] – on General Kilpatrick's staff. So he goes up to Stevensburg to stay and I am left a widow, an item which, during these cold windy nights I find important. "United we sleep – Divided we freeze" is a very truthful representation of the matter.

Williamson by the way, did very handsomely on the raid, led the charge which they made in the night upon the rebel earth-works, from which they dislodged infantry and took between two and three hundred prisoners. There is a vacant Captaincy in the regiment which he ought to have, but which it is very doubtful whether Sawyer will give him. Sawyer is now in temporary command of the Brigade, as Gen. Custer is still suffering from a fall which he had from a carriage last week. Mrs. Custer is here, but I have not seen her.

I have had two rich musical treats during the past week. One evening three of us – a tenor in the regiment, the leader of Kilpatrick's band, and myself got together and drilled all the evening on Mendelssohn four-part songs. For the other, Emma had some songs which she had ordered for herself come by mistake to me, and one day with the tenor aforesaid – who sings quite well – I went up town to a piano and tried them. There was one of Mendelssohns, one of Beethovens and another – all excellent. I shall send them back soon and you may have an opportunity to hear them.

Did I tell you that Kilpatrick had his b<u>an</u>d on the raid, and had them play the national airs with all possible <u>furore</u> [sic] before Richmond?

How you w<u>ill</u> look in b<u>ea</u>vers! I shouldn't think y<u>our</u> longitudinal proportions would be improved in appearance by any such ad<u>diti</u>on.

I am glad to hear of the earnest feeling which you report as prevailing among the boys. O, if Tilden would only start in life guided by a Christian faith instead of an impulsive brain, what a path of bright promise would be open before him!

What you said of Arbutus reminds me of what Mrs. Akers wrote me about a bit of fern. She says that he "who gave it never mistrusted how much he gave me,- A whole summer time and all my childhood over again – So here I have the green leaves tenderly nestled at the throat of my dress and shall be happier all day for them, I feel like fa<u>stening</u> th<u>em</u> b<u>etween</u> m<u>y</u> e<u>yes</u>, as did the Jews the maxims of Moses."

That for perfume to my
goodnight   Ed.

Did you ever see the carte of Mendelssohn?

***

Higley remains on the staff of II Corps along with Company M of the regiment which is now assigned as the escort to General Hancock. He feels another large action is eminent since the sutlers selling their wares and the women selling theirs, are being banished from the camps.

Most of the letter, however, is a treatise on art or perhaps instruction for Noble's own exploration of artistic style and meaning. The somewhat heretical themes of George Sand's work have Higley retreating to his more conventional sensibilities— his "Yankee matter-of-factness." Such "colored descriptions of intrigue" he also finds inappropriate for a future wife or daughter or a son's wandering eye. Yet, his critique of Sand is followed by an animated lecture on the language of music and the spiritual "mystery and grandeur" of its expression. Music or good poetry is not literal—no narrow imitation—but a transcendent emotion brought on through melody or verse "which fills the heart of some awe-stricken, terror-smitten, mortal."

French novelist George Sand.
Wikimedia; by French photograph Gaspard-Félix Tournachon, Dec. 31, 1863.

My dear Noble,

I told you that I had been reading George Sand, and I commence talking about her just here because I may say a good deal and I dont want you to be tired with other things first. – I am not "carried entirely away" by the book because I am able to say. – First – that there are some highly colored descriptions of intrigue which I should <u>not</u> read to my wife and daughters of an evening, and which I should take stringent measures to ascertain that my second son was not reading on the hay-mow – when I thought he was husking corn. Second, once or twice I found myself repelled and shuddering at the fascinating profanity with which a weird sort of Devil-worship was hinted at. And again my Yankee ma<u>tter</u>-<u>of</u>-fac<u>tn</u>ess rebelled against the occasional introduction of the supernatural element, and the trans migration of souls.

But generally, Madame Sand has drawn a picture of chaste purity whose spotless whiteness she was, perhaps, better enabled to portray and appreciate, because her own robes were not untarnished.

And, particularly and especially, she has said upon some of the truest, <u>dearest</u>, <u>wisest</u>, words of Music which I ever met. I am sure I need not fear tiring you upon this subject, and so I want to qu<u>ote</u> a little or rather a go<u>od</u> d<u>ea</u>l.

Consuelo, the heroine, is a great singer who sang a hundred years before Madame Sand, and was contemporary to and a friend of young Joseph Haydn;- the wheelwrights son, who is a character in the book and with whom I was of course delighted to be acquainted. This, which Consuelo's lover says to her, reminds me how often when awkward tongue and pen have been puzzled, I have thought that if I could have ~~had~~ a piano and "Sonata Pathetique," or a "Song without words," I could ~~have made~~ make everything plain to you. "The words of your songs have but little meaning to me; they are but the theme; the imperfect indication on which the music turns and is developed. I hardly hear them; what alone I hear and what penetrates into my very soul, is your voice, your accent, your inspiration. Music expressed all that the human *mind dreams and foresees of mystery and grandeur. It is the revelation of a higher order or ideas and sentiments than any to which human speech can give expression. It is the revelation of the infinite and when you sing, I only belong to humanity in so far as humanity has drunk in what is divine and eternal in the bosom of the Creator. All that your lips refuse of consolation and support in the ordinary routine of life; all that social tyranny forbids your heart to reveal, your songs convey to me knowledge of the winds and waves, before you can at all represent the harmony of nature. This is not a fit subject for music. It has a wider field. All emotion is its domain. Imagine then the impressions of a man abandoned to this torment." (the shipwreck) "a danger, awful, terrible and imminent. Let a musician place himself; that is let a human, vibrating, living soul be fixed amid this distress and disorder, this desertion and despair, then give vent to his sorrow, -and the audience – whether it respond to it or not, will participate in this. It will fancy that it hears the sea, the crashing of the ships, the cry of the sailors and the despair of the passengers. What would you say of a poet, who in describing a battle said that the cannon said boom, boom, and the drums plau, plau? Yet this would be an exact harmonic imitation. It would not however be poetry.- No. Fill yourself, young man, with the idea of a great disaster, in that way you will excite others."*

This, I think, hits Thomas' case exactly. He was seeking in music, for instance in a production like "Night Winds" by Wallace,[35] for a similarity to or "imitation of real noises," for something literally like the sighing winds and rustling leaves and not finding this was prepared to say that no one, were it not for the title page – could perceive any connection between the music and its idea. But if instead of this straining in the wrong direction he had simply left the ears of his soul open, without any exertion of the will – he would have found the weird, sad, minor harmony, continually intertwined with a beautiful, graceful and yet monotonous and oft-recurring chromatic variation, was awaking in his heart the same emotions of melancholy reverie, which the wailing of winds and the mournful rustling of a forest at night would have given rise to.

In the sublime and terrific representations which are given of "the Chaos" in Haydn's "Creation"[36] there is no "exact harmonie imitation" – no "narrow imitation of the real noises" caused by the rushing of waters and the upheaving of mountains. But it is the em*otion*, which fills the heart of some awe-stricken, terror-smitten, mortal who is a witness of such a scene, that rings in those wild, crashing chords, and mingling, responsive, darting scales,- and that carries itself to the heart of every hearer, however ignorant of its meaning.   This view recalls an opinion which I once tried to express of Gottschalk, in whom one finds too little dealing with the soul, and too great a tendency to "fall into the childish pursuit of mere effects of sound."

But enough of this. If I stop here I may not need to apologize.

      I shall probably be for a little while and perhaps longer at the Head Qurs of the Second Corps. Please address me there in "care of Capt J. H. Hazelton" – without any reference to the Regiment on the envelope.[37]

      I am detailed there with Gen. Hancock's escort which is from this Regiment. [38]

      I enclose Mrs. Akers sheet. Your query as to "whether she would like you," can be best ascertained by finding "whether you like her," I think. You perceive that she talks very familiarly and freely of her personal and pecuniary matters, but I dont consider that I am betraying any confidence by showing *you* the letter.

      Thank you for "the Bowl."

      Sutlers are ordered to be out of the army by the 16th. Women are already banished. Hence a movement may be soon anticipated. I have talked more than I should have done, had I not feared that perhaps more tangible and less pleasant themes might crowd upon us soon. We need many more ho*rse*s before we can work, but I believe our stock of pluck and confidence is plenteous.

                  My dear fellow
                    Goodbye

                      Ed

***

Grant's command of the Union armies initiated another reorganization of the cavalry corps of the Army of the Potomac. General Pleasonton was replaced by Phil Sheridan. Alfred Torbert now headed the first division and David Gregg retained command of the second division. Judson Kilpatrick's reputation, however, finally caught up with him following the failed raid and the death of Ulric Dahlgren whose father Rear Admiral John Dahlgren was chief of the navy's ordnance department. Kilpatrick was demoted to a brigade commander and sent west to serve under William Sherman. In his place the third division of Sheridan's corps was given to Brigadier General James Wilson. With the change, Custer's brigade, including the 1st Vermont Cavalry, was transferred to Torbert's division but the shift was temporary for the Vermonters who eight days later were detached from Custer's command and assigned to Wilson's division as the 2nd brigade under the command of Colonel George Chapman along with the 3rd Indiana and 8th New York cavalries. Not only is this unsettling for Higley but the unpopular Colonel Sawyer has returned to the regiment. Sawyer's inept leadership as a brigade commander during the Kilpatrick raid, however, led to his replacement during the mission by Lieutenant Colonel Preston. Bowing to growing pressure, he resigns his commission a week after the next letter, on April 28, 1864.[39]

Colonel George Chapman, ca. 1864.
Library of Congress, LC-DIG-cwpb-01717.

Changes are apparently in the wind at Middlebury College as well, as Higley commiserates with his friend concerning an unidentified snub by the school—perhaps employment of some sort. This appears to lead to Noble's separation from the campus and his short stint as a newspaper editor and writer over the next three years.

Head Quarters Second Corps .
April 21ˢᵗ 1864

My dear Noble,

Your last letter has just reached me coming from the regiment, so I fear that my last roll to you, enclosing Mrs. Akers letters was miscarried. Its discoursing upon Madame Sand and music however would not be congenial to your present excited condition. I don't know what to say to you. I am sure I won't be foolish enough to advise you. I am very sorry. I believe you will not act too hastily. But this I do say, that if the faculty of Middlebury College allow you to leave them – without they come on their bended knees to ask your terms, they deserve the contempt and are unworthy the indignation of honorable men. And of this you may be sure that if Dr. Labaree⁴⁰ so allows you to leave the college which you have honored; the diploma signed by him would be neither credible or desirable to its possessor. But I can't believe that they are so lacking in worldly wisdom not to say moderate decency as to let you leave.

You don't say what Allie purposed [sic] to do.

Fair weather mingles with rain in our weekly programme, and roads are still fables.

Our Regiment are provoked at the removal of Kilpatrick, as are also the whole Division. And to cap the affair instead of giving the command of the Division to Gen. Custer who should have it next; and who is known to the whole country, a new General from the West is given them. Gen. Custer has obtained the transfer of himself and Brigade to the First Division – formerly Buford's – now commanded by Gen.

Talbot [sic].[41] *Williamson will thus return to the Regiment. Our men from the Sixth Corps will soon return also. Col. Sawyer is back again to the regiment I believe. So our hopes of his resigning are again dashed.*

We have a sore thrashing in Arkansas to commence the summers work with. Gen. Stone, the hero of Ball's Bluff "had direction of operation" – and Gen. Stoneman "commanded the cavalry."[42] *Stanton seems determined to keep Banks in trouble in some way. He has been sending him all the broken down Army of Potomac Generals and of course he can't fight successfully. Gen. Ransom who fought so well there, and who would have made a victory out of the fight, had he been allowed his way – is a brother of Captain Ransom of the 3rd Artillery – with whom I served on the raid.*[43] *He is a Vermonter – son of Gen. Ransom who was President of Norwich and was afterward killed at Chapultepec.*

I was going to congratulate you upon your prospective work for the coming year, but "the times are out of joint." I shall wait eagerly for your next message. No one can say how soon this army may move.

Ever yours

E. H. Higley

***

The problems facing Noble still attract Higley's concern and prod his own memory of a singular act of insubordination while at Middlebury which, unsurprisingly, was linked to his passion for music. He had defiantly journeyed to see the celebrated opera star Pasquale Brignoli; this after an admonition by the school's president that he needed to focus on his studies. Now, he finds comfort in the infantry bands in camp, which often play Shubert's "Serenade" which he describes as exuding a certain calmness, as one might experience from choking back a sob. His initial problems with Sand's *Consuelo* seem tamed as he now finds "something grand" in the woman. Higley's latest read predates Sand but is another woman nonconformist, French republican Germaine de Staël, whose writings drew the wrath of Napoleon.

Italian born tenor Pasquale Brignoli. Library of Congress, LC-DIG-cwpbh-02623.

Higley is now part of the corps' Provost Marshal, with twenty-five men detailed to him, responsible for maintaining order in the camps, guarding prisoners or ferreting out deserters. On August 25th, he wrote of twelve rebels who walked off picket duty and surrendered "en mass." "They have been coming over very plentifully of late."[44]

Higley notes increasing preparations in camp, indicating that another action is coming and there is word about Generals Joseph Hooker and Ambrose Burnside, two men whose tactical deficiencies cost them command of the army they still serve. As camp rumors go, Higley has it fifty percent correct. Burnside was positioning his IX Corps along the Orange & Alexandria Railroad, guarding the Union supply line, replacing Meade's troops which would be the spear point for attacking Lee's right flank beginning May 4th—the beginning of the six bloodiest weeks of the Civil War. Hooker was transferred to the west in the summer of 1863 and was in command of one of Sherman's corps as they began their march toward Atlanta.[45]

Headquarters Second Army Corps

My dear Noble,

        Your last letter relieves me from a most anxious uncertainty. I am not entirely satisfied with the result of your fracas, but I think you have taken the best available course. Did you go to Burlington to the concert? I remember well that a Burlington concert – by Brignoli and the divine Carlotti [sic] Patti was the occasion of my only act of insubordination during my college course.[46] - It was the summer after we had been giving concerts and the worthy President was disgusted with so much music and flatly refused me permission to go! He also asserted that music was distracting my attention from study, which in view of my marks which I was then watching with a freshman's eagerness, excited my wrath so much that [I] went straight from his presence with his refusal ringing in my ears and bought a ticket for Burlington, and in an hour was on my way thither. How often have I blessed the impudence on which I did so. I have never heard young Carlo. You must tell me all about him. I shan't be surprised if you should be so dazzled by the fascinating brilliancy of Gottschalk's magic fingers that you may think my late talk of him as lacking in enthusiasm. - No, I don't mean that, for I know that you won't find him all that you could wish. But don't think that I don't admire him. As an artist of bewildering grace and power I regard him as I would a most beautiful ballet dancer, and as a marvel of mechanical power far beyond anything which I ever heard. I am glad that you have heard Mietzke. Unless I am much mistaken you will find much satisfaction in his playing. Sometimes his enthusiasm and vigor lead him to the sacrifice of tenderness, but you feel it is the man's whole soul that is speaking. He was reared on the sturdy, strong old German food – Handel and Mozart and Beethoven. The melody, grace and delicacy which more modern Italian masters have introduced doesn't affect him so much. I hope you heard him play Seraphaels "Wedding March." The gushing, triumphant strains of victorious joy and love which he makes it bring forth can hardly be excelled. I hear a good deal of music here among the infantry bands. A band near here plays often Schubert's "Serenade."

Did I ever play it for you? I think it one of the choicest things – one of the very few, which, in a simple yet studied harmony contain such depths of expression.- I could hear it an hour every evening. It is no happy swains[47] *"Good-night" – or "Sleep on, but dream of me!" Ah, no. It is calm, but a calm which seems choking at the throat, which has just gulped down a sob! It is like*

"Ever be happy, whenever thou art –

Loved by a broken heart!"[48]

And yet through the resignation of an earthly joy beams the calm hope of a surer joy beyond. I have never heard it sung. It seems to me that words would mar it. I presume this affected me peculiarly because I was reading "Corinne." Did you ever read it? I will send it to you if you like. I have been unusually charmed with it. It has constantly reminded me of Miss Shephard, although there is not slightest similarity of style. It seems to me such a book as Lady Geraldine must have written in "Rumor." Who was Madame DeStael?[49] *Or is? I don't know anything about her. In reading the sequel to "Consuelo" I am more than ever struck with marvelous grandeur of that woman's intellectual power. Although I could not accept her philosophy in all particulars I cannot but admire some things in it. In her view of Christ there is nothing of the trusting, clinging, childish faith of the Christian, yet there is something grand in this woman, who dared to deny and scoff at him, and yet, by the might of her me*nt*al stren*g*th kno*w*s him, and ranks him as the m*a*n di*v*ine.*

*Preparations for active service thicken here. Burnside is on the way to join us. Rumors about Hooker are afloat. The weather is pretty good but showers are frequent. You are happy at the F*all*s of course. Please remember me most kindly to your sister. I don't forget that night.*

*You may leave Mrs. Akers budget in E*m*'s care if you please, and forbid her to read it – a*ll *of it at least – to anybody, out of the house.*

As ever

Ed

146

***

Germanna Ford.
Library of Congress, LC-DIG-cwpb-01173.

As noted by Higley, the campaign began in the darkness of early May 4th with Union crossings of the Rapidan at Ely's and Germanna Fords—speed the key to success. Grant would apply pressure on Lee's army on several fronts: German American General Franz Sigel advancing with 6,500 men south in the Shenandoah Valley as General Benjamin Butler with 30,000 steamed up the James River getting midway between the important rail hub of Petersburg and Richmond on May 5th. These were to be Grant's "leg holders" meant to keep in place enough rebel assets to allow Meade success with the main thrust from the north. Grant's first concern was getting through the tangled confusion of pine, scrub oak and thick underbrush known as the Wilderness. It was eight miles of choking gloom that undercut

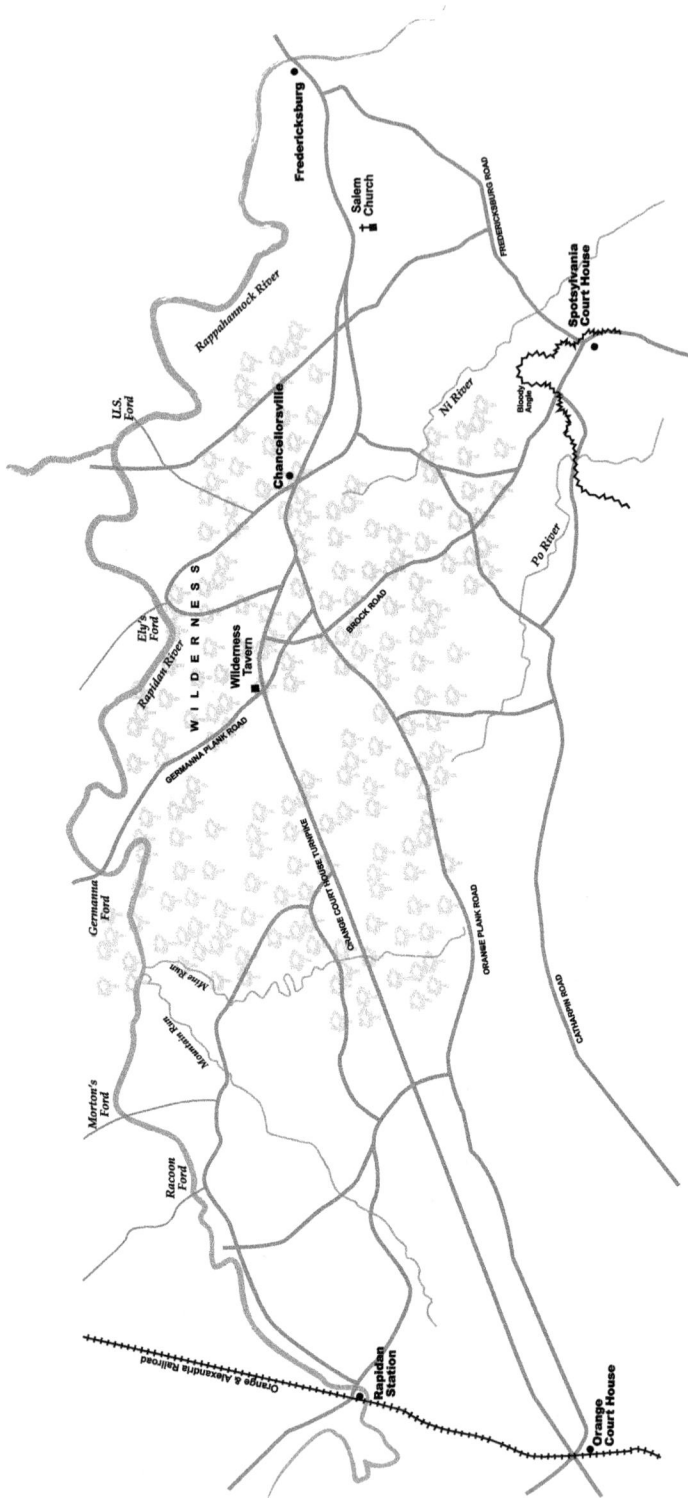

Wilderness campaign and Spotsylvania, May, 1864. Map illustrated by Robin Hanks.

the effectiveness of Union numerical superiority—roughly 115,000 men to Lee's 64,000. Grant wanted the army to clear the area in two days and draw out the rebels to open ground from behind their trenches. Lee did not contest the Rapidan crossing but hit the Union flank as it moved around his right and for two days a nightmarish conflict was waged in the blind, gray snarl where maneuvering or even seeing the enemy was a problem. Adding to the disorder and mayhem, rifle flashes from black powder ignited the underbrush, incinerating wounded men unable to escape the flames. On May 7th, Grant methodically moved his men in a flanking movement around Lee's right taking and securing the crossroads at Spotsylvania, twelve miles further south, setting the stage for the next bloodbath. Union soldiers expected any movement to be the usual retreat and were buoyed by news that they were marching south not north. The news was so welcome that, despite their fatigue, men began to sing as they marched. This in the face of staggering casualty numbers for the Wilderness: 17,500 for the Union and 7,000 for the Confederacy.[50]

The 1st Vermont Cavalry was part of 10,000 Union cavalrymen riding with Sheridan sweeping to the west around Richmond, destroying rail, communication and supply lines, all the while daring Southern cavalry under J.E.B. Stuart to attack. Stuart, despite a stark numerical disadvantage, made his stand on May 11th at Yellow Tavern just north of Richmond. Yankee troopers, many with rapid fire carbines, scattered rebel resistance and killed Stuart, perhaps the most severe blow to Confederate military leadership since the death of Thomas Jackson a year earlier.

The day after Yellow Tavern, Higley is witness to the horrors of an assault at Spotsylvania against a fortified salient dubbed the, "Mule Shoe"—an inverted U which extended a half-mile out on high ground in the middle of the rebel entrenchments. Hancock's II corps, supported by the VI, would attempt a breakthrough. While the overall losses at Spotsylvania over several days would again be horrendous, the removal of twenty-two Confederate cannon from the salient on May 11th was a stroke of luck. Lee wrongly believed that Grant was again flanking south, given reports of movement by Yankee supply wagons, and feared having the guns bottled up if needed quickly.[51]

The Bloody Angle at the battle of Spotsylvania.
From a chromolithograph by L. Prang & Co created in 1887.
Library of Congress--LC-DIG-pga-04038.

As daylight broke through a soup of rain and fog in the early hours of the 12th, Hancock's men raced across the field at the rebel lines with a general convergence at the apex of the salient, breaching it with great initial success; clearing the abatis and breastworks and capturing many of the defenders. Higley writes of the carnage resulting from subsequent counterattacks and in particular the intense butchery at the toe of the Mule Shoe, called thereafter the Bloody Angle of Spotsylvania.   Both flags would fly over the disputed outcropping with fierce hand-to-hand combat where neither side relinquished. "Troops were killed by thrusts and stabs through chinks in the log barricade," wrote Shelby Foote, "while others were harpooned by bayonetted rifles flung javelin-style across it." Battle crazed men in blue and gray would alternately mount the parapet shooting down into the massed enemy on the other side, replenished with rifles passed up by comrades until killed themselves, only to be replaced by another. "Rain fell, slacked, fell again in sheets, drenching the fighters and turning the floor of their slaughter pen to slime," wrote Foote. Bodies lay in piles and heaps before the log barricades at the Bloody Angle. Astonishingly, Higley tells Noble that three days later, as work with the unburied began, soldiers, wounded but alive, are found among the expanse of dead.[52]

Body of a Confederate soldier near Mrs. Alsop's house at Spotsylvania, Virginia. Taken by photographer Timothy O'Sullivan, May 4, 1864. Library of Congress, LC-DIG-cwpb-01185

Four days after the gruesome encounter Higley explains that although constantly busy rounding up stragglers and prisoners, he and his men were not exposed to direct fire except from little used artillery. One rebel captain under his guard, told him that "his regiment had suffered terribly, but the first Yankee he had seen was the one who captured him." His duties took him to all parts of the battlefield where he saw the dying and wounded; "a majority of the wounds are horrible ones. I am sure that there has never been any fighting in this country which approaches in destructive fierceness this desperate and sanguinary struggle."[53] He found the paper used for the next letter in the bullet riddled knapsack of a fallen soldier.

In the field May 16 1864

My dear Noble,

     Your last letter from the <u>falls</u> was shoved under my blanket and into my face about five o'clock this morning. Your previous one of May 2nd came two days ago. These constitute the only mails which we have had since we left Stevensburg on the <u>fourth</u>. A letter from home accompanied yours this morning. It rained very hard last evening and we put up some rails for a shutter but they fell down upon us about midnight. No one was seriously injured and we laid still until morning.

     Yesterday and today have been quiet.- The first days which have been so in <u>ten</u>. I presume the reporters will tell you enough of this wonderful fight. I feel unable to say much about it. I have been so situated personally as to be able to see general movements more than ever before; to be upon different parts of the field, and thus see more of the wounded and the dead. I have heretofore seen and heard enough of battle and slaughter to be enabled to appreciate the descriptive terms which historians use. But here all such terms seem utterly weak and unsatisfactory in portraying the ferocity of this fight. We hardly dare think of our loss. Reliable authorities say that thirty thousand will not cover it. Vermont has lost more in this fight than all her previous losses together I believe. Grant has found a more unfavorable country and a fiercer foe than ever before, but his impregnable obstinacy may yet bring him safe through. Our fighting has been mainly with musketry at short range. Upon anything less than occular evidence we should be inclined to disbelieve some of the actions performed. The lines of battle were sometimes only three or four rods apart. At one time there was an hours fight over a single breastwork, our men upon our side and the foe upon the other. Bullets, bayonets and clubbed muskets alternately were the weapons of slaughter. The rebel loss here far exceeded our own. After they fell back, the dead bodies of their slain lay in heaps. They were not all buried for three days. On the third day, wounded men were found there alive, who had been covered by the dead since they fell. Our Vermont boys said, after the fight, that they made up their minds that "they should all be killed anyhow," and that they might as well die at their posts as be shot in the back. It does indeed seem strange that anyone could have survived so terrible a fire. I send you a sheet of paper which is one of a quire[54] taken from one poor fellows knapsack, which was thus pierced with bullets.

We hardly know whether we have gained a victory here or not. Yet I think it must eventually result in one. I hear from our Regiment that my Capt. (Grover) is wounded, not seriously however.[55]

Our cavalry is now at work in Lee's rear. I wish I was with them.

It is rumored that the sixth Corps is to be broken up and consolidated with other corps. Also that the eleventh Vermont is out here.[56]

Our excellent First Division Band have been playing Faust all the morning to rest us. We captured the famous "Stonewall Brigade" and the whole division to which it belonged on the morning of the 12th. They were very confident and impudent rebels.

This is a miserable apology for a letter but I am tired and "played out." My nervous nature is on a par with this ink.

I presume we shall fight again tomorrow, and I hope soon to write you in better condition and more positively.

You are back at college soon, after your pleasant vacation. There I salute you.

Good bye

Ed

Efforts against rebel lines over the next week after the May 12th fight were fruitless but costly in manpower producing 3,000 more casualties. Butler was bottled up on the James and Sigel had been hit hard and pushed back in the Shenandoah by Confederate General John Breckenridge. Both sides received reinforcements but Grant faced losing a dozen regiments in July when enlistments ran out. On May 19th he began an arcing sprint twenty-five miles south to a rail junction on the North Anna River with Hancock's corps in the lead. Flanking movements to his left, kept his supply lines intact to the Chesapeake where they were protected by the navy. Good reconnaissance and the ease of interior lines allowed Lee time to counter the move, fixing his emplacements on the river's south edge. Repulsed again in a few small probes, Grant then moved downstream, tacking to the left again while having Sheridan's cavalry secure and hold the crossroads at Cold Harbor which he did after an intense cavalry action against Fitzhugh Lee which took most of May 31st. Here Lee and Grant dug in—59,000 Confederates facing 109,000 Federal troops— preparing for another re-creation of a human slaughter house. Grant had planned on a June 1st assault but Hancock's corps arrived two hours late that morning and was too exhausted from an all-night march. Rebel advances on the Union flanks the next day pushed the main attack to June 3rd.57

Higley and his men of the Provost Marshal escaped the savage fire of the front lines, but are constantly engaged

General Winfield Scott Hancock, ca. 1863. Library of Congress, LC-DIG-cwpb-05828.

with particularly Union "skulkers" and "poltroons" as he terms them—deserters whose character may be questionable but not their cunning. Allowed to take themselves to the rear if wounded, a growing number embellish their movements and dress, even to wrapping limbs in the bloody bandages of others. In contrast, Higley often finds a civil comradeship with his rebel prisoners whom he finds intelligent and gentlemanly. Writer W. Storrs Lee, recounts a letter from Higley describing just such a courteous conversation alluded to in the following letter. According to Lee, while herding several prisoners to a holding area Higley noticed a rebel struggling with an arm wound. Asked his condition and finding the man without a bandage, Higley tore strips from his handkerchief to assist the Southerner, adding that he had learned the skill from a college text. What college, asked his captive? Middlebury College in Vermont, said Higley. Where did you enlist? The University of Alabama, came the reply. "I didn't know there was a college in Vermont." "I didn't know there was one in Alabama," Higley responded. Established by the government in 1831, said the Confederate. Middlebury was not so lucky, said Higley, but at one time it had more buildings than the University of Vermont.[58] They both considered a return to their books after the war, talking as if they were just two students entertaining thoughts of a bright future.

> Head Qurs. 2nd Corps
> June 1st 1864

My dear Noble,

I am happy and I don't know but I should say ashamed to state that I am still in the land of the living. When so many have found glorious graves or been crowned for life with scars, it sometimes causes a feeling of chagrin to find oneself amidst it all unhurt. Still I couldn't well help it, albeit I own myself somewhat chided by your letter of May 13th. But provost duty on a battlefield is not by any means dull, at least when connected with general Head Quarters. Some of its associations are not so pleasant however, necessary as they are. It is no wonder that, in an army of a hundred and twenty thousand brave men, there should be a few thousand sneaks and poltroons[59], especially when we remember the days of substitutes and bounties which have just past. My dealings have frequently been with them, indeed I have frequently said that we were fighting Yankees rather than rebels. It has been a good place to study human nature at least. On the second day of the fight in the wilderness we picked up five hundred of these bounty-jumpers and substitutes and took them up to the breast-works in front. Of course wounded men are always permitted to pass to the rear. I have seen men with tragical-looking holes in their pants, limping and groaning along, and when examined by some suspicious provost, and no wound discovered, they would assert that they were wounded by a spent ball! As though the ball which would air a hole in a mans trousers would not pierce his flesh! I have seen men with hands bandaged and dripping with blood, who had wrapped around their _unhurt_ member the linen which had staunched some actual wound, and thus hoped to find a passport to safety. "Oh! my good man!" moaned one skulker whom I had one of my men driving with drawn sabre to the front "don't take me there! Don't you hear that awful fighting! You _know_ I don't want to go there!" And then as the firing grew fiercer and hotter – "I got eight hundred dollars bounty and I'll give it all to ye, to let me back!"

My intercourse with rebel prisoners has been pleasant compared to this. One feels a little of old _chivalry_ in treating foes courteously, when captives. Most of the rebel officers whom I have met have been gentlemanly and intelligent fellows, and I have had some pleasant chats recalling scenes of the war in which we had been _together_ before, and have parted with them, with words of courtesy which seemed somewhat at variance with our mutual positions.

Well, we are getting on. I am writing at our Head Qurs which are only fifteen miles from Richmond. Warren is at Mechanicsville – only six miles from the rebel capitol, and everyone is confident of success. There has been some fighting here for the past two days, resulting in an advance in our position and not very much loss. One man from our detachment – belonging to the escort – was killed, day before yesterday. This is our first loss. We have had three horses shot.

I find it almost impossible to get away from here, and know almost nothing of the fate and condition [of] our boys in other parts of the army. I heard of Capt. Bird's death a day or two after his fall: but not of Cranes; or Kents wound until you told me.[60] I heard from Eaton a few days since. He was then well.[61]

I expect before long to be back to the regiment.

I owe you many thanks for the two sketches which you sent me in your last. Good bye my dear boy.

Ed.

Captain Riley A. Bird.
Photo courtesy of Francis C. Guber Collection.

***

May 1864 was the bloodiest month in American history with the Union losing 44,000 men killed, wounded or missing to the Confederacy's 25,000. The previous four weeks of constant bloodshed had produced both physical and mental damage on both sides creating an early version of post-traumatic stress. Some rebel corps commanders broke down for a time under the pressure. Union Captain Oliver Wendell Holmes wrote that "many a man has gone crazy since this campaign began from the terrible pressure on mind & body." Yet, Grant still believed that Southern morale was at a low ebb and vulnerable to another all-out offensive. Grant had hoped to pull Lee from behind his defenses where Federal numbers could do lethal damage. Lee patiently sought to break the Union army against his massive fortifications—a debilitating attrition which might save the South.

Northern reports of the slaughter associated with the campaign were eroding support for the administration. Southern hopes rested on Lincoln's defeat at the polls in November. Higley's expressed confidence in Grant, in the following letter, belies the sinking confidence among many rank and file closer to the front lines. Despite the great advantage in numbers by the North, Bobby Lee's adaptive maneuvers had warded off defeat. As men prepared to once more cross open killing fields at Cold Harbor, most pinned scraps of paper containing their name and address to the inside of their uniforms in a last hope that their bodies might reach loved ones after their death. Hancock's corps was again in the lead on June 3rd moving against an intricate system of zig-zagged trenches which a newspaper described as, "lines protecting flanks of lines, lines built to enfilade opposing lines." Union forces were able to penetrate the first set of trenches before being pushed back. The loss was 2,500 casualties including eight colonels. Along the seven mile line that day, 7,000 Federals fell. That night Grant painfully said, "I regret this assault more than any one I have ever ordered."[62]

The loss for Higley had been personal: classmate Albert Crane killed at the Wilderness along with Riley Bird. Most recently came the sad news of the death of two of the 1st Vermont Cavalry's most popular officers: Lieutenant Colonel Addison Preston and Captain Oliver Cushman. Five days after the following letter came the mortal wounding of his tent mate and college friend, Jack Williamson, killed during a skirmish near Malvern Hill which presumably Higley took part in as he mentions the return of a paroled Company M officer who was to relieve him of his staff duties. His return to the regiment would be short-lived however, and he will soon begin the last chapter of his life as a soldier.

Lt. Col. Addison Preston.
Photo courtesy of
Francis C. Guber Collection.

Head Quarters Second Corps
June 10 1864

My dear Noble,

Your letter of the 5th has just reached me, and I am seated to answer it in a much more quiet state than any of my recent writings to you have been born in. The chivalry have been driven so near to their hole that Grant seems disposed to sit down, grimly, for a little while at least, and work slowly upon them with the big guns, rather than perpetuate the expenditure of human life, by rushing upon them with the small ones. The first days fighting by which we obtained this position was one of the most severe which we have seen. My little detachment was under an intense artillery fire all day.

"Where will you flank us now?" asked a bright young reb whom we took, a query which pays a pretty high and comprehensive tribute to Grant's month of brilliant works. On the night of that day, and also of the day following, the enemy made a furious assault upon our works, which brought on a scene surpassing in terrific splendor anything in my previous experience. It was also about ten in the night – a dark one – and we were mostly stretched out for rest around Head Quarters when half a dozen muskets fired in rapid succession, startled the stillness which night had gradually brought on, and quickly a volley broke forth along our whole line. Then the cannon belched out, lighting up the sky with all the brilliancy of a pyrotechnic display, while the ominous nature of the illumination seemed to add a lurid, bloody tint to the flashes. Shells and bullets hissed, screeched, sputtered and struck thickly around Hd. Qurs crashing against trees and tearing up the earth, but nothing could shake the equanimity of Hancock, who trusts in his men, as they trust in him. In about an hour the rebels were driven off and then a moment's perfect silence followed the roar, and then the wild cheers of triumphant exultation rang along our lines, thrilling ones heart, in the darkness of night with emotions probably not often experienced in a lifetime. In the second attack Capt. McCune Asst. Pro Mar. on the Genls staff, an officer with whom I have been most associated had his leg broken by a shell.[63] It was amputated just below the knee and he will probably recover. His time was out this month.   Before this you know of the loss of our gallant Col. Preston.[64] What a marked contrast between the manner in which Col. Sawyer went sneaking to his home a few days before we crossed the Rapidan, and the honored grave which Preston has now gone home to fill. In Capt. Cushman of our regiment, who fell the same day, we lost one of our choicest and best.[65] A young sophomore at Dartmouth, in the highest sense a scholar, a Christian and a man he threw his whole life into this war. He left Vermont a Sergeant in Co. "E" and fell the other day a Capt. of the same Co. He was badly wounded at Gettysburg – left for dead upon the field – fell into rebel hands but was considered too near dead to parole. But he recovered rapidly and hurried back to his company. Ordinarily quiet, modest, unassuming- in battle the lion aroused within him, and he was bravest of the brave.
Dear, noble fellow! May we catch his spirit of energy and devotion.
And I believe we shall, I believe that it is part of the power which God

gives to a hero's fall that his remaining comrades gain new energy from his loss. I dont speak, of course, of an army commander upon whom everyone depends. But I think that our regiment, bereaved of its idolized Colonel and many of its best officers and men, will today instead of being demoralized by its loss, make a braver, better fight than ever before.

I saw Capt. Edwards of our regiment yesterday.[66] Williamson and Smith are well. I am pleased to know of Kent's condition. I don't know whether I told you how heavily Crane's loss affected me. His strong, dear brain would be of so much use to the country in days that are to come, that I hardly expected he would fall. I hope to go back to the regiment soon – perhaps in a few days. Yet I think my address had best be here still. There is an officer here to relieve me, who has just been exchanged from captivity. He belongs to this company and as soon as all the necessary orders can be effected and obtained, I can get away.

Our regiment hopes to get back to Custer's Brigade from which they have been detached. Nobody likes Gen. Wilson – Kilpatrick's successor.[67] Sheridan has left him behind while he goes on his present raid from which we have not heard. The regiment is ten miles from here, near Bottoms Bridge.

I am sorry at the unpromising appearance of the class-tree. I confess that I have thought – but little of trees and flowers of late. The scenery here is not inspiring. We passed some pleasant country on our way down. At Chancellorsville (we slept there) one thing struck me. All over the old battle ground are clumps of forget-me-nots, nestling in the furrows where the shells plowed, and growing all around where so many poor fellows laid in their blood and suffered. And we passed over Chancellorsville to the Wilderness! What a mute appeal those little blossoms made to us; preparatory to the coming fray! I gathered some of them for you but lost them before I could send. There were a good many bones around, and all night as I lay there I could almost fancy that the little flowers were whispering for them "Remember! Remember me, tomorrow!"

Rumor, since I began to write, says that we are going to move again to the James. You may imagine that the old believers in

McClellan's military ability have none the less admiration for Grant because he has taken <u>Mac's</u> route. The military wisacres of the nation have been at logger heads since the war began over the comparative merits of the overland and peninsular highways to Richmond. Grant steps in and coolly adopts them b<u>oth</u> <u>at</u> <u>once</u>; goes overland to the peninsula! Grant forever! Have patience up there. We shan't have Richmond by the fourth of July. But we're b<u>ound</u> <u>to</u> <u>win</u>!

In that faith
Yours ever

E. H. Higley

Captain Oliver T. Cushman, n.d.
Photo courtesy of Francis C. Guber Collection.

***

In his June 1st message to Noble, Higley admits to a common soldier's remorse: how could so many be lost or changed by this conflict, and I stay unharmed? In less than three weeks, his altered fortune will immerse him in the suffering he's escaped. We can only imagine the torment Higley felt at the loss of his close friend Jack Williamson since his letter of June 10th offers the last words from him until his accounts as a prisoner of war. Some of these are from a journal kept by prisoner Higley and others were written for his editor friend Noble following his March 1865 release.

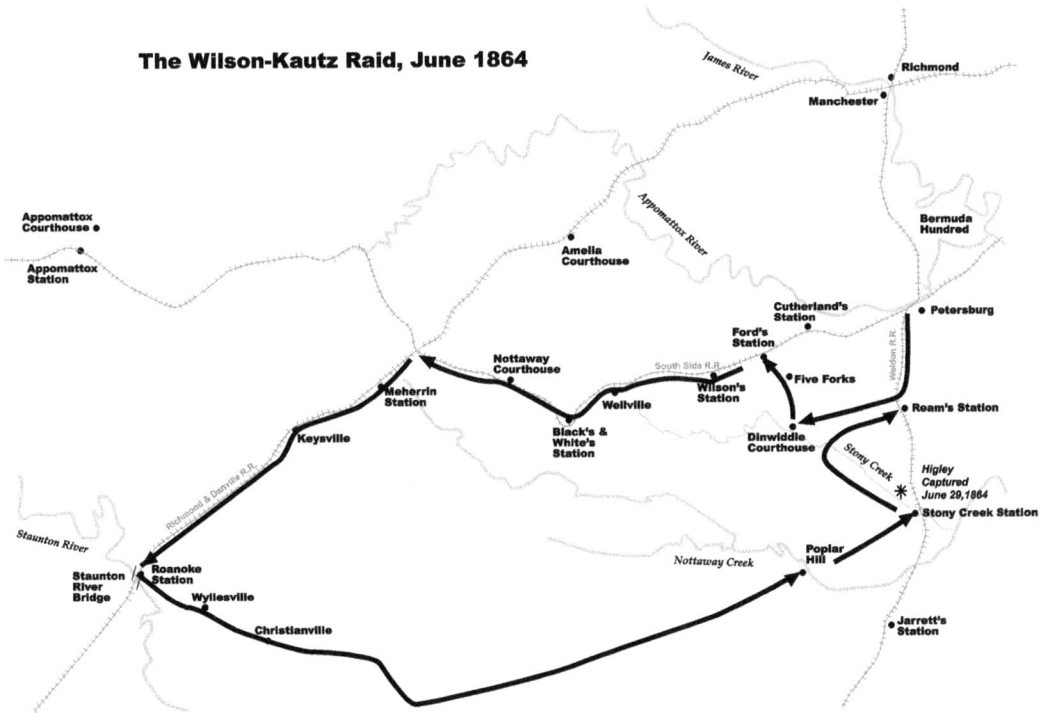

The Wilson-Kautz Raid, June 1864

Raid led by Brigadier Generals James H. Wilson and August Kautz in late June 1864. Map Illustrated by Robin Hanks.

Higley's capture came as Wilson's division, including the 1st Vermont Cavalry, covered the last flanking movement of Grant's campaign. Two Union corps held ground at Cold Harbor while three others slipped south to reach and cross the James—a twenty mile swing which would take them across the river and put them on the doorstep of Petersburg with its vital rail links to Richmond. Wilson's troopers secured Wilcox's Landing while a pontoon bridge was laid for the approaching infantry.

With the Army of the Potomac entrenched before Petersburg Grant directed Wilson, now reinforced with riders under Brigadier General August Kautz of Butler's department, to raid south and west of Petersburg, striking at the Petersburg & Weldon and Southside railroads. They began their task at 1 a.m. on June 22nd with 5,000 riders and were almost immediately harassed by Fitzhugh Lee's Confederate cavalry. Skirmishing was ongoing by the time they reached Dinwiddie Courthouse but over the next twenty-four hours the Federals wreaked havoc on rail and rolling stock needed to supply the rebel capital, additionally destroying mills and bridges as well as stores of grain, cotton and tobacco. A larger encounter at Nottoway Courthouse cost the regiment three dead and 21 wounded.[68]

Turning south they were met by infantry supporting protected artillery at the Staunton River bridge at Roanoke Station. Blocked from crossing, Wilson left Roanoke in flames

General James H. Wilson.
Library of Congress, LC-DIG-cwpb-06208.

and turned east, heading back to Petersburg. At Stony Creek, however, the Yankees found themselves confronted by Fitzhugh Lee again, this time reinforced by infantry. In a sunset attack by Confederate Wade Hampton's division on June 28th, Higley and the 1st Vermont Cavalry dismounted and quickly threw up makeshift breastworks. An initial Union advance after dark was met with withering fire from carbine and artillery. Sporadic fire continued through the night pinning men behind their hastily constructed works. At daybreak the division began pulling back a mile to the west and the road to Petersburg. During the movement, Colonel Chapman's brigade, including the Vermonters, was cut off. The Confederates threw regiment after regiment at the bluecoats, dug in behind the newly constructed earthen barriers, and maneuvered around to their flank and rear. A retreat by the men handling the brigade's horses left most of the brigade afoot and resulted in a hurried retreat by the overwhelmed Yankees. Some reached the horses and made for the division eight miles distant, while a few under Major Wells fought their way through and escaped. But sixty men, including Higley, classmate Sergeant Dwight Smith and Captain Eben Grant of Company I, were all captured. Higley wrote later of the stern reality of losing your freedom. "Our introduction to Southern hospitality was no exception to the general rule. A rifle barrel, gleaming unpleasantly near,--an invitation to surrender in terms more emphatic than polite,--and the ceremony was over."[69]

Disarmed, the Yankees were marched six to eight miles under a heavy June sun until they reached the "worn-out" trappings of a railroad. Any remaining possessions, watches, money or jewelry, were scavenged by guards along the way. They were loaded on flatcars and boxcars for transportation. "We found ourselves cramped, crowded, intertwined and twisted together in most disagreeable confusion," Higley wrote. Higley later wryly remembered the quilt of men as they tried to allocate a piece of floor for themselves. One "dark, close night" a nervous fellow "seized hold of, and commenced vigorously *scratching*, his companion's leg," wrote Higley, "and, when remonstrated with therefor, sighed forth—'Well, we *are* mixed up! *I thought that ar' leg*

165

was mine.'"[70]

They reached Weldon, North Carolina having gone twenty-four hours without food when "a few bags of cornmeal were brought to the door of the shed in which we were crowded," wrote Higley. Hungry men scrambled for anything to carry the grain—"pockets and coat linings were torn out, stocking-legs were amputated and every spare bit of cloth appropriated" with each man getting his precious share. Making something of their paltry allowance was another problem. Sheet iron was bent and fashioned into something akin to an oven and mixing pan from which came a dough dried over fire. Higley muses that, given his new circumstances, it would have served him better to have carried a skillet or kettle into battle rather than a musket.

Delayed in South Carolina on July 4th, they spent a hot sweltering night with Higley noting that it was "a year since I was in Washington, clean and comely, sipping my ice cream and soda water, attending celebrations and hearing fair music. Quo tempora mutantur! And yet today I am happier than a year ago."[71]

After 850 miles and a week's transit, they arrived at Camp Sumter near Americus, Georgia, better known as Andersonville. They had heard the stories of the terrible place and reports of its high death rates, wrote Higley, but hoped that the depictions were exaggerated. "But when we looked over from the railroad into that huge pen, swarming with its masses of suffering men, when we inhaled the odors of filth and death reeking from it,—our hearts sank within us." Hoping to disprove the worst truth, Higley asked a nearby guard about the gossip. "There's only forty-two been fetched to the dead house to-day, but we hain't got 'em all out yet," was the soldier's indifferent reply. Forty-two was the same number of Vermont enlisted men who were led away to their fate in the noxious confines of Andersonville; less than half would see the green mountains of their fair state again. Higley and Grant were "the possessors of shoulder straps," and as officers were taken to Camp Oglethorpe sixty miles away in Macon, Georgia on July 9th.[72]

166

Loud cries of "Fresh Fish!— "Fresh Fish!" greeted the newcomers when they first arrived, as veterans of this earthly hell—mostly bare-foot and bare-headed— shuffled toward them dressed in tattered uniforms patched from pieces of anything available. All were Federal officers; "veteran colonels and majors, captains and subalterns" who "had once stood resplendent in all the elegance of bullion and broadcloth, the showy dignitaries of parades, reviews and court-martial," now vestiges of their former selves.

Two days later Higley wrote of the numbing routine: "we sleep, cook, eat, wash our shirts, and ourselves, are counted by the prison keeper like so many sheep and that is all." Armed sentries dotted at intervals the stockade walkway sixteen feet above the inmates, with cannon positioned to silence any disturbance. "There was none of the romance of granite walls, massive, bolted doors and iron-grated windows"—no "Monte-Christo" experience gleaned from the pages of a Dumas novel which animated boyish minds in better days.

"A small brook ran through one corner of the enclosure, which served as wash-tub and sewer for the camp, and here could constantly be found a crowd of nude Yankees endeavoring to scrub themselves or their clothing into a state of cleanliness." Most of the 1,500 officers had been given planks to create makeshift shelters. Latecomers like Higley and Grant were lucky enough to find a corner of a shed occupied by members of the 1st Vermont Cavalry captured the year before. Rations were "a pint of unsifted corn meal, a few beans, two spoonfulls [sic] of rice and some atoms of salt and vinegar daily." Necessity made the men skillful with recipes. They "bake cornbread, fry corncakes, boil mush, and bean soup and alternate these dishes as best we can," he wrote; "vapid, mealy, tasteless monotony of the whole." A Confederate approved black market sporadically offered apples or an onion if one could obtain a bit of cash, otherwise visions of his mother's buckwheat cakes and buttered biscuits decorated with maple molasses or honey occupied Higley's dreams. Noble was also in his thoughts. "If ever I am permitted to resume communication and connection," Higley wrote, "I shall wish to send or say many things to you, O, Noble; my heart's friend, of whom I have so frequent thoughts, and whose weekly message I so greatly miss."[73]

Grant's campaign against Richmond forced the removal of prisoners to Macon and Andersonville. Sherman's penetration into Georgia again excited Southern concerns along with a late July Union cavalry raid on Macon, Georgia coinciding with Higley's arrival in camp. A decision was made to again move the prisoners to the better security of Savannah or South Carolina. On July 27th Higley and others were again packed into rail boxcars which left Macon, Georgia for Charleston, South Carolina at midnight. Twenty-four hours and 165 miles later— roughly half way between Savannah and Charleston— opportunity was seized by Higley and 38-year-old Captain William Beeman who jumped from the moving car at midnight escaping into a lowland of swamps. This was a country of rice plantations and the humid malarial sloughs which took a high toll on those slaves condemned to work them but handsome profits for their white owners.

Higley and Beeman walked the area looking for a way to the sea but realized that they were surrounded by a "belt of swamps" and retraced their steps back to the railroad cut to get a new bearing. Spying a lone black they revealed themselves, seeking directions about road positions and rivers. Learning little, they hole up in the swamp again until after dark and after a short walk came upon the plantation's "negro settlement" quieted for the evening. They slipped cautiously between the shacks, but were "accosted by one of the dusky inhabitants who seemed laboring under the weight of some intelligence which he longed to communicate." They again asked about a route to the coast but were bewildered by the man's unintelligible speech. Blacks in the coastal plains of South Carolina and Georgia spoke a dialect called Gullah—a creole language which incorporated English and a mixture of west and central African tongues which probably accounts for Higley's reference to the slave's "broken jargon." Hearing hoof beats, the slave gestured for them to wait and ran to a nearby gate. In another moment, wrote Higley, "a couple [of] confederate cavalry trotted into the street and we had barely time to whisper to each other 'we are gone up' when with cocked carbine they called on us to surrender. We were betrayed by the negroes. They had reported us to the overseer on our first appearance who had dispatched word to a cavalry camp near by."[74]

They reached the Old Charleston city jail on August 8th—a most villainous place according to Higley. The "nastiest, dirtiest, filthiest, lousiest place I ever was in," according to A.O. Abbott of the First New York Dragoons who left Macon just after Higley. Upon arriving, he heard that 70 officers had attempted to escape from the train but most were caught with some mangled by the dogs. The sudden increase in population resulted in a curtailment of rations shortly after Higley's arrival in Charleston. "Yesterday, our ration of beef was changed to one of lard, a spoonful and a half to a man, and today instead of bread were are offered some rice! Think of it—lard and rice for N. E. officers, captured in honorable war, to eat," Higley complained in his journal.

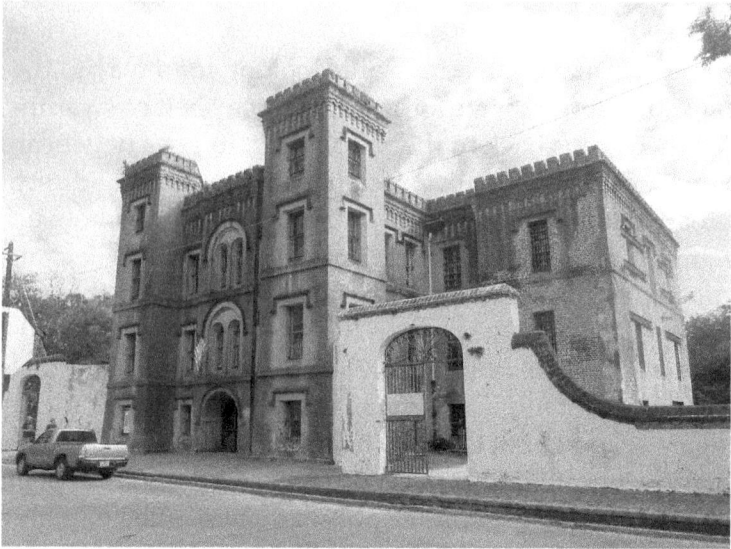

Old Charleston City Jail.
Wikimedia; created October 19, 2013.

The building itself was a "massive, ancient edifice, built in a unique style of architecture, with octangular towers and projecting angles," wrote Higley. The building held political prisoners, Confederate deserters and accused felons besides the growing number of Union captives. An estimated 600 Federal officers were packed onto the acre of its inner yard. A few tents were provided but most slept on the ground "unprotected by any covering." Abbott wrote that "the ground was literally covered with lice" and swarming with vermin, according to Higley, who added that "the water which we drank came from a cistern which stood in a repulsively close proximity to the sewer, and had about it a flavor of death, which seemed to feed, rather than ally, our feverish thirst."[75]

Death was commonplace and disease inevitable including for young Higley who quickly came down with fever; perhaps Yellow Fever. His journal entries are absent for twenty-two days and then only to record his weakened condition with short static updates. The illness does get him removed to nearby Roper

Hospital which Abbott later described as "paradise" compared to the raw jail yard. Higley described the first part of his illness as a blur "seen through the dim, dreamy vision of a brain weakened and at times blinded by fever." But, one memory stood out for the young lieutenant "as a light shining in a dark place . . . forms of woman, fair, pale women, dressed in flowing, black robes, moving gently about among us, bending tenderly over the sufferer's couch, speaking words of cheer, and cooling with soft hands the heated brow." They were a "Romish organization"-- the Sisters of Charity. "If Sodom was saved for ten righteous men," wrote Higley, "Charleston should stand forever in honor of these heroic women."[76]

Roper Hospital, Charleston, South Carolina, 1865.
An earthquake in August 1886 destroyed the building.
Library of Congress, LC-DIG-cwpb-03023.

The outbreak of Yellow Fever among the prisoners worried rebel authorities that it would spread to the surrounding civilian community. The Yankee hospital was therefore moved several miles out of town to Rykersville. This unfortunately limited the good sisters to only intermittent visits and introduced Higley to a deviant with a medical license, Dr. George Rogers Clark Todd, the brother of Mary Todd Lincoln. C.W. Brunt of the 1st New York Cavalry was in Rykersville at the same time as Higley and reported Todd to be a "profane, obscene, and brutal man. In his madness he would pound and kick the Union officers, and caused some to be bucked and gagged for spitting on the floor." "One of the most brutal and inhuman rebels whom I was ever unfortunate to meet," wrote Higley. "He used to come in occasionally and swear at a colored corporal of the 54th Massachusetts who had lost his leg at Fort Wagner the year before, or to threaten some sick man with a shooting, for violating some trivial regulation of the hospital."[77]

Many of the prisoners kept in the main building's upper floors were from the 54th and 55th Massachusetts—members of free black regiments, some captured during the storming of Fortress Wagner on July 18th, 1863. Captain Samuel Timson from the 95th New York Infantry wrote that there were twenty-one black soldiers from the 54th in the city jail. "They were never to be exchanged, but were to be reduced to slavery." They were all that remained from those captured at Wagner, Timson wrote. "The rest were bayoneted and shot after they surrendered." They were often given little to eat and used for the harshest labor such as cleaning and shoveling out the human filth. However, despite the abusive and inhuman treatment, soldiers such as Abbott found them "intensely loyal" and remarkably stoic about their condition. There are many accounts of the uplifting effect the singing of these black soldiers had on the other prisoners. "They were beautiful singers and usually between sunset and dark would come to the windows and sing to drive the blues away," said Abbott. They would sing Union songs, wrote Timson, "pouring their melody through their prison bars for the entertainment of the Union officers in the prison and below."[78]

Such few uplifting moments, however, were short respite to the daily misery. "O those were terrible days," Higley recalled months later. "To lie there, faint and languid, and see men dying, daily, all around, dying alone and uncared for,—to hear their calls for water and for aid, to hear the last messages for the loved ones at home, given to those who never thought to reach home for themselves,--to hear their pathetic pleadings with comrades, who expected soon to follow them to the same nameless grave, that *they* might be sent to lie in the old church yard with their fathers,—to see every morning the *'dead cart'* with its ghastly freight driven at a mad gallop away to the 'Potters Field,'—to see the victims of the Andersonville tortures brought in,--who were now no longer men, whose bodies and garments had become fused together in a mass of living corruptions—these things filled those days with scenes of horror, from the recital of which I am fain to cease."[79]

Higley's compiled service records show he was transferred to Camp Asylum on the northwestern edge of Columbia, probably in December 1864. Roughly 1,200 Union officers used the former

Camp Asylum prison in Columbia, South Carolina, n.d.
Library of Congress, LC-DIG-pga-01185.

state lunatic asylum until the camp closed on February 14, 1865 the day before Higley's 22nd birthday. Camp Asylum had several new barracks although some men had to endure the weather in outdoor pits.[80] As Sherman's army closed in on Columbia in mid-January 1865, prisoners were hurriedly moved to an open field in Charlotte, North Carolina. From there Higley's records show that he was paroled at the Northeast Ferry just south of Wilmington, North Carolina on the Cape Fear River the first part of March 1865. We have no record of Higley's thoughts or actions from September 29, 1864 until April 11, 1865 with his renewed correspondence to Noble.

A writer for the *Burlington Free Press* reported on the arrival of prisoners, including Higley, from Wilmington to Camp Parole in Annapolis, Maryland on March 6th. "Poor creatures, it makes one shudder to see so many of them as they arrive here, once healthy men, looking so thin and emaciated, and almost destitute of sufficient clothing to cover their nakedness. . . . It was very gratifying and amusing to hear the men shout and hurrah, as they are greeted on their arrival by the Band of the Post Hospital, playing the national airs of the land of the free."[81]

Camp Parole, Annapolis, Maryland, May 5, 1865.
Library of Congress, LC-DIG-pga-04081.

NOTES:

[1] **Philippics:** A Greek term used by the statesman and orator Demosthenes, meaning "a verbal denunciation characterized by harsh, often insulting language; a tirade."

[2] **Special Order 191**, issued June 25, 1863, offered incentives for soldiers re-enlisting prior to the expiration of their three year terms, as long as they had served at least nine months. Men received an extra month's pay, a signing bonus of $402 and a 30-day furlough. The men were classified as "Veteran Volunteers," and if three-fourths of the regiment re-enlisted, a Veteran Regiment. See: *What I Saw, From 1861 to 1864, Personal Recollections of John M. Paver, 1st Lieutenant Company C and R.Q.M. 5th Ohio Vol. Infantry* (Indianapolis: Scott-Miller Company, n.d.), 46-47.

[3] **Charles Kingsley** was born in Devon, England June 12, 1819. His literary work ranged from historical romances to poetry and children's literature (*The Water Babies*, 1863) and novels highlighting the plight of the poor (*Alton Locke*, 1850). He advocated for improved sanitation, adult education and "growth of the cooperative movement" rather than political change. In 1859 he became Queen Victoria's chaplain and in 1869 a professor of history at Cambridge University.

"The Sand of Dee,"(ballad poem) was one of his most well-known works which lamented the drowning death of a young girl as she tended her cattle. Its two middle stanzas are:

> The western tide crept up along the sand,
> And o'er and o'er the sand,
> And round and round the sand,
> As far as eye could see.
> The rolling mist came down and hid the land.
> And never home came she.
>
> 'O is it weed, or fish, or floating hair--
> A tress of golden hair,
> A drowned maiden's hair,
> Above the nets at sea?'
> Was never salmon yet that shone so fair
> Among the stakes of Dee.

See: Vivek Abhinav, "Charles Kingsley," *Encyclopedia Britannica*, 7-3-2013, Web, February 3, 2014, http://www.britannica.com/EBchecked/topic/318730/

George A. Mietzke (1835-1901) was a composer, pianist and vocal instructor in the Rutland, Vermont area. He was a prize graduate of the Leipzig Conservatory in Germany, before emigrating to the United States in 1857. Higley would spend two years at the Conservatory in the 1880s. Mietzke lived and taught for a time in New York state, but is living in the Rutland area by 1866 where he was a main influence in introducing the study of music to their school system—the first in the state to do so. He received an honorary Master of Arts degree from Middlebury College in 1862. In 1873 he organized Vermont's first musical festival which continued for seven years with great success. Edwin Higley performed with Mietzke at the 1873 festival. In 1890 he moved to North Adams, Massachusetts where he was organist and musical director for the First Congregationalist Church. He was well known throughout New England and his compositions were widely played. In 1874, Mietzke agreed to direct the music department at Castleton Seminary. He later moved to Rockville, Connecticut and became organist and musical director of the Union Church. He died in Hartford, Connecticut November 26, 1901. See: *Springfield* (Massachusetts) *Republican*, November 28, 1901; *The Rutland Globe*, May 2, 1874 as quoted in Helen K. Davidson, *"Tidbits from Then and Now," The First 600, June 10, 1999 to December 15, 2010*, Rutland Historical Society, 91; *Catalogue of the Officers and Students of Middlebury College*, 486.

[4] Many Union soldiers had enlisted for three years and were due to leave the army in 1864 which was of great concern to the Lincoln administration and Congress which did not go the way of the Confederacy of forcing re-enlistment but relied on inducements such as found in Special Order 191. In the end, 136,000 veterans did re-enlist although 100,000 thousand men chose to go home. See: McPherson, *Battle Cry of Freedom*, 719-720.

[5] Transcriptions of Higley Correspondence, January 20, 1864.

[6] **Cipher:** A person who has no power or is not important. **William F. Johnson** of Middlebury originally enlisted in Company I of the 1st Regiment of Vermont Volunteers (Infantry) in April 1861 as a three month volunteer. The regiment was stationed in and around Fortress Monroe on the tip of the Virginia peninsula until mustered out on August 15, 1861. He re-enlisted on December 31, 1863 and was promoted to commissary sergeant on November 19, 1864. See: *Revised Roster of Vermont Volunteers And Lists Of Vermonters Who Served In The Army And Navy Of The United States During The War Of The Rebellion, 1861-1866* (Montpelier, VT: Press of the Watchman Publishing Company, 1892), 23, 357.

[7] **Louis Moreau Gottschalk** (1829-1869) born in New Orleans, was a pianist and composer known for his romantic piano works. He wrote roughly 300 compositions in his lifetime and by the 1860s was the country's best known pianist. His opera company in 1862 and 1863 often included soprano Carlotta and violinist **Carlo Patti**, siblings of the famous opera coloratura soprano **Adalina Patti** (1843-1919) who debuted her career in New York City in 1859. Carlo Patti was known as a "superior violinist of bohemian temperament." Carlo and Gottschalk were known as some of New York's "male beauties." By the time of the concert Higley refers to, Carlo had created some controversy. Gottschalk was a well- known supporter of the Union but early in the war Patti had joined the Confederate army for a short time, only to desert out of boredom and tried to reach Havana on a blockade runner. Captured by a Federal gunboat, he was released from jail through the intervention of Gottschalk's manager. However, rumors of his participation with the rebels spread. See: S. Frederick Starr, *Louis Moreau Gottschalk (Music in American Life)* (Urbana-Champaign: University of Illinois Press, 2000), vii, 317-319, 341-342; *The Columbia Encyclopedia, Second Edition, Volume IV*, 1497.

[8] Transcriptions of Higley Correspondence, January 26, 1864; W. Storrs Lee, *Father Went to College*, 141.

[9] Custer married Elizabeth Bacon on February 9, 1864.

[10] See: *The War of the Rebellion: A Compilation of Official Records of the Union and Confederate Armies*, Series I, Volume XXIII, 114-120.

[11] **Gouverneur Kemble Warren** (1830-1882) graduated from West Point in 1850 and was assigned to the corps of topographical engineers, and surveyed areas of the west. With the onset of the Civil War, Warren commanded a brigade in the Peninsular Campaign of 1862. He is best known for seeing the vulnerability of the Union left wing on the second day at Gettysburg and diverted troops to protect the Round Tops. In August 1863 he was given command of the Army of the Potomac's II Corps. He led the corps in October 1863, defeating the Confederates of A.P. Hill at Bristoe Station. In March 1864 he was given V Corps which he commanded during the Wilderness Campaign leading to the siege of Petersburg. However, he was removed by Major General Phil Sheridan after the battle of Five Forks on April 1, 1865 when accused of procrastination and delay of action; although later exonerated of the charge. See: *The Columbia Encyclopedia, Second Edition, Volume V,* 2109.

[12] **Eugene Wilbur**. See: FN 50, Letter, Higley to Noble, October 5, 1863 in this work.

[13] **Charles Edward Prentiss** (1843-1906), was born in Weathersfield, Vermont and prepared for college at the Columbian College (preparatory department) in Washington, D.C. He graduated from Middlebury College in 1864 but did spend a year as a clerk at the U.S. Quartermaster's Department in 1862-1863. After the war he was a medical student at Georgetown University, graduating in 1868. After jobs in various government positions, he practiced medicine in Washington from 1878 to 1882. He became an Assistant Librarian at Middlebury College in 1896 holding the position until his death on March 5, 1906. See: *Catalogue of the Officers and Students of Middlebury College,* 219.

[14] **Pennons**: Swallow-tailed streamers typically attached to the head of a lance as an ensign; i.e. pennant.

[15] Legibility of the word Higley used after crossing out "satin" is difficult to decipher, but it is the editor's opinion that the phrase Higley was using was "silk muslin." A 1915 publication for the creation of costumes cites the use of soft silks; ". . .silk muslin, muslin, organdie," etc. for historical and romantic plays where hats would also be trimmed in "silk muslin." It also suggested that for plays of the Civil War, women's evening dresses use "silk muslin, satin, or tarlatan." Called Mousseline de soie by the French, it was considered firmer than chiffon. See: Constance D'Arcy Mackay, *Costume and Scenery for Amateurs: A Practical Working Handbook* (New York: Henry Holt and Company, 1915), 169, 174.

[16] For the time being; temporarily.

[17] An examination of Vermont newspapers shows **S.C. Moore** as a pianist and organist from Burlington, Vermont who had a large presence in the area in the 1860s and 1870s, and is often associated with various musical conventions held

throughout the state. He is frequently associated with H. I. Proctor, another pianist from St. Albans, Vermont. See, in part: *Burlington Free Press*, August 26, 1859 and *Vermont Phoenix*, September 14, 1866.

[18] **Sigismond Thalberg** (1812-1871) was born in Geneva Switzerland and was considered a rival to virtuoso pianist Franz Liszt. He began performing in Viennese salons at the age of 14. His mother Baroness von Wetzlar created his name after bearing him out of wedlock by Prince Moritz Dietrichstein. "Thal" means valley in German. "Berg" means mountain. Robert Shumann wrote of Thalberg that "he was famous for the elegance both of his person and of his playing." See: Robert Shumann, *Shumann on Music: A Selection from his Writings*, (Henry Pleasants, translator and ed.) (Mineola, New York: Dover Publications, Inc., 1988), 175-176.

Irish born **William Vincent Wallace** (1812-1865). Composed his first march at the age of eight for his soldier-father's regiment. By 16 he was the first violin in Dublin's Theatre royal orchestra. Hearing the great violinist Paganini inspired him; constant practice made him a virtuoso. Biographer Catherine Mackerras wrote that "as a man he was charming but unprincipled, and his habitual untruthfulness makes it hard to determine the real facts about him." See: Mackerras, "Wallace, William Vincent," *Australian Dictionary of Biography*, Web, February 7, 2014, http://adb.anu.edc.au/biography/wallace-william-vincent-2769.

[19] **Felicita von Vestvali** (1829-1880) was another favorite of theater goer Abraham Lincoln. Lincoln's enthusiasm for Vestvali brought him twice in one week to hear her in *Gamea, or the Jewish Mother* and the following week for two other musical dramas. See: Donald, *Lincoln*, 570. The *Daily National Republican* newspaper shows Vestvali performing *Gamea* on January 26, 1864 and beginning on January 29th, debuting her performances in *Maffio Orisini* and *The Brigand* at Grover's Theatre in Washington, D.C. Known as "Vestvali the Magnificent," she "was also an unusually visible lesbian," according to author Tony Howard. Born Anna Marie Staegemann in Stettin, Poland she became an internationally known actress and opera star. Her performances of Hamlet were as much lauded as they were controversial. Howard wrote that "Vestvali's Hamlet was not only a dreamer . . . she made him heroic and vividly represented his energetic will, his pressing, piercing decision toward action." She had come to America in 1855 and found great acclaim for her talents but returned to Europe in 1867. See: George Owen Willard, *History of the Providence Stage, 1762-1891* (Providence: The Rhode Island News Company, 1891), 171; Tony Howard, *Women as Hamlet: Performance and Interpretation in Theatre, Film and Fiction* (Cambridge: Cambridge University Press, 2007), 56-57.

[20] Ullery, compiler, *Men of Vermont: An Illustrated Biographical History of Vermonters and Sons of Vermont*, Part III, 83; Foote, *The Civil War, A Narrative: Fredericksburg to Meridian*, 910.

[21] **John Gregory Smith** (1818-1891) was born in St. Albans, Vermont and graduated from the University of Vermont in 1838 and Yale Law School in 1841. He became a trustee of his father's railroad company—the Vermont to

Canada Railroad—and was in the Vermont House of Representatives from 1860 until 1862 and successfully ran for governor in 1863. He was re-elected in 1864. Following the Confederate raid across the Canadian border on October 19, 1864, he formed the Frontier Cavalry and a militia unit to protect the state's northern boundary. The rebels robbed the banks of St. Albans and got away with $210,000. See: Albert Ricker Dowden, *Vermont History*, Vol. xxxii, No. 2 (April 1964), 79-97.

Possibly former governor **Frederick Holbrook** (1813-1909), who was born in Connecticut but settled in Brattleboro, Vermont in 1833. An agriculturist, Holbrook was elected to the State Senate in 1859-1860. He was elected to the governorship in 1862 on the Republican ticket and oversaw the raising of Vermont troops at the outbreak of the Civil War. The Draft Rendezvous at Brattleboro was named Camp Holbrook after the governor. Under his direction, Vermont was the first state to provide hospitals for soldiers with the major facility again in Brattleboro. See: Ullery, compiler, *Men of Vermont: An Illustrated Biographical History of Vermonters and Sons of Vermont*, Part III, 198-199.

[22] This is possibly **Edward S. Dana** who graduated from Middlebury College in 1876. Federal Census records show that Dana held clerk positions within various offices of the Federal government from 1862 to at least 1870, but worked primarily in the Pension Office although Higley wrote Patent Office. An 1866 news article announced his appointment as assistant clerk to the U.S. House of Representatives. The reference to New Haven is likely New Haven, Vermont where another Middlebury 1858 graduate **George Washington Squire** (1833-1864) was born. See: *Catalogue of the Officers and Students of Middlebury College*, 194, 254; *Boston Recorder*, November 30, 1866.

[23] **Evarts B. Kent** (1843-1924) was born in Benson, Vermont on March 12, 1843 and graduated from Middlebury College in 1865. He prepared for college at Castleton Seminary and entered Middlebury in 1861 as did Higley. As Higley wrote this letter, records indicate that Kent, on February 6, 1864 had enlisted in Company A of the 6th Vermont Infantry. He was wounded during the Battle of the Wilderness on May 6, 1864 and discharged from the service on February 25, 1865. After Middlebury he attended Harvard, Auburn Theological Seminary and Andover Theological Seminary and became a pastor in Sterling, Massachusetts and various other communities. See: *Catalogue of the Officers and Students of Middlebury College*, 223.

[24] Musician **Karl Anschütz** (1813-1870) was born in Coblentz, Germany and became conductor of the royal musical institution and its orchestra and musical director in approximately 1837. After a successful tour of performances in London, he came to the United States in 1857 with Ullman's Italian opera. In 1862 he founded the German opera in New York and was active in the New York Conservatory. He was known for his work with Beethoven's Ninth Symphony. Washington area newspapers show that Faust was performed in the city throughout the year by Anschütz. See: "Karl Anschütz," *Appletons' Cyclopædia of American Biography*, James Grant Wilson and John Fiske (eds.) (New York: D. Appleton and Company, 1888), 80.

[25] Foote, *The Civil War, A Narrative: Fredericksburg to Meridian*, 909-917; Collea, *The 1st Vermont Cavalry*, 211-216; Jeffrey Marshall in *The War of the People: Vermont Civil War Letters*, Jeffrey D. Marshall (ed.) (Hanover: University Press of New England, 1999), 203.

[26] Transcriptions of Higley Correspondence, March 2, 1864.

[27] Thoroughbreds.

[28] **Tamagent**: Originally used in medieval Europe as an imaginary deity of violent and turbulent character, often appearing in morality plays, the term was incorporated into literature and plays as a ranting, bullying person; violent, overbearing and later shrewish women.

[29] **Henry Herbert** (1843-1865) was born in Philadelphia and attended Middlebury College from 1859 until 1862 but never graduated. He was a member of the Chi Psi fraternity. He joined Company H of the 2nd U.S. Sharpshooters and was mustered in at Camp Holbrook in Brattleboro on December 31, 1861. Herbert rose to the rank of captain but resigned shortly after the Battle of Antietam in September, 1862. A year later he enlisted as a U.S. volunteer and was appointed as captain of Company G of the 6th U.S. Colored Troops. He died at Goldsboro, North Carolina on May 15, 1865. The Middlebury catalog of students and faculty erroneously lists his year of death as 1863. See: *Catalogue of the Officers and Students of Middlebury College*, 216; National Archives and Records Administration (NARA); Washington, D.C.; *Compiled Military Service Records of Volunteer Union Soldiers Who Served With the United States Colored Troops, 2nd through 7th Colored Infantry including 3d Tennessee Volunteers (African Descent), 6th Louisiana Infantry (African Descent), and 7th Louisiana Infantry (African Descent)*; Microfilm Serial: *M1820*; Microfilm Roll: *73*; *Philadelphia Inquirer*, May 20, 1865, pg. 5.

[30] **Sylvester Baron Partridge** (1837-1912) was born in Evans Mills, New York and graduated from Middlebury College in 1861. He enlisted as a private in the 92nd New York Volunteers and rose to 1st lieutenant in 1862. In 1863 he became the Chief Signal Officer for XXV Army Corps. He was promoted to brevet captain in 1865 and resigned that year. In 1868 he was ordained after attending the Newton Theological Seminary and was a missionary to Siam and Swatow, China until 1908. Returning to the U.S. he settled in Hamilton, New York. His work included translation of most of the New Testament into the Chinese of Tie-chiu. He died in Hamilton in 1912. See: *Catalogue of the Officers and Students of Middlebury College*, 205.

[31] **John Bankhead Magruder** (1810-1871) born in Winchester, Virginia graduated from West Point in 1830 a year behind future Confederate generals, Robert E. Lee and Joseph Johnston. His displays of daring during the Mexican American war won him the brevet rank of lieutenant colonel. He is stationed in Southern California during the 1850s where, as Captain Magruder serving under Samuel Heintzelman, he leads troops against the followers of Cupeño Indian leader Antonio Garra, helping to crush the rebellion of 1851 near San Diego. He resigned his commission with the coming of the Civil War and joined the Confederacy as a colonel but rose to brigadier general by the time of

the Peninsular Campaign in the spring of 1862. He may be best known for the tactics at that time against George McClellan which stalled the Union attack up the Virginia peninsula toward Richmond. At Yorktown, 13,000 rebels faced roughly 55,000 Federal troops. James McPherson wrote that Magruder, "a lover of the theater . . . marched his infantry in endless circles and moved his artillery noisily," convincing the Yankees that the forces facing them were much larger than they actually were. Even though President Lincoln demanded McClellan break the enemy lines, the cautious general dug in for an extended siege only to discover a month later that the Confederates had abandoned their positions just as the Union prepared for a barrage of heavy cannon. The delay gave time to move Southern troops to fortify the defense of Richmond. Known alternatively as a "renaissance man" of "wit and polish" or a "severe disciplinarian with a hot temper," he was dubbed "Prince John." After the war he became a major general in the army of Maximillian's imperialist Mexican regime. With the fall and execution of the emperor in 1867, Magruder settled in Houston, Texas where he died in 1871. See: McPherson, *Battle Cry of Freedom*, 426-427; George Harwood Phillips, *Chiefs and Challengers: Indian Resistance and Cooperation in Southern California* (Berkeley: University of California Press, 1975), 92-93; Gary Gallagher and James Robertson as quoted in Arnold M. Palovsky, *Riding in Circles, J.E.B. Stuart and the Confederate Cavalry, 1861-1862* (Southhampton, N.J.: Published by the author, 2010), 373; *The Columbia Encyclopedia, Second Edition, Volume III*, 1198.

[32] *Hard Cash* was first published in 1863 under the title *Very Hard Cash* by English novelist and dramatist, **Charles Reade** (1814-1884). He was an avid defender of causes in which he believed and began a series of propagandist novels such as *Hard Cash*, which exposed the injustices inherent in the English system of insane asylums. The book highlights the lax policies for committing and warehousing a person, often without mental problems, and the lack of scientific pursuit in the field or training. See: *Columbia Encyclopedia, Second Edition, Volume IV*, 1646.

[33] **George Sand** was the pseudonym for the French novelist Amandine Aurore Lucie Dupin, baronne Dudevant (1804-1876). After divorcing her husband Baron Dudevant in 1836, she supported herself and her children by writing 80 novels during her life, all finding broad popularity. Her initial focus on romantic themes changed later in life to works showing concern for social reform especially more social liberties for women which her work *Consuelo* represents. Controversy often surrounded her sexual involvement with men such as Chopin, Franz Liszt and Jules Sandeau (whose name she abbreviated for her pen name). The English translation of *Consuelo* was first published in 1846. It explores the musical life of the talented Consuelo whose innocence and talent provide her strength through many adventures. See: *Columbia Encyclopedia, Second Edition, Volume IV*, 1747.

[34] Officers in charge of military police and thus responsible for military discipline in a large camp, area, or city.

[35] *Softly Ye Night Winds*: An 1851 nocturne for piano and voice by William Vincent Wallace. Lyrics were written by Mary E. Hewitt.

[36] *The Creation* or *Die Schöpfung*, an oratorio written by Joseph Haydn between 1796 and 1798 and considered by many to be his master work. It celebrates the

creation of the world as told in Genesis and Milton's *Paradise Lost*. See: Anthony Tommasini, "No Requiem for Earth, Only Celebration Haydn's 'The Creation,' at Carnegie Hall," *New York Times*, December 24, 2012.

[37] **John H. Hazelton** (1838-1878) enlisted in Company H on November 19, 1861 as a sergeant. He was promoted to 2nd lieutenant in October 1862 and 1st lieutenant on April 1, 1863. He was made captain of Company M on July 6, 1863. Company M was assigned as escort for General Hancock and staff in the spring of 1864 after he had been given command of II Corps of the Army of the Potomac. See: Historical Data Systems, comp. *U.S., Civil War Soldier Records and Profiles, 1861-1865* [database on-line]. Provo, UT, USA: Ancestry.com Operations Inc, 2009. Original data: Data compiled by Historical Data Systems of Kingston, MA .; Ancestry.com. *Vermont, Vital Records, 1720-1908* [database on-line]. Provo, UT, USA: Ancestry.com Operations, Inc., 2013. Original data: State of Vermont. Vermont Vital Records through 1870. New England Historic Genealogical Society, Boston, Massachusetts.

[38] Major General **Winfield Scott Hancock** (1824-1886) showed an interest in military affairs from an early age. Born near Lansdale, Pennsylvania, his father was a lawyer and deacon in the Baptist Church. He was named after Brigadier General Winfield Scott, a veteran of the War of 1812. He entered the army's military academy in 1840 and remained in the army for the next 45 years. Graduating in 1844 eighteenth out of twenty-five of his West Point class, he was assigned to the 6th Infantry and served two years in the west. He served under Winfield Scott in the Mexican American War. After the war he was stationed in St. Louis, Florida and Fort Leavenworth, Kansas during that state's violent days prior to the Civil War. In 1858 he was assigned to Los Angeles, California where he forged strong friendships with several men whom he would face during the national conflict including Albert Sydney Johnston, Richard Garnett and Louis Armistead, his closest friend whom he met in 1844. The men gathered at the Hancock home on a summer evening early in 1861—a tearful farewell party before the Southern sympathizers headed to the Confederacy—a fact Hancock chose to overlook. Two years later Hancock commanded the center of the Union lines at Gettysburg during the third day attack. Rebel brigade commander Armistead received a fatal wound at the famous stone wall hoping to see his friend one more time, only to learn Hancock had been taken from the field severely wounded as well. After the war Hancock served in the west and in New Orleans and finally as head of the Department of the East centered at Governors Island, New York. He was the Democratic candidate for president against James Garfield in 1880. He died at Governors Island in 1886 still in charge of the Military Division of the Atlantic. See: Jones, *Generals in Blue and Gray*, Volume 1, 309-322.

[39] Collea, *The 1st Vermont Cavalry*, 222.

[40] **Reverend Benjamin Labaree** (1801-1883) was born in Charlestown, New Hampshire and prepared for college at Kimball Union Academy of that state. He graduated from Dartmouth in 1828 and was ordained in 1831 after attending the Andover Theological Seminary. He later earned a degree from the University of Vermont (1841). He taught in Tennessee becoming a Professor of Ancient

Languages from 1832 until 1836 and became president of Jackson College in Columbia, Tennessee in that time leaving the post in 1837 and resided, pastoring and lecturing on Moral Philosophy and International Law, in New York, Massachusetts, New Hampshire and finally at Middlebury College where he became the longest serving president of the college from 1840 until 1866. See: *Catalogue of the Officers and Students of Middlebury College*, xxviii.

[41] Although Higley clearly writes the officer's name as General Talbot, this is certainly a misspelling. **Alfred Thomas Archimedes Torbert** was given command of the cavalry corps' 1st Division on April 10, 1864, which had been John Buford's until his death in December 1863. It is likely that Higley only heard the name of General Buford's replacement and did not see it written.

[42] **Charles Pomeroy Stone** (1824-1887) was an 1845 graduate of West Point and served as an ordnance officer in the Mexican American War and later as Chief of Ordnance for the Department of the Pacific. He resigned in 1856 and worked as a surveyor for the Mexican government but with the Civil War he left for Washington where he helped secure the capital as Inspector General of the District. By August 1861 he was a brigadier general of volunteers serving in the Shenandoah Valley and the Bull Run Campaign. He commanded Union forces during the ill-fated Battle of Ball's Bluff in October 1861 attempting to dislodge Confederates from Leesburg, Virginia which cost the Union 1,000 casualties including Lincoln's close friend and Oregon Senator Edward Baker. Fallout from the defeat led to Stone's arrest and six month imprisonment although no charges were filed against him. He was not reassigned until May 1863 and then as Chief of Staff to Nathaniel Banks who commanded the Department of the Gulf during the Red River Campaign of March to May 1864. The campaign was a failed attempt to secure more of Louisiana and seize local cotton stocks by driving up the Red River. Stone was demoted to colonel of the regular army on April 4, 1864 and although serving for a time during the siege of Petersburg, resigned from the army in September 1864. He later served 13 years as the chief of staff in the Egyptian army. He died in Washington, D.C. See: Ted Ballard, *Battle of Ball's Bluff, Staff Ride Guide* (Washington: Center of Military History, United States Army, 2001), 67-68.

[43] **Dunbar R. Ransom** was born in North Carolina in 1831 but raised in Vermont. His younger brother was **Thomas Edwin Greenfield Ransom**. He attended the U.S. Military Academy from 1847 to 1850 when he resigned. He graduated from Norwich University in 1851 and was then appointed as a 2nd lieutenant in the 3rd U.S. Artillery in 1855. Dunbar served on the west coast and as a 1st lieutenant and participated in actions against northwestern Indian tribes in 1858. With the outbreak of the Civil War, he was given command of a 3rd U.S. Artillery battery in 1861, with the rank of captain. He participated in the battle of Second Bull Run with the 5th U.S. Artillery. He was in command of several batteries at Gettysburg when badly wounded. He returned to the Army of the Potomac in charge of Battery C of the 3rd U.S. Artillery and took part in the Bristoe and Mine Run campaigns in late 1863. Ransom is listed as participating in the Kilpatrick-Dahlgren raid in March 1864. Higley was assigned to that battery during the raid and although credited with lobbing the first artillery shells into the Confederate

capital, he wrote Noble on March 17, 1864 (in this work) that despite Richmond being in range of their incendiary shells, they concentrated on the breastworks in their immediate front. See: *The Reports of Committees of the House of Representatives for the 2nd Session of the Fifty-Third Congress, In Five Volumes*, volume 2 (Washington: Government Printing Office, 1893-1894), Report #518; Also: Ullery, *Men in Vermont*, part III, 83. General Thomas Ransom had command of XIII Corps in the Red River Campaign and the XVI Corps under William Sherman in the campaign which took Atlanta in the fall of 1864. During Sherman's march through Georgia, Ransom commanded XVII Corps of Sherman's army. See: Benedict, *Vermont in the Civil War*, Volume II, 789.

[44] Transcriptions of Higley Correspondence, April 25, 1864.

[45] Foote, *The Civil War, A Narrative: Red River to Appomattox* (New York: Vantage Books, 1986), 136-137; McPherson, *Battle Cry of Freedom*, 675. Just two days prior to initiating Grant's plan, Higley wrote that "I have been playing ball very hard for two days and my arm is so sore that I can hardly write." See: Transcriptions of Higley Correspondence, May 2, 1864. Baseball was popular entertainment for soldiers in Civil War camps and it is not uncommon to see references to such games in diaries and regimental histories. See: George B. Kirsch, *Baseball in Blue and Gray: The National Pastime During the Civil War* (Princeton: Princeton University Press, 2003), 37.

[46] **Pasquale Brignoli** (1824-1884) was born in Naples, Italy and came to the United States in 1855. *The Encyclopedia Americana* said that Brignoli "for 30 years was one of the most popular opera tenors in this country in spite of the fact that he was an awkward, mediocre actor. His voice was unusually flexible and its carrying power very great." One critic said that while he had the voice of an angel he had the manners of a codfish. However, celebrated American poet Walt Whitman was a fan of the Italian tenor and composed a poem called "The Dead Tenor" only a few days after the singer's death on October 30, 1884. Writing of the artist, Whitman said that, "I doubt if a singer ever lived, a tenor, with a sweeter voice than Brignoli . . . I never thought of his manners when I heard him sing: they were not present; they were easy to forget." According to one of Brignoli's obituaries, he had some strange superstitions including never starting a performance on a Friday and always rubbing the hump of any hunchback he met for good luck. He was closely associated with the star Adelina Patti although Higley incorrectly cites her sister as Carlotti instead of Carlotta. See: *Enciclopedia Americana*, Frederick Converse Beach (ed.), (New York: The Americana Company, 1904); *Walt Whitman: Selected Poems, 1855-1892*, Gary Schmidgall (ed.), (New York: St. Martin's Press, 1999), 513; The *New York Herald*, October 31, 1884, pg. 5.

[47] A male admirer or suitor.

[48] A line from "Ever Be Happy, the pirate's farewell;" a ballad from the opera *The Enchantress* by Irish composer Michael William Balfe (Philadelphia: Edward L. Walker, 1849). The lyrics were written by Augustine Duganne.

[49] **Germaine de Staël** (1766-1817) was another free thinking female writer of a slightly earlier period than artists like Elizabeth Sheppard and George Sand.

Born in Paris, Anne Louise Germaine Necker (her full name) was of French/ Swiss ethnicity, who was shaped by discussions of art, literature and politics in her mother's salon. Her marriage in 1786 was arranged to Swedish diplomat Baron Staël-Holstein. Helen Jenkins wrote that Madame de Staël's salon during the upheaval of the French Revolution, "was the rallying place of the 'Constitutionals,'" such as Lafayette who hoped for a constitutional monarchy or republic. Driven from Paris by the reign of terror and separated amicably from her husband, Staël joined other exiles in London. Upon her return to Paris, she became an ardent critic of Napoleon after his rise to power and the enmity between the two was well known. A trip to Italy inspired the novel *Corinne, or Italy* in 1807. The book's prose, concerning a love affair between an Englishman and an Italian performer, thinly obscures a political message against French imperialism promoted through the nationhood of England and Italy. Infuriated, Napoleon ordered all initial copies of the book destroyed. Forced to again flee France she returned in 1815 where she died two years later. See: Helen Philleo Jenkins, "Madame da Stael," in *The Congress of Women; Held in the Woman's Building, World's Columbian Exposition, Chicago, U.S.A., 1893, Mary Kavanaugh Oldham Eagle (ed.), (Chicago, Ill: Monarch Book Company, 1894), 686-690.

[50] McPherson, *Battle Cry of Freedom*, 723-726, 728; Foote, *The Civil War, A Narrative: Red River to Appomattox*, 146-147; Foote, *The Civil War, A Narrative: Red River to Appomattox*, 215.

[51] Ibid, McPherson, 728-729.

[52] Foote, *The Civil War, A Narrative: Red River to Appomattox*, 221; Benedict, *Vermont in the Civil War: A History of the Part Taken by the Vermont Soldiers and Sailors in the War for the Union, 1861-5*, Volume I, (Burlington, VT: The Free Press Association, 1886), 446.

[53] Transcriptions of Higley Correspondence, May 13, 1864.

[54] **Quire**: a collection of 24 or sometimes 25 sheets of paper of the same size and quality: one twentieth of a ream.

[55] **Andrew Jackson Grover** (1832-1917) was born in Harvard, Massachusetts and enlisted as a 1st lieutenant in Company E of the 1st Vermont Cavalry on October 16, 1861. He was promoted to captain of Company K on February 2, 1863. On May 5, 1864 he was wounded in the Battle of the Wilderness. He died in 1917 and is buried in Hartford, Vermont. An 1880 census shows him married and selling clothing in Hartford. See: "Grover, Andrew Jackson," *Vermont in the Civil War*, Cemetery Database, Web, February 11, 2014, http://vermontcivilwar.org/get.php?input=2655.

[56] The 1500 men of the 11th Vermont joined the Vermont Brigade in time for the assault on Confederate lines at Spotsylvania. The brigade, part of Sedgwick's VI Corps, consisted of the 2nd, 3rd, 4th, 5th, and 6th Vermont regiments and would see some of the toughest fighting of the campaign. The brigade had approximately 2850 men at the beginning of the Wilderness campaign. They were in the lead on May 12th and they would be at Cold Harbor days later. By the middle of June 1864 it is estimated that the Vermont Brigade had been reduced to only 1200

soldiers. See: Benedict, *Vermont in the Civil War*, Volume I, 414, 434.

[57] McPherson, *Battle Cry of Freedom*, 732-733; Foote, *The Civil War, A Narrative: Red River to Appomattox*, 281, 288.

[58] W. Storrs Lee, *Father Went to College*, 141-142.

[59] **Poltroons**: spiritless cowards.

[60] **Riley A. Bird** (1836-1864) was born in Bristol, Vermont and enlisted on October 15, 1861 into Company A of the 6th Vermont Infantry—the same regiment which included Higley's friends **Albert Crane** and **Evarts Kent**. Bird was promoted to captain on November 1, 1862. He died May 5, 1864 during the Battle of the Wilderness as did Crane. Kent was wounded in the same battle on May 6th. George Benedict wrote that "Captain Riley A. Bird (of Bristol) of Company A, a soldier of rare merit, especially distinguished himself on the first day, and died before its close. He was first wounded in the head, and advised to go to the rear, but with the blood streaming down his face he sternly and even angrily refused, saying that it was 'the business of no live man to go to the rear at such a time.' Soon a second musket ball struck him in the thigh. He retired a few steps, sat down, took off his sash, bound it round his leg, and then resumed his place in the line. A third bullet pierced his heart, and he fell dead with the word which he was cheering on his men cut short upon his lips." See: George Grenville Benedict, *Vermont in the Civil War:* Volume I, 224-225. See also: "Riley A. Bird" *Vermont in the Civil War*, Web, February 11, 2014, http://www.vermontcivilwar. org/units/6/obits.php?input=497.

[61] This is likely **Henry Augustus Eaton** (1838-1864) who was born in Granville, Vermont and left Middlebury College in 1862 and was commissioned a captain in Company A of the 16th Vermont Volunteers in August of that year. He was severely wounded on the third day of the Gettysburg battle and mustered out of the service on August 10, 1863. After his recovery, however, he joined the 17th Vermont Volunteers as a captain of Company D on March 4, 1864, and was elevated to major August 12, 1864 and finally lieutenant colonel. He died in action during the siege of Petersburg, Virginia on September 30, 1864. See: *Catalogue of the Officers and Students of Middlebury College*, 208.

[62] McPherson, *Battle Cry of Freedom*, 732-735.

[63] Assistant Provost Marshal **Alexander M. McCune** (1835-1864) joined the 71st New York Volunteers in New York City on May 10, 1861. He was mustered in as 2nd lieutenant of Company F but was made 1st lieutenant May 19, 1862 and Adjutant on May 31st of that year. He is discharged for unspecified reasons on August 2, 1862 but is commissioned a 2nd lieutenant in Company K of the 74th New York Volunteers on September 18, 1862. He made 1st lieutenant on March 7, 1863 and was promoted to captain of Company G on December 14, 1863. The nighttime assault Higley describes in his letter took place on the evening of June 5, 1864 as the army dug in for several days around the battlefield of Cold Harbor. General Hancock recorded McCune's injury in his report adding that the captain was hit while standing in the doorway of Hancock's tent. "The shot and shell raked the headquarters fearfully," Hancock wrote, "and scattered all servants,

teamsters, etc." See: *The War of the Rebellion: A Compilation of Official Records of the Union and Confederate Armies,* Series I, Volume XXXVI, Part I, 182, 346, 368. After McCune's leg was amputated he was taken to the Armory Square Hospital in Washington, D.C. where he died on June 19, 1864. See: *New York in the War of the Rebellion, 1861-1865,* compiled by Frederick Phisterer, (Albany: J.B. Lyon Company, state printers, 1912), 2731, 2777.

[64] Colonel **Addison Webster Preston** (1830-1864), was born in Burke, Vermont but moved to Danville at an early age and would enlist from the village on October 15, 1861, being mustered in on November 19, 1861 as captain of Company D of the 1st Vermont Cavalry. He was promoted to lieutenant colonel on September 16, 1862 and to full colonel on April 29, 1864. He attended Brown University at the age of 21 but ill health forced his departure and he sailed to Australia and California where he spent several years. He was in business at Danville when the war commenced and helped recruit Company D of the 1st Vermont. He often had command of the regiment for the twenty months prior to his death given the frequent absences of particularly Edward Sawyer. On June 3rd, the regiment was supporting Burnside's IX Corps on the far right side of the Union line and met resistance from Fitzhugh Lee's troopers in rifle pits in a wooded area near Haw's Shop. Seeing men in between the lines, Preston approached on foot thinking them Yankees only to be struck near the heart with a musket ball.

George Benedict wrote of Preston that, "as a man he was frank, hearty, genial, quick of thought and action. As a fighter he was brave to a fault, impetuous, eager to strike, ready to go himself wherever he sent his men, and unwilling to leave any place of danger as long as there was anything to be done. . . . Had he lived a few days longer he would have been promoted to a brigadier generalship; for he stood very high with his superiors, and they were only waiting for his appointment as colonel, to give him higher rank and more responsible duties." Custer said of him: "There lies the best fighting colonel in the Cavalry Corps." See: Benedict, *Vermont in the Civil War,* Volume I, 645-646, 649; *Revised Roster of Vermont Volunteers And Lists Of Vermonters,* 214-215, 220, 234.

[65] Captain **Oliver Tucker Cushman** (1841-1864), born in Hartland, Vermont left Dartmouth College with the war's start and enlisted as a sergeant in Company E of the 1st Vermont Cavalry on October 12, 1861 and was mustered in November 19th. He was promoted to 2nd lieutenant on April 10, 1862 and 1st lieutenant on February 1, 1863 and finally captain on March 17, 1863 (the same day as the ill-fated Herndon raid which was wrongly blamed on Higley). He was severely wounded in the face on the third day at Gettysburg. Benedict wrote that Cushman "was recognized as one of the finest young men and best soldiers in the regiment—gallant, patriotic, high-spirited and faithful to every duty. He was severely wounded at Gettysburg, receiving injuries which would have justified him in resigning; but instead he hastened back to his regiment almost before his wound was healed, and served till he met his death." See: Benedict, *Vermont in the Civil War,* Volume I, 646; *Revised Roster of Vermont Volunteers And Lists Of Vermonters,* 238.

[66] Captain **Ellis B. Edwards** (1842-1920) enlisted in Company A of the 1st Vermont Cavalry in October 1861 and was mustered in as a 2nd lieutenant on

November 1st of that year. He was promoted to 1st lieutenant on July 16, 1862, the same day Higley was promoted to 2nd lieutenant of Company K. On February 7, 1863 Edwards was promoted to captain of Company A following the resignation of Ellis' friend Joel B. Erhardt. Following the war the two men became close associates in New York politics and engaged in several real estate ventures primarily in the area around New York City. Erhardt was president of the New York and Northern Railroad with Ellis as a superintendent of the company until both men resigned on June 30, 1888. Erhardt then ran unsuccessfully for mayor of New York City as a Republican, but was appointed as U.S. Collector of Customs from 1889 to 1891. An 1892 article in the *New York Times* reported that Edwards was associated with Erhardt and "in politics, has owed much to the ex-Collector in business and for personal favors, and in turn has trusted Mr. Erhardt as implicitly as one friend can trust another, and has obeyed him as a soldier obeys his General." Erhardt died in Manhattan in 1909. Edwards and his wife Adah apparently retired to Zephyrhills, Florida where Edwards died on March 3, 1920. See: *Revised Roster of Vermont Volunteers And Lists Of Vermonters*, 214, 223,735; *New York Times*, September 9, 1909 and April 19, 1892; Federal census returns for 1900, 1910 and 1920.

[67] Major General **James Harrison Wilson** (1837-1925): a native of Shawneetown, Illinois, he attended McKendree College for a year before entering West Point where he graduated sixth in a class of forty-one in 1860. An able student he was made a 2nd lieutenant in the army's elite Topographical Engineers and served briefly in the Pacific Northwest. With the beginning of the war, he became part of the Port Royal expedition and later made aide-de-camp for George McClellan during the Maryland campaign culminating with Antietam. Promoted to 1st lieutenant he was chief engineer for the Army of Tennessee until early 1863, when as a lieutenant colonel he was assigned as inspector general and assistant engineer of the Union army at Vicksburg where he became friends with Ulysses Grant. Upon Grant's recommendation, Wilson was chosen to head the cavalry bureau in Washington, D.C. in October 1863, with the rank of brigadier general despite the fact that he had no experience with cavalry. Wilson, however, gets high marks as an organizer from biographers, weeding out graft and supplying many regiments with new repeating Spencer carbines. He wins the job as a division commander in April 1864 again on Grant's request which produced the scorn of more senior officers. Six months later Grant promoted Wilson again to major general and assigned him as commander of William Sherman's cavalry corps in the Military Division of the Mississippi. The rank of major general in the regular army would be secured by Wilson after cavalry under his command captured Jefferson Davis on May 10, 1865. Biographer Jerry Keenan wrote of Wilson that "of medium build, he was a fine physical example of young manhood. A contemporary described him as a 'slight person of light complexion and with a rather pinched face.' An intense young man with a full measure of arrogance, Wilson was driven by an almost ruthless ambition to succeed." The controversy surrounding the Kilpatrick-Dahlgren raid of February and March 1864 tarnished Kilpatrick and he was reassigned to Sherman's western command on April 17, 1864 and demoted to a brigade commander. His divisional command was given to James Wilson with Grant's cavalry corps now headed

by Major General Phil Sheridan. Initially Custer's brigade, including the 1st Vermont, was re-assigned to the 1st Division commanded by Alfred Torbert but quickly the 1st Vermont was shifted back to the 3rd Division under the command of Colonel George Chapman which created a good deal of discontent particularly among members of the Vermont regiment. See: Keenan, *Wilson's Cavalry Corps: Union Campaigns in the Western Theater, October 1864 Through the Spring 1865* (Jefferson, NC: McFarland & Company, Inc., 1998), 3-10, 211-218; Collea, *The 1st Vermont Cavalry*, 222-224.

[68] Benedict, *Vermont in the Civil War*, Volume II, 647-651; McPherson, *Battle Cry of Freedom*, 739-744.

[69] Ibid., Benedict, 652-654; Higley, "Concerning Southern Prisons," *Noble Scraps*, (first paper). These are from a scrapbook with a collection of undated newspaper articles kept by Day Noble. Many are articles or reviews written by him. Three lengthy articles were written by Higley describing, with some detail, his time as a prisoner of war from June 1864 to March 1865. It is more than likely that these articles were published in 1865 after Higley's release and at a time when Noble was employed as an editor and writer for the *Vermont Record* newspaper. The articles will herein be referenced as *Noble Scraps*.

[70] Ibid., "Concerning Southern Prisons," *Noble Scraps* (first paper). In his memoirs A. O. Abbott described the rail lines of the South: "Their rolling stock was nearly worn out, the rails broken, splintered, and battered, the ties rotten, and, altogether, it was a dangerous matter to ride at all upon them, to say nothing of speed." See: A.O. Abbott, *Prison Life in the South: At Richmond, Macon, Savannah, Charleston, Columbia, Charlotte, Raleigh, Goldsborough and Andersonville During the Years 1864 and 1865* (New York: Harper & Brothers, Publishers, 1865), 43-44. This lieutenant of the First New York Dragoons was removed from Camp Oglethorpe at Macon at the same time as Higley and spent time in some of the same facilities as the Vermonter including the Charleston City Jail.

[71] Transcriptions of Higley Correspondence (Diary), July 4, 1864; Higley, "Concerning Southern Prisons," *Noble Scraps* (first paper). **"Quo tempora mutantur;"** Latin for the times are changing, and we are changing with them. Higley is remembering the shame of a year ago when faced with charges of cowardice in the face of the enemy. He found captivity preferable to that embarrassment.

[72] Higley, "Concerning Southern Prisons," *Noble Scraps* (first paper). **Andersonville Prison** operated from February 1864 to March 1865 and became one of the most notorious camps for brutality and a high mortality rate. Meant to hold 8-10,000 prisoners on, in the end, twenty-six acres, an estimated 45,000 men were imprisoned during its operation with the August 1864 population put at 32,000. Nearly 13,000 men died there of malnutrition, contaminated water, disease such as dysentery and no semblance of medical care. The camp's commander Henry Wirz, was the only man in the Civil War to be charged, tried, convicted and executed for war crimes.

Camp Oglethorpe in Macon, Georgia was opened in 1862 on fifteen to twenty acres and primarily meant for Union officers. The Old Floral Hall which was at the center of what had been the county's fair grounds housed roughly 200 men, generally of the higher rank. It was surrounded by a 16-foot stockade similar to the one at Andersonville. Higley's arrival there coincides with a raid on Macon by General George Stoneman in the waning days of July where the general was taken prisoner. However, it prompted Confederate authorities to move their prisoners from Oglethorpe and Andersonville. By the end of September 1864 Oglethorpe basically ceased to exist. See: Henry Segars, *Andersonville: The Southern Perspective* (St. Petersburg, FL: Southern Heritage Press, 1995), 2-3; *New York Times*, August 14, 1864; "Camp Oglethorpe," *National Park Service*, Web, February 21, 2013, http://www.nps.gov/history/history/online books/civil war series/5/sec7.htm; Transcriptions of Higley Correspondence (Diary), July 9, 1864

[73] Higley, "Concerning Southern Prisons", *Noble Scraps* (second paper); Transcriptions of Higley Correspondence (Diary), July 11 and 21, 1864.

[74] Transcriptions of Higley Correspondence (Diary), July 28, 29, August 8, 1864. Higley writes his account after being taken to the Old Charleston jail. The captain with him, **William Mills Beeman** (1826-1918) was born in 1826, probably in Hartford, Connecticut but joined the 1st Vermont Cavalry from St. Albans, Vermont in October 1861 as a 1st lieutenant of Company B. He was promoted to captain a year later and was captured on October 11, 1863 at the battle of Brandy Station where Higley had been engaged as part of rear guard skirmishers for the division. Beeman was paroled on December 10, 1864 and returned to his family in St. Albans that year in poor health after his long imprisonment. He moved his family to Hartford, Connecticut in October 1865 and again opened a watch and clock repair shop which he was still working at the age of 90. He died in Hartford in 1918 at the age of 92. See: *St. Albans Messenger*, March 9, 1916; "William Beeman," *Ancestry.com*, personal stories excerpted from an unidentified 1908 Hartford newspaper, Web, February 22, 2014; "Beeman, Wliam M.," *Vermont in the Civil War*, Cemetery Database, Web, February 22, 2014, http://vermontcivilwar.org/get.php?input=415. While there are many more instances of slaves assisting escaped Union prisoners to freedom, it is not unprecedented that blacks might, either through fear or reward, betray escapees. See: William Dusinberre, *Them Dark Days: Slavery in the American Rice Swamps* (Oxford: Oxford University Press, 1996), 6-8, 74-75, 133.

[75] Higley, "Concerning Southern Prisons" *Noble Scraps* (third paper); Abbott, *Prison Life in the South*, 104, 113; Transcriptions of Higley Correspondence (Diary), August 8, 1864.

[76] Higley, "Concerning Southern Prisons" *Noble Scraps* (third paper); Abbott, *Prison Life in the South*, 114.

[77] **Timson** as quoted in Luis Fenollosa Emilio, *A Brave Black Regiment: History of the Fifty-Four Regiment of Massachusetts Volunteer Infantry, 1863-1865* (Boston: The Boston Book Company, 1894), 416; Higley, "Concerning Southern Prisons" *Noble Scraps* (third paper). **George Rogers Clark Todd** was the youngest of Mary Lincoln's biological siblings, born in July 1825 in Lexington, Kentucky. He died in Camden, South Carolina in 1902. Michael Burlingame writes of Todd that he "referred to himself as the 'black sheep' of the family, that he did 'not get

along with people,' and that he was 'very egotistical and extremely jealous of his professional reputation. Very peculiar and eccentric. Drank whisky to excess.'" Burlingame adds that Todd told "dubious tales about his role in divvying up the last of the Confederate treasury in 1865, and he also claimed, most improbably, that he had visited the White House early in the war and aroused the president's suspicions about his loyalty." See: Michael Burlingame, *Abraham Lincoln: A Life, Volume I,* (Baltimore: Johns Hopkins University Press, 2008), 179.

[78] Timson as quoted in Emilio, *A Brave Black Regiment,* 414-415; Abbott, *Prison Life in the South,* 107-108.

[79] Higley, "Concerning Southern Prisons" *Noble Scraps* (third paper).

[80] Camp Asylum was the former state lunatic asylum on the northwestern edge of Columbia, South Carolina protected by 12 foot walls. Prisoners were kept there starting in December 1864. See: Chester B. DePratter and James B. Legg, "Columbia's Two Civil War Camps: Camp Asylum and Camp Sorghum," *Scholar Commons,* Volume 15, Issue, 1 (2011), 20, Institute of South Carolina Archaeology and Anthropology, Web, February 24, 2014, http://scholarcommons.sc.edu/cgi/viewcontent.cgi?article=1049&context=sciaa staffpub.

[81] *Burlington Free Press,* March 17, 1865. Men normally received a 30 day furlough after being processed in Annapolis. Higley's first letter to Noble on April 11 will be from Castleton.

—PART TWO—
RETURN TO CIVILIAN LIFE

Chapter Five: 1865-1871

Resurrexit

Our hearts, like April brooks, break into singing,
>   For the brave lad was lost, and he is found;
Home he comes from Southern prisons, bringing
>   For us new life to every sight and sound.

The old house lightens with his face's shining
>   That puts to flight the shadows and the chill;
The mother's heart hath rest from weary pining,
>   One great rich joy doth all the household fill.

The neighbors come with smiling gratulation
>   The pleasure runs from kindly heart to heart;
O, God! That up and down the troubled nation
>   Some other homes have only loss and smart!

For them the slow black night of pain and doubting
>   Will never flush and change to our sweet day
Would Heaven their lads had died mid battle shouting
>   Leaping to death in glorious way!

So horrible for men to feel life oozing
>   From heart and nerve in festering waste,
Both victor glow and home caresses losing,
>   And cowards grown, who belching guns had faced!

Our lad is saved. Now gracious shielding
      God give him when he mounts to horse once more,
And charges where the beaten foe is yielding,
      And shares in final victory's blaze and roar.[1]

Poem by Calvin Day Noble (under the pseudonym of Carl Day) for the Vermont Record upon news of the release of Edwin Higley.

The robust and energetic young man who had followed his sense of honor to the battlefields of Virginia three years earlier was not the soldier who arrived at Camp Parole on March 6th. A "mere shadow" of himself wrote one scholar. Officially he still waited to be exchanged for active duty again but a leave of absence permitted his return to the green hills of Castleton. There, friends reported that even his mother did not recognize him. Loved ones feared for his mind as well saying that he sat about in a stupor for weeks. On April 5th, local physician Dr. Joseph Perkins examined Higley. His official report found him unable to travel and unfit for duty by reason of general debility. A visit from friend Noble, however, earned a positive response from Higley on April 11, 1865. "Your visit here resurrected me from a slough of intellectual and abstraction to say nothing of higher and better things."[2]

That same evening in Washington President Lincoln, bowing to demands by an enthusiastic crowd, spoke from a window of the White House. Lee had surrendered two days prior and throngs of people with banners and bands hemmed into the semicircular avenue before the President's home. A resolute Lincoln spoke of rebuilding the country—a plan for reconstruction. Choosing his words carefully, the president had written out his talk. His young son Tad scooped up the pages which fell from his father's hand as he spoke. We would treat the vanquished with charity, and, for the first time publicly, Lincoln recommended suffrage for black men who had served the Union in the war or were educated. Hearing those words in the crowd that evening was Confederate zealot and celebrated actor John Wilkes Booth. Booth promised

John Wilkes Booth, n.d.
National Archives photo no. 64-M-19.

a fellow conspirator that it would be Lincoln's last speech.[3]

Booth made good on his threat three days later, destroying the joy Northerners felt at the end of the bloody conflict. On April 17th Higley wrote of the shock and Booth's betrayal, characteristically drawing on his vast knowledge of the performing arts and its personalities. He had seen Booth act many times. First impressions of the actor pleased Higley, he said, since "having been brought upon the stage; he was perfectly familiar with all its tricks and customs, has a fine figure and a good share of his family natural ability. But when he attempted great characters of Hamlet or Macbeth it was easy to see that the soul was wanting. Where, in his brother Edwin, there was deep and earnest scholarly thought and study, together with the most delicate appreciation and sympathy with every shade of the poets meaning, all thrown into the intense, passionate impersonation of his character, with this other it was all ranting affectation. Mrs. Akers was especially disgusted with him. Curious that the last thing which I heard him play was Macbeth. Heard him say 'This Duncan hath borne his faculties so meek, hath been so clear in his great office, that his virtues will plead like angels, trumpet-tongued, against the deep damnation of his taking off!' Strange that a man who could ever have been even slightly impressed by such powerful representation of the terror that follows guilt, could ever have dyed his hands with the 'damned spots.'"[4]

As Higley waited for official word of his exchange, he struggled with the idea of remaining in the army and asked Noble for his "sober advice" on the subject. Higley's reasons for joining were very clear, but the idea of returning to the halls of Middlebury was now clouded by the very personal experiences of the past two years, both good and bad. "The military history of all officers will stand on the official records of the state and country forever," he wrote. "If I leave the service now, when my posterity look up my record it will read thus—'Commissioned 2nd Lt.—First Sergeant jumped over him—left the service.' It will also read—'Dismissed the service—restored through political influence—never promoted thereafter.' It is this last thing which I care for more particularly. If after leaving the service as I did, I receive advancement it is good evidence that any dismissal was inconsistent with my military character."

Colonel Wells and others were holding a position for Higley which greatly pleased him; "the pleasure it would be to me [to] serve under such men as Wells and Custer, the pride I would feel in returning with the old veterans to whom I have become so much attached, and who have given me so many pleasing evidences of attachment to me, my reluctance to lay aside this glorious army blue—and you have one side of the question." The commitment, however, would be for three years if mustered into the peacetime army. Duties would entail garrison and patrol around Virginia. Brother Allie had taken a year off from college to re-enter Middlebury with Edwin; "college life cannot but be worth more to both of us if we go on together," Higley acknowledged. And then there was the call of an artistic soul. "After this month filled with so many musical and intellectual enjoyments, after intercourse with so many people of culture and refinement," Higley confessed, "the prospect of returning to the profanity and roughness of camp life has some repulsive features. The dealing out of stern martial law and justice to the iniquitous inhabitants of the Old Dominion, although just in keeping with my present retaliatory disposition, might not be particularly beneficial to ones nature and sensibilities."[5]

Five days later the government put an end to Higley's indecision with General Order #82. It said, in part, that "all company and staff officers of volunteer regiments, absent from their commands on account of physical disability, or by virtue of leaves of absence granted them, be honorably mustered out of service, to date from the fifteenth of May."[6] At first angered that the choice was taken from him, he wrote Noble that despite the need faced by the country, an army career was certainly more honorable than before the war but, "nothing could be more contrary to my desires and repugnant to my feelings than the life of lazy rowdyism in which the majority of our regular officers indulged in the 'good old days' of the 'Union As it was.'" Now he waited at Camp Parole to receive his muster-out papers.[7]

Returning home Higley's healing progressed surrounded by the music and artistic stimulations he craved. Requests to contribute his recollections to the *Vermont Record* where Noble was an editor, were deflected for the time being. "I solemnly intend to perpetrate something for its columns some day," Higley wrote, "for it tickle[s] my vanity to see myself in print as much as anyone's."[8]

The retirement of Middlebury President Dr. Labaree offered some hope that there would be "new professorships in future," which clearly had been an interest to Noble. Higley is still torn over returning to school or pursuing his first love. "I sometimes have a wild half impulse to 'throw physics to the dogs,' go to Boston for a year, and Germany two years, study music, and be happy. I have money enough – plenty – to do it." In a gesture of their close friendship, Higley thanks his friend for his long support and inspiration. "I consider that I owe my musical growth—if there has been any—and I know there has, more to you, than to any one during the last three years. You made me acquainted with Mendelssohn, and talked to me of Madame Sand, and this has led the way to Chopin and Beethoven."[9]

Family, visiting friends and honorariums lifted Higley's spirit.

Castleton Seminary honored Higley at their commencement ceremonies in July by making him Marshall of the event. "It was no trifling affair for a young man of retiring disposition, to find himself in the aisle of the church with eighty-seven young ladies; dressed in white; with blue sashes; and with roses in their hair – floating around him," he wrote.[10]

With the fall came classes at Middlebury. Initial

Composer and musician Felix Mendelssohn, 1895.
Library of Congress, LC-USZ62-122746.

misgivings about receiving instruction from Brainerd, a former classmate, were soon set aside. He wrote Noble in September that, "it is impossible for me to tell you how pleasant Brainerd makes the relation between us; -what a union of delicacy and cordiality, so that here is not the slightest occasion for any feeling of sensitiveness or mortification to arise, concerning the change in our relative positions. It seemed before I came here as if there must necessarily be something which would be unpleasant, in reciting to him." Years later Brainerd remembered how Higley re-entering college "submitted with becoming grace to the instruction and discipline of a former classmate."[11]

Higley settled into the routine while still harboring dreams of Boston and a real musical exploration. In true sophomoric fashion

Higley, although not personally a participant, joined in the satisfaction of other second year students who locked a cow in the freshmen recitation hall one evening which rendered the room unfit for use the next morning. "We Sophomores feel sublimely grand in the consciousness of having done a "big thing." How do such exploits look from your stand point?" he wonders of Noble.[12] The hazing resulted in retaliation by

Ezra Brainerd, n.d.
Photo courtesy of Middlebury College Archives.

freshmen which escalated to a dangerous level. Following the bovine episode, freshmen made a point of displaying revolvers to the upperclassmen "and vaunted their intention to use them if the occasion demanded," Higley wrote Noble. When a sophomore's chickens were stolen as the main course for a freshmen feast, the action, Higley said, required that it not go on without some disturbance. The plan was to pin the freshmen in the room and secure the door preventing its use as an exit. Expecting such a raid, two armed freshmen stood watch in the hallway. Springing from an upstairs stairwell, the sophomores surprised the lookouts; "they were drenched, soaked, blinded, by successive and well-thrown pails of water and as they continued to come the freshmen almost involuntarily shrank into the room, and a quick rush brought the door to a close and strong hands kept it there," Higley wrote. The sophomores held the door shut but realized the doorknob was fixed for removal by the chicken thieves. They screwed a wooden handle in place which, when secured by rope to the stairwell, would prevent any escape. "Meanwhile a wild mixture of curses and cries came from within that they would fire through upon us if we did not leave the door," Higley said. "These threats I regarded as mere bombast and continued busily to work, when the cowardly rascals actually fired, and the ball came through the door and embedded itself in the hard handle of the screw-driver which I held in my hand!" Undaunted, the sophomores finished their task even as four additional shots rang out. The only escape for the freshmen was by the room's window where they were again assaulted with buckets of water from the floor above. Luckily, most of the faculty's ire over the incident was aimed at the freshmen gunslingers.[13]

Given Higley's actual war experiences, the college antics and their disproportionate result, seem an odd reversal for the former officer who noted the startling change in his life. "Do you remember receiving letters from me of two years ago this date?" he asks Noble. It was the anniversary of the desperate fight at Brandy Station. "It sometimes almost makes me dizzy to look at the abrupt series of events which have brought me from those circumstances to these."[14]

Noble decided to take employment as the literary editor of the *Houston Telegraph* newspaper and began his trip to Texas down the main waterways of the Ohio and Mississippi Rivers that fall. By early November Higley had decided to follow his passion—it was to be Boston that winter. He would get rooms with Brains (Ezra Brainerd) and sister Emma. "So just fancy how we shall grow!" he delights. "How we shall go to the opera and the theater and the lectures and all the wonders of the New Athens, and you can imagine enough to fill this sheet of possible and probable joys connected with such a consummation. Now may no unforeseen disaster dash the cup from the lip!" He highlighted his excitement with lines from Robert Browning's poem, "Abt Vogler:"

> But God has a few of us, whom he whispers
> in the ear.—
> The rest may reason and welcome; 'tis we
> musicians know![15]

Higley commiserated with Noble with "appreciative sympathy" concerning the "beautiful devils" his friend had encountered in the former rebellious state of Texas. Higley had come across similar unrepentant belles in the secessionist hamlets of northern Virginia. "I have met women who were most emphatic in reiterating the intense joy which would fill their souls, could they see my brains smashed in, my heart cut out, and my blood inundating promiscuously the sacred soil—who nevertheless would give me an excellent dinner, and when, in one or two instances, wounded officers or men fell near their dwelling I have known them cared for with the most tender attention. So I do not anticipate any physical danger for you, although I shudder at your being compelled to rely upon such unwomanly natures for companionship and friends."[16]

On Christmas Eve of 1865 Higley wrote from the coveted quarters of Boston. The three of them now joined by a Miss Hall, had found "nicely furnished" apartments on the sixth floor of the "elegantly kept" Evans House facing Boston Common. It was warmed by steam and featured marble center tables and bureaus; "and then such a view – the harbor, Ft. Warren, the spires and hills all about the city, and such glorious sunsets that we are delighted with our quarters." "We have bread and milk or bread and butter for breakfast, at nine, and go out to dining rooms for dinner at five or six," Higley noted. And, by necessity for Higley's new life, they had purchased a second hand piano.[17]

He studied now with Edward Oliver of the Mendelssohn Institute. "He is a thorough scholar and gentleman and completely realizes my ideal in his knowledge and appreciation of music as a soul-language," Higley wrote glowingly. "He has studied many years in Germany; was a pupil of Czerny's – and taught Conservatory

Washington Street, Boston, Massachusetts in 1874 or 1875.
Image from a lithograph by G. A. Klucken.
Library of Congress, LC-USZC4-5167.

there. I have taken but three lessons of him, and yet it seems as if I had come from darkness into light (although but the beginning of light) still I wonder how I could have been so ignorant, and yet have pretended to know anything of music before."[18]

He embraced a demanding routine but one which clearly invigorated him. "I practice two hours upon the piano and one upon the organ," he wrote. "We have our regular hours at the piano here and everything goes by clock-work I assure you. Breakfast at nine – then I practice an hour; then Brainerd and I read Greek an hour; then I go to the organ – and then another hour at the piano. Evenings we have to ourselves for general aesthetic and social cultivation." His spare time was filled with the works of Charles Dickens, John Ruskin, Jean Paul Richter and Socrates. That evening they would hear the great singer Euphosyne Parepa in Handel's *Messiah*. "My dear fellow I wish I could insure you such a pleasant holiday season as we are having, but I can only give my most earnest "Merry Christmas" and "Happy New Year" although both will be past when you read these lines. . . . The snow has turned to rain – You have the best of us on the roses at least – roses at Christmas!"[19]

201

The winter in New Athens, as Higley thought of Boston, passed too quickly for the maturing musician. From a New Year's Eve performance of Mendelssohn's *Elijah* to a January outing of *Ernani*, Higley was in the element he dreamed of. He derived inspiration from artists such as Parepa, Carlotta Zucchi and Adalaide Phillips who brought to life the operatic works of Verdi or Mozart and he reveled in the instruction of Mr. Oliver whose teaching he considered providential. "I firmly believe that there is no man in this city no, nor, in America, whose instructions would be worth so much to me, or to anyone, as his. Just think,- he k<u>new</u> Men<u>dels</u>sohn well,- (he showed me a letter from him which he had, so that I have seen a letter wr<u>itten</u> <u>by</u> Sera<u>phael</u>'s <u>own</u> h<u>and</u>)—he was intimate with Clara Schumann, whose father was at one time his instructor, and as a man is of the largest kind, warm-hearted—religious—refined, and deeply learned."[20]

By the top of March Higley had returned to Middlebury College for the spring term. He believed Boston had done much in shaping his future. Music was not what his father hoped for Higley and he didn't wish to embitter his father, so instead would let things take their course, "trusting that

Parepa Rosa, ca. 1867.
Image from a lithograph by Thomas Sinclair.
Library of Congress, LC-USZ62-89643.

202

I shall gradually work into my proper sphere, what-ever that may be," he confided to Noble.   Higley learned from Noble's sister "Frank" of his friend's worsening health and scolded him for not entrusting that news to him.

It was a time of political illness in Washington between President Andrew Johnson and the Radical Republicans. Johnson's leniency toward the South infuriated many in the North.   The elections in the fall of 1866 would be a referendum on the Fourteenth Amendment giving black males the vote, and on Reconstruction itself. Higley wrote Noble that he had ignored politics since the war until the last two or three months "but now with our drunken President sworn to 'stand by' the traitorous South instead of the loyal North," he said, "I begin to feel very much as I did five years ago." Higley agreed with Noble that the South should have representation in the Congress but not necessarily all Southerners, many of whom he felt were unwilling to admit defeat. Drawing on latent feelings from his war experience, Higley wrote that "rather than see any man who has reddened his hands and blackened his heart by any association with the rebellion, admitted to vote upon the future policy of this government, which he had so labored and plotted to destroy,— I would rather a hundred times see the whole horrid war acted over again. I was greatly surprised at the sudden termination of the war, because I had been so long in personal contact with rebels that I know that they were far from that state of submission or rather extermination which alone could secure for us a peaceful country. And I now see that their apparent submission was merely a characteristic, cowardly maneuver to obtain by sneaking devices, what they were unable to do in open fight. They are indeed 'Constitutionally crazy' and I can see no way in which we can safely live, without such a disfranchisement as shall compel their emigration or their living in solitude and exclusion, until they die out and a healthier race has filled their places.   I am very sorry that Congress does not assume a definite and decided ground, but I hope above all things that they will cease regarding the feelings of these Southern rascals." He doubted that Noble would print his remarks in the *Telegraph*, despite the fact that he felt its readers should know the "conservative" Northern sentiment.[21]

The term at Middlebury ran its course uneventfully. Higley tutored underclassmen and provided organ lessons to some in the community. The time between letters from Noble had lengthened and Higley feared sickness was the reason. "If you are sick, away there—the very thought is terrible. I believe I can sympathize with you, by virtue of a lonely sickness which I had in Charleston two summers ago—but I will not believe any such contingency for it clogs my attempt at writing, as I will choke down all misgivings and talk as though there was nothing to prevent you from hearing." He continued to hope, however, for his friend's removal from the ungracious South. "I was extremely glad to read the outburst of radicalism which you gave me in your last, for I will own that it has pained me much to see your articles side by side with so much of the venomous insolence which appears in the Telegraph. O, why must you stay there, working for that unappreciative herd of rascals, without sympathy or freedom? Two years ago to-day [July 30] I was out in the swamps of South Carolina listening to the baying of their blood-hounds, and now you must be feeding their sensitive souls with literary dainties and sweet-meats!—Well you get gold out of them—thanks for that—get all you can."

There had been some inquiry, Higley wrote, of Noble returning to accept the position of the Tutor's chair at Middlebury the following year but Higley volunteered that some among the more orthodox on campus considered Noble an apostate. "But I have no superstitious reverence for that word orthodox," wrote Higley, "although I cleave to it, in most things myself. But I have no fears that anything of this kind which might be said of you would affect me in the least—for I have a personal knowledge of you which precludes the possibility of my getting another one at second-hand."[22]

Perhaps it was Noble's growing infirmity or perhaps it was the news of his mixed reputation at his alma mater which bruised his self-esteem for he asked Higley in a subsequent letter, "do you love me?" In a September response, Higley wrote, "I hope that the question was not asked with any real sense of ignorance on the subject, but I am filled with shame that I should ever have suffered it to be asked at all. But since the question has been put, perhaps I can do nothing better than to answer it and say—my dear fellow that I <u>do</u> love you, as I have done for years,—love you as I have never loved any one else, and that nothing gives me so much satisfaction as the consciousness, which I always have that you love me in return."[23]

Noble's next letter brought the news Higley hoped for; his friend was leaving Texas and returning home. "If I could only step over the continent so as to take your hand as you step off the steamer at Cairo!" Higley wrote. "But I breathe freer for you at the thought of your exode from your present isolation and surroundings." The October 24th date of Higley's letter brought back memories of his letter to Noble from the "old stone house" on the Bull Run battlefield—"one of the most arduous and exciting weeks which I ever experienced in campaign life. The contrast presents itself very vividly to my mind between the rough, uncouth wildness in which I wrote that letter—seated on a cracker- box –and writing, with my sabre on, on the window seat of that old dismantled house; -- and now clean and cozy in the quiet elegance of this

Cairo, Illinois wharf boat, 1864
Library of Congress, LC-USZ62-62366.

room-- I wish you could see how pleasant it is this evening. I am all alone.—Allie has slipped home for a week of work and visiting—and the mellow light sets off the pictures—my ivy which is running all over the window, and the carpet, the piano, and all, so as to make a very pleasing picture."[24]

Higley's last letter of 1866 came from Malone, New York, just a few miles from the Canadian border. Higley agreed to operate a singing school there and in nearby Ft. Covington. "The two facilities are eighteen miles apart, and there is only an open stage for conveyance between them. So I am in for numerous cold rides before the winter is through with. But I have pleasant work in the main so far. I have several private scholars in piano and singing in both places."

1867

Before leaving Malone for Middlebury's spring term, Higley wrote Noble that "Malone is a queer place. It has vast quantities of wealth—a good deal of style—but very little advanced culture." In a seeming revision Higley confesses that his classes were "thinly attended" but the people of Malone sought to reward Higley's efforts with a concert meant to enhance the little pay he received. An attentive crowd filled one of the local churches and an article describing the event praised not only Higley's organ performance but contained a resolution thanking the musician for "elevating the standard of vocal and instrumental music in this vicinity." Higley noted that "everything went off harmoniously and the receipts of the concert were ninety-two dollars."[25]

There continued to be news of Noble's failing health although few details were offered by Noble to his friend which was a source of concern for Higley. "My dear boy how my heart aches for you suffering under this long burden of weakness and pain! I wish you would tell us more about yourself, and cease forever to feel that I can fail to be interested and anxious about your bodily condition upon which so much depends. Is it fever or nervous derangement or what that now clings to you?"[26]

Noble declined an invitation to deliver the Master's Oration at the Middlebury Commencement for which Higley expressed his regret. For Higley, however, the stars were properly aligning. He was performing in "private theatricals," formed a Shakespeare Club and, of course, maintained his practice sessions on the organ. "The entertainments of which I spoke have drawn me so much into society here at rehearsals etc. that I have barely had time to attend to the regular curriculum and hardly that," he wrote. "There is a great deal of good feeling, which makes the days go on pleasantly. But there is no one whom I seem to get very near to," Higley admits, although he is growing closer to Brainerd.[27]

In late fall of 1867 Noble accepted a position with the Swedenborgian Church in Cleveland —The New Church of Jerusalem—despite the continuing problems with his health and in hopes he would improve with a different climate. Noble discovered the views of Emanuel Swedenborg from his maternal grandfather James Jewett, according to a family genealogy. These untraditional views certainly played a part in his reputation as an apostate and very likely colored his relationship with the conservative Middlebury. His decision did prompt a letter from Brainerd on October 28th, the first in quite a long time. Brainerd's studies at Andover Theological Seminary had relaxed his religious views and he acknowledged Swedenborg's importance as a "the first great apostle" of this "New Church" but with reservations: "While I admit the reality of Swedenborg's intromission into the spiritual world, I am so far from regarding him as infallible, that I believe his books full of scientific & philosophical error," he wrote. "All his treatises and adventures in the other world are very highly colored by his own individuality."[28]

It is not Noble's quest of new religious thought which Brainerd questions in Noble but the substance of Swedenborg's views: "In philosophy and the pursuit of general wisdom we must pay due

Andover Theological Seminary, 1904.
Library of Congress, LC-DIG-det-4a11522.

attention to the mighty achievements of all the great minds of the world," Brainerd wrote. However, he adds that "we ought not I think, to retail Swedenborgian aphorisms as many are content to do, but to present these truths as we have worked them out in our own thoughts and experiences. . . . The question of inspiration has puzzled me greatly for over a year, and though my opinions are still somewhat unsettled, I cannot hold to Swedenborg's doctrine on this point without some modifications." Brainerd had studied the more free thinking theologians of the day and believed any ministry he assumed would embrace this broader philosophy of the liberal church rather than the so-called "New Jerusalem Church."

Brainerd has no desire to breach his friendship with Noble and his letter ends on a conciliatory tone. "I wanted to give you my latitude & longitude in that broad globe of religious opinions, & to assure you of continued friendship for you and sympathy in the work you are about to undertake. Though our fields may be somewhat different, I feel that we are both laboring for the overthrow of scholastic theology and for the spread among men of those higher views of God and His Providence which He has graciously imparted to the growing intellect of the Grand Man— our human race."[29]

Higley wrote a month later following term examinations at Middlebury with his usual apologies for tardiness. "Will you, at this late day, accept the assurance of my never-changing interest in all your ways and thoughts, and my constant and undiminished trust and affection for yourself?" Higley asked. While pleased that Noble had escaped the tainted confines of the Confederacy and has now, "found a more congenial atmosphere in which to breathe," he treads lightly on Noble's newly professed vocation with the New Church. Higley had not seriously considered Swedenborgianism's tenets. "But I have sympathized most heartily with that kind of thought which has been of late prominent among many of the leading literati of this country, which takes a larger view of the meaning and mission of human life, and all that dignifies and cultures it, and which claims that all the voices of Nature and Art are but interpretations of the Divine Essence to those who will listen. . . . I presume with all my orthodox family connections I should never wish to change my present communion, and I feel as yet no desire to do so. But I have known what your inward feelings were for these years, and I have loved you too much to permit this change in your outward course to affect me."

It is neither the rigors of school nor considerations of religion which has delayed Higley's correspondence, but new found love—"the absorbing power with which I have drawn toward a woman's heart," he delightedly states. "And lately, for a few weeks, I have been permitted to believe that the spell has not merely drawn me toward but into such a wealth of affection as words seem weak to depict."

Higley's message of joy is also one of reassurance for a friend who is to embark on such an altering change in his life. "Of course I am not cold blooded enough to attempt to express to you all the

Edwin Hall Higley, 1873.
Photo courtesy of Middlebury College Archives.

gladness which this experience has brought me. If you are ever similarly blessed, you will know how to forgive my inattention to you—although I have never felt, and never expect to feel any diminution in the warmth of my friendship for you. This passion has been growing upon me for nearly a year, as some words which I dropped concerning Jennie Turner last summer might have indicated to you, and I have led a life of mingled hope and dread and fear which only increases my present happiness.--I could not have spoken these words to anyone less dear to me than you are." [30]

It is not known where Noble took his studies for the New Jerusalem ministry but most likely in Cleveland. Although classes were held in Waltham, Massachusetts beginning in the summer of 1866, Noble's name does not appear in those records for 1866 or 1867. In September 1867 he is a licentiate allowed to preach in the Ohio Association of the New Church where he succeeds Willard G. Day. [31]

Despite continued oaths of unconstrained friendship, the
number of letters extant in the Riverside Metropolitan Museum's
collection falls off precipitously after 1867. There are three letters
in mid to late 1868. On July 5, 1868, among news of trout dinners,
Middlebury professors and favored concerts, Higley asked, "how
does your clerical life become you? Are you growing rotund and
ready for the degree of D.D.?" It is easy to feel that the strain
of distance, new relationships and perhaps ideology, has begun
to create a subtle separation. "Now that I am about to step out
into the world I feel a strong desire to again renew the ties which
have existed between us," Higley wrote. "I have never found and
never expect to find a friendship so rich to me as yours has been. I
hope you will find time to write to me, and that before long I shall
see you face to face."

The last two letters of 1868 are from Boston where Higley, now a
graduate of Middlebury, is again immersed in the cultural, social
and most importantly, musical life of the city. This time he lives
on his own, telling Noble that he boards with a very hospitable
Mrs. Root. "I sleep in a sort of a closet, with a window in it,
which opens out of another room, and thus am waiting further
developments." In place of Mr. Oliver is the New England
Conservatory where he just started his instruction in September.
In the meantime he becomes more acquainted with the city and its
citizens and seeks employment as an organist for one of the area
churches. Brains has not taken to the pulpit but the podium as a
professor of Rhetoric and English Literature at Middlebury.[32]

In Cleveland Noble was ordained by Dr. John Randolph Hibbard
of Chicago on November 1, 1868 as a pastor of the New Jerusalem
Church. The last letter to Noble in 1868 comes just before
Thanksgiving with the news of Brainerd's marriage where Higley
will be a groomsman on December 1st. Higley's term at the
Conservatory is coming to an end but Higley is impressed with
the level of musicianship by teachers in the character concerts

New England Musical Conservatory, 1904.
Library of Congress, LC-DIG-det-4a11362.]

which happen once or twice a week.   The last concert of the term
will be performed by the Conservatory's pupils.   Higley has been
asked to play a solo on the school's great organ. "Only think,--the
great grand instrument, which has been for years one of my bright
ideals of perfection, upon which I have looked with reverence,
and to whose thrilling harmonies I have listened afar off, -- is now
to be handled with mine own hands, and its deep diapason are to
answer to the tread of my feet!"[33]

1869

By January 1869 Higley found a position as organist and director of music for the First Parish Congregational Church of Charlestown near Boston where he moved. His salary was $400 a year. He gave lessons in the church's basement and at singing schools in Medford but still studied Harmony at the Conservatory where he often played the "Great Organ" at concerts. Brainerd and his new wife Fanny visited Higley in Boston where Brains became very ill for two weeks. Higley and Fanny doted on Brains until well and then spent "a gay, happy winter going about to places of enjoyment together and . . . I read him your ordination sermon, and we spoke after and affectionately of you," Higley told Noble.[34]

In April 1869 Noble directed the building of a new chapel in Cleveland—Chapel of the Morning Star—which was finished and dedicated in July. The first service was held on July 25th and the eighty seats of the sanctuary were generally filled on following Sundays. "The year has been one of many difficulties," Noble reported in October 1869, "but I have the gratification of believing that something has been done towards a permanent establishment of the New Church in Cleveland." He tended to congregations in Cleveland and East Rockport, and delivered three sermons in Chicago that year. Two of the twenty-six people Noble baptized that year included Clarissa Wilcox and his sister Frances Emeline Noble Swift—the "Frank" of such interest in Higley's earlier letters who married Foster Elliott Swift in 1859. The widow Clarissa Wilcox and her daughter by the same name lived in the household of James Jewett in 1860 along with Noble. It appears that Noble attended the commencement at Middlebury in August 1869. At the alumni meeting he was chosen as program poet for the commencement the following year.[35]

None of the three letters written in 1870 from Charlestown, Massachusetts, are more than three paragraphs in length. "I expect to be married on the 2nd of June next, and I want to ask if you can officiate as groomsman for me on the occasion. I know you have planned to come East in that month and I hope you can arrange to give me the joy of your presence at that time," Higley asked Noble on May 5th. Higley responded to Noble's reply in a three sentence letter on May 24 saying that, "of course we could not wish to put you to so much inconvenience as your presence with us on the 2nd of June would necessitate."[36]

Noble's trip to the east in June took him to Providence, Rhode Island for the 36th anniversary conference of his fraternity Delta Upsilon of which Higley also belonged. The meeting was held June 1st and June 2nd –Higley's wedding day in Middlebury. Noble was chosen to be an officer for the following year's gathering in Hudson, Ohio, as "Poet" for the conference. Higley's last letter on July 18th states that he will meet with Noble at Middlebury's upcoming commencement. Advertisements in Cleveland newspapers show that Noble's lecture schedule was consistent through1870 except for the month of August when Middlebury held its commencement for the summer term.[37]

It may have been at this August meeting that Noble announced his own wedding plans. He would marry Hannah Gorham Phinney in her hometown of Waltham, Massachusetts. She was the twenty something daughter of the very large family of George Phinney and his wife Cordelia. Her father was the editor and printer for Swedenborgian journals of the *New Jerusalem Messenger* and *New Church Messenger*. Noble and Hannah were married on Christmas Eve of 1870. We do not know if Higley attended but it seems probable.[38]

In September 1870 Noble agreed to a position substituting for an ailing Reverend Hibbard at the New Church parish of South

Mission in Chicago while Hibbard was away in Europe. The Illinois Association of the New Church was founded in 1839 and Hibbard is credited with spreading the word of Swedenborg throughout the state on horseback with his missionary work. In 1842 the State Superintendent of Schools, I. S. Britton, a New Church member, is reported to have introduced Abraham Lincoln to the religion. Springfield, where Lincoln was a young lawyer, had a number of New Church families. American poet and Springfield native, Vachel Lindsay, wrote that the intellectual life of the Middle West was influenced by "the exquisite sharp-edged Swedenborgian culture." "Springfield, without knowing it," he said, "was 'brought up a Swedenborgian.'"[39]

Noble assumed the ministry for two congregations after Hibbard's departure with sermons in the morning and afternoon. His service was to continue until at least October 1872. A reporter visiting the South Park Avenue temple where Noble preached described the "quiet, homelike feeling that seems characteristic of the Swedenborgians and the Quakers. The plain neatness of the room, its small dimensions, the flowers on the altar, the expression of the faces of the auditors, and the earnestness of their singing all contributed to this effect." Noble is described as "a slight man, of medium height, with a pale, intellectual face, which contrasts with his black eyes, beard and hair. You know him to be a student and a man of culture from his manner and appearance before you have heard him speak. His voice is full and rich and, like face and gesture, offers no hint of harshness or angularity. His sermons are written and he reads them with the careful inflection and emphasis of an elocutionist, and with a subdued reverence that never rises to theatrical declamation or frenzied appeal. His congregation is intent upon the matter of his sermon, from which his manner does not distract their attention. His power is one of insight, delicate appreciation, and nice distinction. In his choice of words and arrangement of sentences, he shows the marks of the same culture and polish that his appearance suggests."[40]

His appointment was not without some controversy, however, as well as significant challenges. On September 20, 1871 an executive committee of church officials, headed by Jonathan Young Scammon, who established the New Church in Chicago, met to discuss an article which appeared in a Chicago paper. Written by a self-proclaimed "spiritist," it declared that Noble was in full sympathy with their spiritist beliefs. The committee, which oversaw the conduct of the Chicago Society of the New Church, decided to interview Noble about these allegations. The transcript of what transpired at that interview was lost when the great Chicago fire erupted on October 8, 1871 destroying the Marine Bank building where the committee met in Scammon's office. A sole memorandum of the committee's secretary declared that "Mr. Noble was informed that the committee must insist on a positive declaration, and promise, that he would in the future give up social intercourse with a class of people that would lead him astray, poison his mind, and unfit him for the holy office of a minister of the Lord's New Church." While there is no record of Noble's reaction to the committee's demand, one writer believed that Noble gave his pledge since he remained employed by the Chicago Society as an acting pastor and there is no further evidence of any association between spiritists in Chicago and Noble.[41]

The great Chicago fire of October, 1871.
NW corner of Washington
& LaSalle Sts.
Library of Congress, LC-USZ62-57045.

The Great Chicago Fire of October 8th through the 10th left 100,000 people homeless, consumed 18,000 buildings and caused $200 million in damages. The blaze also destroyed the New Church's main house of worship, the Adams Street temple, along with the city's central business district. The Marine Bank building with Jonathan Scammon's office was destroyed along with his home. According to one writer, "a wilderness of smoking ruins filled the place where the wealth and greatness had stood."[42]

1871

The first of only two letters written in 1871 inquires about Noble's life and thoughts with a fond overture to Hannah. "Jennie sends love to you both. Did we not have the promise of something from her pen? How does she enjoy the honors and onera of being the minister's wife?" asked Higley. Still in Charlestown, he and Jennie are putting on small musicals for the children of their Sunday School class. Programs sent to Noble in 1867 show Jennie participating as a singer and actress in performances at Malone at which Higley was a central organizer and performer.[43]

The last letter from Higley in the Riverside collection comes nearly ten months later on December 16, 1871 where Higley seeks Noble's advice for a crucial decision: "I have keenly felt during the past year the realization of a fear you once expressed to me that 'the practice of music as a profession would interfere with the study of it.' At the close of the last year I was unable to see that I had made any real advance in the line of ability as a performer, and I could see that I have given almost no time to the practice which would enable me to improve. And it was necessary for me to admit that a few years spent in this way would settle me into a mediocre position in my profession; a prospect which is discouraging to me not because I have any hunger for fame, but because it would shut me out from almost all real or satisfying opportunities for influence. For the class of pupils which I have been able to attract, has been (with a few bright exceptions) disheartening and repulsive in the extreme. Incorrigible children of shallow parents, and illiterate seamstresses and occasional shoddy aristocracy have formed a large share of the 'field' in which I have labored. And there can be few kinds of drudgery more hopeless and devoid of intellectual or artistic quality than to teach such people how to apply their hands to the mechanism of some instrument."

Although content to follow the Lord's lead in respect to his music, he received an offer from Brainerd which would offer reasonable security and time to pursue his artful measure. He would teach Greek to the college students of Middlebury and continue to improve his musical skills, just away from Boston. "So I have accepted this new position with no purpose of giving up my devotion to music or because my enthusiasm for it has abated one jot; but with the expectation that within five years I shall return exclusively to it. . . . I have made a very first-personal letter for I know how fully I had your sympathy when I first took my profession and I do not wish to lose it now. Of course I have a love for classical literature and learning which will make the class-room work one which I shall enjoy. . . . Give our warm love to Pansie and please write to me when you can. We shall stay here until the middle of February. We remember last Christmas, as the year comes around again. I wish you could attend the oratorio this year."[44]

Ever truly yours

Ed.

NOTES:

[1] *Noble Scraps*, n.d. Higley refers to this poem in a letter to Noble on December 17, 1866 after learning that Noble has returned from his position in Houston, Texas. "I have half a mind to perpetrate some lines on 'Resurrexit,' this morning. I am sure that there is as much occasion therefore as existed twenty months ago where such an effusion appeared in my honor in the Vermont Record," said Higley.

[2] Ward, "Edwin Hall Higley, An American Classicist," 80; Billings, *An Address in Memory*, 5; Edwin H. Higley, *Compiled Military Service Record*, First Vermont Cavalry, Company K, Civil War, RG 94, National Archives and Record Administration, Washington, D.C.; Letter Higley to Noble, April 11, 1865, Evans Collection, Riverside Metropolitan Museum.

[3] Noah Brooks, *Washington In Lincoln's Time*, (New York: The Century Company, 1895) 254-256; Donald, *Lincoln*, 588.

[4] Letter Higley to Noble, April 17, 1865, Evans Collection, Riverside Metropolitan Museum.

[5] Letter Higley to Noble, May 1, 1865, Evans Collection, Riverside Metropolitan Museum. Higley's compiled military service record shows that he received brevet promotions following his discharge from the army. General Order no. 67 on July 16, 1867 (five years to the day of his promotion to 2nd lieutenant) promoted him initially to 1st lieutenant and then captain effective from March 13, 1865. General Order no. 91 on October 9, 1867 increased the rank to major.

[6] *Report of the Adjutant and Inspector General of the State of Vermont from Oct. 1, 1864 to Oct. 1, 1865* (Montpelier: Walton's Steam Printing Establishment, 1865), 19.

[7] Letter Higley to Noble, May 13, 1865, Evans Collection, Riverside Metropolitan Museum.

[8] Letter Higley to Noble, June 7, 1865, Evans Collection, Riverside Metropolitan Museum.

[9] Letter Higley to Noble, July 6, 1865, Evans Collection, Riverside Metropolitan Museum.

[10] Letter Higley to Noble, July 26, 1865, Evans Collection, Riverside Metropolitan Museum.

[11] Letter Higley to Noble, September 10, 1865, Evans Collection, Riverside Metropolitan Museum; Ezra Brainerd in *The Undergraduate*, vol. XVII, no. 8 (May 1892), 119.

[12] Letter Higley to Noble, October 12, 1865, Evans Collection, Riverside Metropolitan Museum.

[13] Letter Higley to Noble, October 22,, 1865, Evans Collection, Riverside Metropolitan Museum.

[14] Letter Higley to Noble, October 12, 1865, Evans Collection, Riverside Metropolitan Museum.

[15] *The Undergraduate*, vol. XI, no. 2 (Nov. 1885), 12; Letter Higley to Noble, September 1, 1865, Evans Collection, Riverside Metropolitan Museum; Letters Higley to Noble, November 4, 1865, December 9, 1865, Evans Collection, Riverside Metropolitan Museum. The full stanza by Browning is:

> And what is our failure here but a triumph's evidence
>> For the fulness of the days? Have we withered or agonized?
> Why else was the pause prolonged but that singing might issue thence?
>> Why rushed the discords in, but that harmony should be prized?
> Sorrow is hard to bear, and doubt is slow to clear,
>> Each sufferer says his say, his scheme of the weal and woe:
> But God has a few of us whom he whispers in the ear;
>> The rest may reason and welcome; 'tis we musicians know.

[16] Letter Higley to Noble, December 9, 1865, Evans Collection, Riverside Metropolitan Museum.

[17] Letter Higley to Noble, December 24, 1865, Evans Collection, Riverside Metropolitan Museum.

[18] Ibid. **Karl Czerny** (1791-1857) was an Austrian pianist and a pupil of Beethoven and a teacher of Franz Liszt. See: *The Columbia Encyclopedia, Second Edition, Volume II*, 498.

[19] Ibid. **John Ruskin** (1819-1900) was an English author and critic, raised by strict evangelical parents. During tours of Europe with his family he developed a love of nature and painting. He studied at Oxford and his first book *Modern Painters* was published in 1843 and would lead to five volumes of the work by 1860. That same year his interest turned to political economy on which he produced several books which attacked the mercantile foundations of Great Britain. In 1870 he was made the first professor of art in England and became a successful lecturer until a mental collapse in 1878. Continuing to write, he became unbalanced after 1889. See: *The Columbia Encyclopedia, Second Edition, Volume IV*, 1718. **Jean Paul Richter** (1763-1825) was a German romantic novelist who produced *Titan* in the early 19th century. His writings influenced other German writers as well as the composer Robert Schumann. See: *The Columbia Encyclopedia, Second Edition, Volume IV*, 1675. **Madame Euphrosyne Parepa** (later Parepa-Rosa) (1836-1874) was born in Edinburgh, Scotland to Baron Georgiades De Boyesku and soprano Elizabeth Sequinn. Her father died when she was an infant and her mother took to the stage to support the family. Parepa's talents became obvious at a young age and she gave her first public appearance. She was fluent in English, French, Italian, German and Spanish when eighteen years old. She remained in England from 1859 to 1866 but the death of her first husband led her to accept one of the numerous offers to sing in the United States. She arrived in the U.S. in September 1866, two months before Higley watched her perform. Eugene Cropsey wrote that Parepa had "a rich and flexible voice, melodious and pure, free of any coarseness or shrillness and her singing was thoroughly enjoyable." Edwin Higley wrote that "to me, who never heard [Jenny] Lind, all other singing which I have heard seems like pale, reflected moonlight by the side of the pure, sparkling, radiant, soul-filling sunshine of this great genius." See: *New York Times*, January 23, 1874; Eugene H. Cropsey, *Crosby's Opera House, Symbol of Chicago's Cultural Awakening*, (Cranbury, N.J.: Associated University Presses, 1999), 112: Letter Higley to Noble, December 24, 1865, Evans Collection, Riverside Metropolitan Museum.

[20] Letters Higley to Noble, January 7 and 21, 1866, Evans Collection, Riverside Metropolitan Museum.

[21] Letter Higley to Noble, April 1, 1866, Evans Collection, Riverside Metropolitan Museum.

[22] Letters Higley to Noble, June 6 and July 30, 1866, Evans Collection, Riverside Metropolitan Museum.

[23] Letter Higley to Noble, September 27, 1866, Evans Collection, Riverside Metropolitan Museum.

[24] Letter Higley to Noble, October 24, 1866, Evans Collection, Riverside Metropolitan Museum.

[25] Letter Higley to Noble March 11, 1867, Evans Collection, Riverside

Metropolitan Museum.

[26] Letter Higley to Noble May 3, 1867, Evans Collection, Riverside Metropolitan Museum.

[27] Letter Higley to Noble July 1, 1867, Evans Collection, Riverside Metropolitan Museum.

[28] Boltwood, *History and Genealogy of the Family of Thomas Noble of Westfield, Massachusetts…*, 180; Letter, Ezra Brainerd to Noble, October 20, 1867, Evans Collection, Riverside Metropolitan Museum.

[29] Ibid., Letter, Brainerd to Noble.

[30] Letter Higley to Noble, November 27, 1867, Evans Collection, Riverside Metropolitan Museum.

[31] Rev. C. Th. Odhner and Rev. Dr. William Whitehead, *Annals of the New Church, Volume II, 1851-1890* (S.I. : s. n., 1976), 101, 106, 108.

[32] Letter Higley to Noble September 23, 1868, Evans Collection, Riverside Metropolitan Museum.

[33] *The New Jerusalem Magazine, Index to Volumes I-XLIV, 1827-1872* (Boston: The General Convention of the New Jerusalem Church in the United States, June 1872), 169; Letter Higley to Noble November 21, 1868, Evans Collection, Riverside Metropolitan Museum.

[34] Letters Higley to Noble, January 19 and June 1, 1869, Evans Collection, Riverside Metropolitan Museum.

[35] *Journal of the Sixteenth Annual Session of the Ohio Association of the New Church held at East Rockport, Ohio, Oct. 15-17, 1869* in *New Jerusalem Messenger Magazine, Volume 42* (Boston: C. A. Dunham, 1869), 10, 16-17. Noble is chosen president of the Association for1870; *Burlington Weekly Free Press*, August 20, 1869. Noble's other sister Amelia is also in the Mid-West at that time possibly because of Noble's move. She married her husband Henry Streeter on March 11, 1868 in Cairo, Illinois which was a central dock for steamboats piloting the Ohio and Mississippi Rivers. Streeter and Amelia will join Noble in Riverside, California in 1875. See: Elmer Holmes, *History of Riverside, California with Biographical Sketches of the Leading Men and Women of the County who have been Identified with its Growth and Development From the Early Days to the Present* (Los Angeles: Historic Record Company, 1912), 323.

[36] Letters Higley to Noble, May 5 and 24, 1870, Evans Collection, Riverside Metropolitan Museum.

[37] Letter Higley to Noble, July 18, 1870; *Middlebury Register*, June 14, 1870.

[38] See: *Journal of the Massachusetts Association of the New Jerusalem Church*, Oct. 7, 1869 in *New Jerusalem Messenger Magazine, Volume 42*, 21; *New Jerusalem Messenger*, Volume 20, no. 1, (January 4, 1871), 8. Census records and Massachusetts marriage records provide a range of possible birth years for Hannah Phinney from 1845 to 1852.

[39] Marguerite Beck Block, *The New Church in the New World: A Study of Swedenborgianism in America* (New York: Henry Holt and Company, Inc., 1932), 122-123. Bryant Higgins of Olney, Illinois gave an affidavit that he knew that Lincoln and two other men regularly met and spoke of Swedenborg's works. A *New Church Messenger* in 1915 published a letter from Robert Todd Lincoln which refuted Higgins' story but did confirm that his father and later he himself became good friends with Jonathan Young Scammon who established the New Church in Chicago. "If in the years of his close friendship with my father he talked of and quoted Swedenborg a mere fraction as much as he did later with me, my father became familiar with the subject." Robert Lincoln said that he never heard his father speak of Swedenborg or the New Church. See: Letter, Robert Todd Lincoln to Rev. Richard Hamilton Keep, October 30, 1914 printed in *The New Church Messenger*, Volume 108, no. 5 (February 3, 1915), 94-95. **Vachel Lindsay** (1879-1931) was born in Springfield, Illinois and traveled the country paying his way by selling his poems and drawings. His readings and lectures popularized much of his work but stifled him creatively and he committed suicide at his home in Springfield in 1931. Lindsay may also have been a convert to Swedenborgianism. American poet and teacher Lewis Turco wrote that "the major Modernist poets engaged in conversations and arguments . . . the relevance of religion, the loss of a sense of God — it is what drove Wallace Stevens, it's what motivated T. S. Eliot in his early poems; his later poems were rationalizations and justifications for returning to the fold of traditional religion. It's what drove Vachel Lindsay, who was an American mystic, a New World Swedenborgian, and Robert Frost, who was an Emersonian." See, *Columbia Encyclopedia, Second Edition, Volume III*, 1139; Turco, "The Poetry of Emily Dickenson's Letters," *Poetics and Ruminations*, (August 2007), Web, April 2, 2014, http://lewisturco.typepad.com/poetics/2007/08/the-poetry-of-e.html.

[40] Rudolph Williams, *The New Church and Chicago: A History* (Chicago: W. B. Conkey Company, 1906), 188.

[41] Williams, *The New Church and Chicago: A History*, 188-191. Noble officially resigned his pastorate by October 16, 1871. See: *Journal of the Sixteenth Annual Session of the Ohio Association of the New Church Held in Pomoroy, October 27-29, 1871* (Boston: John C. Regan & Co., Printers, 1872), 19.

[42] Ibid., Williams, 175-176. Jonathan Young Scammon was president of the Chicago Marine and Fire Insurance Company and the Marine Bank and a noted philanthropist. The great fire of 1871 and another in 1874 ruined him financially. He died a poor man on March 17, 1890. See: Block, *The New Church in the New World*, 121-122.

[43] Letter Higley to Noble, February 28, 1871, Evans Collection, Riverside Metropolitan Museum; Concert programs from 1867 are kept with the Higley letters of that year in the Evans Collection.

[44] Letter Higley to Noble, December 16, 1871, Evans Collection, Riverside Metropolitan Museum.

Epilogue

In the winter and spring of 1872 a division developed within the Chicago Society of the New Church of Jerusalem with dissenters on the south side of the city upset over the administration of their parish. With Rev. Hibbard still in Europe, they appealed to Noble to continue his ministry. Supporters wrote in a letter to the Society's executive committee that "we know and appreciate the earnest wish of a majority of our number, amounting in many cases to a determination to retain Mr. Noble in Chicago." The committee declined until Rev. Hibbard could be consulted. Twenty-six supporters of Noble thereby pledged their resources and formed the Second Swedenborgian Society of Chicago on November 13, 1872. Noble accepted their invitation as pastor returning from Waltham to Chicago. He held the Church's first service on Sunday October 6th. "The free loan of Swedenborgian books could be obtained" at Noble's home on Indiana Avenue. A published notice declared that "the seats of the Sunday service are free, the service being sustained entirely by voluntary offerings and subscriptions."[1]

Noble's ministry did capture the attention of Chicago newspapers in 1873 for his discussion from the pulpit of the secularization of the Sunday Sabbath. The *Chicago Times* reported that while the day no longer called for "foolish acts of deprivation"—staid hours of religious contemplation common to our Puritan past- -priests and preachers, kept it as, "God's own day." Noble's "liberal utterances" were therefore all the more surprising, said the *Times*, since they came from a preacher. Sunday, said Noble, was no more God's own, than any other day. "He declared that a man might work on Sunday if his family needed bread. Christ was more liberal than that eighteen hundred years ago, but that was before there was any such institution as the Christian Sabbath." Noble's preaching mirrors the discussion on the subject with Higley in February 1864. The *Chicago Times* wrote that Reverend Noble "had unconsciously entered upon a field of investigation where his labors may be productive of good results to the world..." Enough to make a transcendentalist like Emerson proud.[2]

Around February 1, 1874 Noble contracted scarlet fever which kept him from his pulpit. Regaining his strength by mid-March, he left for Georgia seeking a climate which might prove beneficial and abate his deteriorating health. His resignation was read to his congregation on March 15th although his salary continued until May 1st.[3]

Georgia proved unsatisfactory and Noble decided on Riverside, California as a new home for himself and his growing family. It is unknown why he eventually picked Riverside but perhaps knowledge of other Swedenborgians and spiritualists in the western community drew him to the distant colony. Leaving his family in Waltham to enjoy the comfort of Hannah's parents, he set out on the cross country trek. His travels were chronicled in newspaper articles written either for his former Vermont employer or perhaps for a paper in his new home. The articles, unfortunately, lack those specifics. The trip with its irritating discomfitures and delays is described with some detail. There was Pittsburg with the "heavy grinding influence of its coal and oil industries;" Cleveland which "hastes to become a milder and more endurable Pittsburg;" Chicago rising from the ashes of its last great fire and the outposts of Council Bluffs, Iowa and Omaha, Nebraska. The "sharp, bare, fierce look," of Cheyenne, Wyoming led to "the harsh iciness and furious Rocky Mountain gale;" from Ogden, Utah through the Sierra Nevadas to Sacramento and finally San Francisco. Noble wrote that Boston citizens used to comfortable order, "would be shocked beyond measure at the screaming, jostling, insulting crowd of public carriers which here besets the traveller," [sic] at the bustling California port. With no rail lines yet reaching Southern California, Noble paid a twelve dollar fare which put him aboard a congested coastal steamer bound for San Pedro near Los Angeles. "The travel to Southern California at this season is immense and all the boats are crowded," he explained. "Invalids make a large portion of it, and although something of one myself I cannot say that I relished the sights and sounds which met me at every turn throughout the swarming ship."[4]

Los Angeles, California, 1880.
Library of Congress, LC-DIG-ppmsca-15851.

He found Los Angeles and its 15,000 inhabitants of little attraction "outside of its vineyards, orange groves, and more than Italian atmosphere. . . . The town itself is irregular and rather rickety looking, with some hills to break its monotony . . . . The sun was shining and a delicious dreaminess, or shall I say laziness, pervaded the quiet town." Noble's excitement increased as he made the last leg of his long 4,000 mile journey. From Los Angeles he went to the Mission San Gabriel and Spadra (near today's Pomona).[5]

Noble reveled in the stark landscape of his new destination, with its towering mountains and fields of color. He composed descriptive columns about the "vast plains and brown billowy hills," which produce, if rewarded by winter rains, "floral splendors" of "Turk's Cap," "fringed gilia with its tubular throat" and "rose-colored claytonia" and many more.[6]

His poetry spoke of family and love but also the new features of a
new land such as:

"Arrowhead Brook"

BROOK, sky-born 'neath mountain pines,
And nursed by mountain mothers,
Let loose your heart in cooling foam
To cool the hearts of others.
From mottled rock and mossy vale
Leap, like a child enchanted;
The ferns your airy pathway point
With emerald lances slanted.
Laugh low, laugh loud,
Child of the cloud!
We, too are children with you.
You fall to rise
Within our eyes—
Immortal life we give you!

Riverside, California, corner of Main and 8th streets, ca. 1876.
Photo courtesy of the Riverside Metropolitan Museum.

He purchased 20 acres to the west of Riverside on what was known as the Government Tract. The arrival of wife and family from the east six months later resulted in a lengthy article letting readers eavesdrop on the experience. Their house became their sanctuary—"Church of the Household"— since distance and lack of a "Spanish pony" impeded their attendance at the only church in the small Riverside village. Leaving the area around Spadra, Pansy was captivated by the "majesty" of the mountains. "They were not mountains to be loved and mentally caressed, like the dear old green hills of New England, but temples to worship in, priests to receive a sacrament from," Noble wrote. Coming to the "wide, swift, treacherous" Santa Ana River, the horses plunged a half dozen feet down to the ford and across and then up to the level of the Riverside plain. "What a lovely sight greeted us ...," Noble remembered. "A smooth, wide green plain flowed off through round, rocky hills. Half a mile away from us, burnished by the low mellow sun, lay Riverside amid its green hedges, flower gardens, and young orange orchards. Its neat white houses, its one white church-spire, its wide, quiet streets, its store and post-office, and its trim hotel, gave it exactly a New-England look."

Riverside founder John W. North on Pine Street, 1875.
The white church-spire of Riverside's church can be seen in the background.
Photo courtesy of the Riverside Metropolitan Museum.

They arrived at their new home, if incomplete, around dusk and rested on the eastern veranda for an evening meal with the "precious smell" of the young orange orchard, "subtly mingled with the odor of the jasmine and heliotrope that climbed about our heads." Their household church had been christened, Beulah Cottage. The next morning, Noble and Pansy walked the property imagining how the landscape would change and progress with the spread of vineyards, orchards and gardens. "Our little home will grow with ourselves," Noble told his wife. "We can put of ourselves into it."

Pansy responded slowly and very solemnly, "after she had looked all over the low, rough cottage ornamented only with vines, all over the little farm, where only the smallest beginnings of orchards and gardens and shrubbery stood then over the wide plain, where other rude homes just like our own were planted, and finally around the whole vast circle of mountain walls roofed by a glowing, spotless sky, 'Yes, work and worship can be one here; here church and home can be one. I am satisfied.'" "You see," wrote Noble, "we had begun life over again in a new land, a land so sweet and sunny . . . that we seemed to have gone east instead of west, and to be in Palestine instead of Southern California."[7]

Noble felt they had brought culture with them to the Riverside community. They started Dovenook, a private school of fine arts and language; a piece of Middlebury in the California desert. "Cultivated people make the very best pioneers for the same reason that they make the best soldiers," penned Noble. "They have veritable, superior strength of mind and heart which gives endurance, courage, skill, and judgment where these are all especially needed."[8] A year after their arrival, they were joined in Riverside by Day's brother Reverend William Cyrus Noble and his brother-in-law Henry M. Streeter who had married Noble's younger sister, Amelia. William Noble would assist in officiating the wedding of Mission Inn owner, Frank Miller and Belle Hardenburgh in 1880.[9]

Deteriorating health caused Day Noble's withdrawal from most school activities by 1880 but he still managed some secular and religious undertakings despite his illness.   Riverside newspapers record Noble giving an oration on the nation's centennial in 1876, marrying William Huckaby and Martha Ann Casteel in 1880 and christening the granddaughter of Eliza Tibbets, Daisy Summons and Tibbets' adopted Negro daughter Nicey at Noble's home in either 1874 or 1875. Eliza Tibbets had been raised in the Swedenborgian Church and was well-known in Riverside as a powerful medium and a communicator with the other side through her spirit guide, "Floating Feather."[10] Other local spiritualists included Riverside co-founder Dr. James Greves, state geologist Professor William Denton, and sisters Mrs. Seibold and Mrs. Annie Denton Cridge and by implication, Annie Cridge's husband Alfred. It was an intellectual community, wrote Tom Patterson, "to which an appreciable minority of educated people were attracted at the time." Some suffered from the same lung ailment as Noble.[11] A Swedenborgian Church would not be officially organized in Riverside until 1886, a year after Noble's death, with the arrival of Reverend Barry Edmiston whom Noble had worked with at the Chicago Society church.

The health of Hannah Noble rapidly deteriorated in 1884 and she died on April 22, 1885 of tubercles (nodules) on the throat, a product of her own battle with consumption. Day Noble soon followed, passing away July 12, 1885. A childhood friend, E.W. Dennison, wrote that Day's spirit had always been hampered by a "feeble physical frame." Noble's illness, he feared, sent him to the raw landscape of California and secluded him from the music and literature which had been so much a part of his life in the east and deprived him

Dr. James Porter Greves, n.d.
Photo courtesy of the
Riverside Metropolitan Museum.

of that spiritual stimulation. But just weeks before his death, Dennison remembered, Noble had the opportunity to again enjoy "some fine music." Noble wrote of the experience that, "I thought I had been somewhat starved all these years, but I find that I have been well fed, and that the infinite love knows more than one way to feed a soul."[12] Before leaving for Texas in 1866 Noble offered a poem to friends at a gathering for him. He wrote of what home meant to him. One stanza read:

> Love makes the home, and makes the spot
> It stands on warm and fair;
> The bleakest hut or lowliest cot
> Is glorified if love be there.
> He misses not earth's grandest art
> Who carries Eden in his heart.[13]

Dennison felt that despite the suffering, Noble's "gifts of heart and soul shone clear and bright."[14]

Edwin Hall Higley, 1875.
Photo courtesy of Middlebury College Archives.

Higley joined the faculty of Middlebury in 1872 as a professor of Greek and German but was a consistent presence among the choirs and drama clubs of the campus. "The Choral Society is very thriving this term under the leadership of Prof. E. H. Higley. More college boys than ever attend," reported a college publication in 1878.[15] He continued his personal progress on the organ as well. "The advent of a new eight hundred dollar organ in the chapel, with a selected choir and the generous aid of Prof. Higley, renders our chapel exercises unusually interesting this term," the school newsletter proclaimed in the spring of 1879.

"Prof. Higley plays a voluntary each morning and the choir sing some carefully prepared music. . . . These efforts are keeping alive the spirit of song in our College, which we are sorry to say is not thriving amongst the mass of the students."[16]

The school faced some challenges by the mid-1870s as noted by one of its alumni who saw Higley as a counter to the decline. Bishop Julius W. Atwood wrote that when he entered Middlebury in 1874 "it had fallen upon evil days. Dartmouth, Amherst, Williams, Union and the University of Vermont, with larger and increasing endowments, drew from the same territory. It no longer had instructors of eminence as in earlier days. It had been without a president for some time, but it never lowered its standard of scholarship or requirements for entrance. There was, however, a group of fine young professors in my days, of wide and varied scholarship: Ezra Brainerd, Edwin Higley and McGregor Means."[17]

Dr. S. Orlo Jefferson also remembered the "sad, silent man" who guided his studies in Greek at Middlebury. "He possessed an unusual striking personality. Tall, erect, fair hair, and a remarkably intelligent strong face," wrote Jefferson. "But beneath all this was a cold, silent demeanor which seemed foreign to all else found in him." There were rumors, Jefferson recalled, that Higley's prison confinement had "shattered his nerves." One student may have attempted to exploit the artistic sensitivities of the professor. Unprepared for class, he "hired an organ-grinder to grind out his cheap music directly under the stipulated window," which was that of Professor Higley's classroom, said Jefferson. Jefferson reported that an exasperated and angry Higley "dashed to the window gesticulating and threatening in every known tongue, but failed to dislodge the persistent intruder," and instead Higley dismissed the class for the day. Professor Higley "could never conduct a class with such unbearable music floating into his room," noted Jefferson.[18]

In 1882, he resigned from Middlebury in order to follow another long dreamed pursuit of studying music in Germany, despite entreaties from many at the college. He spent two years in

Leipzig Conservatory today.
Commons.Wikimedia, taken by Appaloosa

Leipzig, Germany at the Royal Conservatory studying music and Philology and while there one of his compositions was awarded a prize. "He was the first American to have a piece played by the Liepzig university orchestra," a colleague remembered. He brought back the best of his German visit: "German sentiment and almost naïve simplicity, the music of ballad and of organ, an old idealistic philosophy and a love for a natural life such as he had always lived."[19] He made another musical pilgrimage to Germany, this time Berlin, while on sabbatical for a year in 1894 and 1895. Returning home, he became organist for St. Andrews Church in Ayer from 1898 until his death.[20]

Upon his return to the United States in 1884 he accepted a teaching position at Groton School in Massachusetts which had just opened under the leadership of Endicott Peabody. At Groton, he continued pursuing a musical career, teaching only twice a week, and remained the organist at Central Church in Worcester until becoming full time at Groton in1886 when he also became Groton's choir master and school organist. Although later offered the position of president of Middlebury College, he chose to remain at Groton.[21] Dr. William Thayer of Groton remembered that "Mr. Higley came in fair and foul weather, sometimes walking from Groton School to assist with training of the choir."[22]

Groton School. Image is a photocopy of a photograph from The Brickbuilder, Volume 12, No. 5, 1903, p. 113. Library of Congress, HABS MASS,9-GROT,4—1.

"The Major, on account of his long yellow mustache, was nicknamed 'The Walrus' and 'Tuskers' and 'The Growler,'" reported former student Frank Ashburn. However, Ashburn felt the sobriquet of "Growler" unwarranted since Higley "was always kindly, though at first reserved."[23] The "old growler" is how one student referred to him in correspondence to his parents in October 1897. Almost a year later Franklin Roosevelt wrote that he had Mr. Higley in History (Roman), and it was rather dry. Roosevelt had done poorly in his earlier Greek classes and Higley's class was a chance to catch up with the other students; a daunting task as he noted in December 1898: "In Greek we have Mr. Higley and it is a foregone conclusion that all . . . will fail." Roosevelt passed with C's, however, in both Greek and History that term.[24]

Roosevelt's opinion of "the growler" changed by the spring of 1899 when he volunteered to assist the professor. "You will be surprised to hear that I am to be a new missionary," he wrote his parents. "There was a lack of organ-players for the various mission houses in the neighborhood, so I volunteered and tonight I am to drive over with two other boys and Mr. Higley to hold service at Rockey Hill in a little schoolhouse which is about 6 miles from here." Roosevelt wrote that he and three other boys picked up Higley who was to deliver the address that evening and all four sandwiched in a two seated wagon and lumbered through a blinding snow storm to the "little bit" of a schoolhouse. However, the schoolhouse was empty, with area citizens apparently heeding the bitter weather that evening. Locking up the building they made their way back to Groton but Roosevelt reported two days later that they were to again make the journey in hope of finding a larger congregation.[25]

His love of nature led Higley and a company of professors and students to camp on Knight's Island in Lake Champlain most every summer, accompanied by the occasional state politician or college president. Higley was not noted for his outdoor skills but for the quality of his person. Sherrard Billings quoted one of the campers in a tribute to Higley. "There never was a member whose arrival was more cordially welcomed than that of Prof. Higley;

Franklin Roosevelt at Groton School, 1900. Commons.Wikimedia; modified image from the Franklin D. Roosevelt Library by userSoerfm.

not for his skill as a hunter or fisherman, nor for his efficiency as a sailor or as a cook, but because of his charming character, his absolute sincerity, his loyal friendship, his unassuming good sense, his rare talent as a singer and a writer of admirable songs for special occasions."[26]

Edwin Hall Higley (standing, third from right) with faculty at Groton School, 1898. Photo courtesy of Groton School Archives.

The Higleys had no biological children of their own but in 1888 they adopted a baby girl. Massachusetts records show a July 1888 decree changing the baby's name from Mary Buchanan to Margaret Edna Higley.[27] Reared in Groton, Margaret grew into a beautiful woman well situated in the heady social circles of the prestigious area. One newspaper described her as being "remarkably pretty" with "blond hair, blue eyes, exquisite coloring, and a raquish, captivating way that made her absolutely bewitching. She was the social belle of the very aristocratic little academy town of Groton." She apparently was also headstrong and willful. Sent to the Lasell Seminary in Auburndale when 15, she was sent home after a year for "misconduct." Her parents then sent her to a Montreal convent but illness brought her back home in the spring of 1904. After turning 18 she refused to return to Montreal and after quarreling with her parents disappeared from Groton. Others reported later that her father's insistence on marriage to a man she did not love drove her first to Boston then later New York. She reportedly had been engaged to Harry Lake but the name of a former boyfriend, Harold Barnard, was also suggested by the press. Margaret's mysterious disappearance however, "cast a gloom over the whole community" of Groton, "almost as profound as if her death or suicide had been announced. . ."[28]

Dismay turned to shock on January 2, 1905 when newspapers carried the story of her quick courtship and marriage to 20-year-old Samuel Blanchard Rose, son of prominent New York City attorney Abram J. Rose. She had met the young man through friends while in New York. Higley's position at the prestigious Groton along with the public reputation of Abram Rose gave the story interest and papers from New York City and Boston to as far as La Crosse, Wisconsin and Denver, Colorado carried the details of the family upheaval and scandal. Abram had attempted to stop the marriage citing the youth of Samuel and Margaret but was unsuccessful.[29]

Adding to the embarrassment for the families were the details of Samuel Rose's young yet checkered past, as he explained openly to the *Boston Herald*. "Gambling has been my undoing," said Samuel. "I have gone on a ruinous pace lately. Why, I have lost $12,000 on the races since November. I inherited this money and have thrown it away. I am heartily ashamed of myself." Samuel Rose pledged himself to settling down and said he had reconciled with his father. He was considering positions either as a lawyer or broker in Manhattan. His father, Samuel said, did not object to Miss Higley. "He knows she is of one of the best families in Massachusetts and that she only left home and came here with a chaperone because her father wanted her to marry another." Edwin Higley, throughout the very public discourse on his daughter, chose not to comment.[30]

Higley's foundational understanding of the world was changing—in his personal life and his professional life. The coming of the new century saw an erosion of the educational tenets which had so defined his beliefs and persona. David Walker Howe wrote that "the Greek and Roman classics . . . occupied a place in defining American culture exceeded in importance only by the Enlightenment and Christianity." Its writers and poets had influenced the political and philosophical framework of the country's founders and continued in the 19th century to shape American architecture, statuary and grammar, and even its place names. "A classical education represented the synthesis of reason and virtue," said Howe. "Classical learning became a vehicle for self-cultivation," he wrote, "for the pursuit not of public influence or civic participation but of personal perfection"—a virtuous citizen for the new republic.[31] Scholar Carl Richard called antebellum America—the America which produced Edwin Higley and Day Noble— a "golden age of the classics" in the American educational system. The American Civil War changed that. By 1900 Greek had virtually disappeared as a requirement for admission to New England's colleges and universities," wrote Allen Ward.[32] America saw rapid progression in mass media, transportation, expanded suffrage and literacy. In the post-war era, more educational institutions embraced modern languages, practical skill building and utilitarian pursuits above what would generally be called the Humanities.

In 1906 Higley questioned the shifting focus by historians to one of sociology, institutions and constitutions "who thus write histories of civics rather than civilizations." While acknowledging that these have their place in historical analysis, he wrote that, "an important part of the historian's task is to show us the faiths and moral standards of a people; the ideals they held in regard to loyalty, honor and self-sacrifice."[33] The remarks were written for the first meeting of the Classical Association of New England in April of that year. Scholars from many of the Northeast's finest colleges, concerned at the trend away from the classics, had met in

May 1905 which gave rise to the organization to foster the study of the classical world. Edwin Higley "represented the best of their type," according to Ward.[34]

"The student needs to know what the ancients believed about themselves, in order to appreciate ancient literature and the vast amount of later literature and art which has been inspired by it. . . . Many classical narratives, whose literal veracity is suspected, should still form part of the mental furniture of every intelligent person," wrote Higley. "History can be made to appeal not only to the memory but also to the sentiment," he said, "and to the sense of the picturesque."[35] Perhaps Higley had in mind the Roman orator Cicero who wrote that "history is the witness that testifies to the passing of time; it illumines reality . . ."[36]

Higley came down with a bad cold in May 1916 but insisted on continuing with his work. Growing worse, he conceded to Jennie's demands that he see a doctor. The diagnosis of pneumonia finally put him in his bed but his condition worsened. On May 16th he seemed to improve slightly only to have his breathing suddenly stop. Ironically he had already resigned his teaching position for the upcoming year. Endicott Peabody wrote a friend that "I only wish now that I had made a point of seeing him more frequently and talking more with him for he was a mine of learning and was always ready to enlighten one on the problem that one might bring to him. He was the most lovable of men. I am afraid he did not know how much we cared for him, but perhaps it is clearer to him now." His easy nature, said Peabody, and lax discipline allowed some students to take advantage of the professor but Peabody knew that Higley's "magnificent character" would afford a deep and lasting influence.[37] Rev. Sherrard Billings said that it was not so much Higley's brilliant intellect that he thought of, but "his rare soul." Death in connection to a man like Edwin Higley seemed "impotent and cheap."[38]

Grafton Minot was one prankster student who, by his own view, had acted "outrageously" in Higley's class. Responding to word of the professor's death, Minot wrote that despite the antics the "bashful and retiring" Mr. Higley "took a live interest in us from the first, and by the end of the year I know he cared a great deal for us." Minot was among the upperclassmen who were invited to the Higley home for Sunday tea. The house with its low ceiling and white woodwork and old-fashioned New England furniture held a "big piano with a picture of Beethoven hanging above it," Minot wrote. "Mrs. Higley sat facing the door, behind a steaming tea kettle and mountains of hot things to eat, around her we were grouped with a sprinkling of masters, and the Major opposite, talking with those about him or listening to what was said. Then, if we had luck, we sometimes could persuade him to play to us, or to talk to us of history, of those men whom he had known personally at the time of the civil war, and sometimes even of what he himself had done then. But he was always embarrassed to tell us about himself, and often to talk; he much preferred to sit quietly listening to those about him. . . .

"It was there that we came to know them both so well and in such a delightful way, for they were both so endlessly kind to us that we shall never forget it all our lives. Their continued remembrance of us and their real interest in our doings after we had left school is one of the most touching things that I have ever encountered. . . . it is only after the friend is gone that we feel the extent of our loss."[39]

Edwin Hall Higley with pet, ca. 1910.
Photo courtesy of
Middlebury College Archives.

Edwin Higley outlived his friend Calvin Day Noble by thirty-one years. But perhaps Noble was thinking of his friend Higley when he penned the lines of his poem, "The Mountain Man" many years earlier:

He builds his soul to noble height
Who builds it on a mountain plan,
Whose granite will and deeds of light
Reveal his measure of a man.
His feet are set on sunny plains
'Mid fruitfulness and work and calm,
But morn and eve his soul attains
The rosy height of prayer and psalm.

He drinks the melted snows of God
That purify his lifted head;
For brother-souls who soar or plod
His love becomes his daily bread.
In freedom flies his eagle thought
Skyward or earthward as he wills;
From distant lands and worlds is brought
The knowledge that his spirit fills.

In range with other souls he stands,
Yet lifts alone his tranquil head.
From off his mind he breaks the bands
That bind the dead past to its dead.
The winds of battle round him blow,
But steadfast calm is in his breast—
Humanity his work below,
The Eternal One his starry rest!

Calvin Day Noble, n.d.[40]

Middlebury President John Thomas said that "I doubt if there was
a single alumnus of Middlebury College more sincerely respected
or genuinely loved." A school board member said Professor
Higley was "the noblest Roman of us all."[41]

NOTES:

[1] Williams, *The New Church and Chicago: A History*,200-204.

[2] *Chicago Times*, November 30, 1873, pg. 6.

[3] Williams, *The New Church and Chicago: A History*,205.

[4] Noble, "The Golden Land," *Noble Scraps*. This is a fourteen part series describing in some detail his travels along the transcontinental railroad to San Francisco where he boarded a steamer for Los Angeles and finally horse and buggy to reach Riverside. The articles are undated.

[5] Ibid., Part VII.

[6] Noble, "Flowers of Southern California," *Noble Scraps*, Riverside Metropolitan Museum Archives, Riverside, California.

[7] Ibid.

[8] Noble, "Frontier Culture," *Noble Scraps*.

[9] James H. Roe, *Notes on Early History of Riverside, California* (unpublished manuscript), Riverside Public Library, Riverside, California, 15; Tom Patterson, "Dovenook's unique role," *Riverside Press Enterprise*, October 19, 1980. "Diary of Two Decades: Phonographic Resume of Events in our Valley in the year 1880," *Riverside Daily Press*, March 20, 1897, p. 6.

[10] *Press and Horiticulturist*, July 3, 1880, pg. 3; "Diary of Two Decades: Phonographic Resume of Events in our Valley in the year 1876," *Riverside Daily Press*, Dec. 1, 1896, pg. 2; Mary North Shepard as quoted in Patricia Ortlieb and Peter Economy, *Creating An Orange Utopia: Eliza Lovell Tibbets and the Birth of California's Citrus Industry* (West Chester, PA: Swedenborg Foundation Press, 2011), 70-71. Tom Patterson, "Spiritualist introduced séances, navel orange farming to Riverside," *Riverside Press-Enterprise*, July 14, 1984.

[11] Tom Patterson, *A Colony for California* (Riverside, CA: Press-Enterprise Company, 1971), 106.

[12] E.W. Dennison, *Riverside Press and Horticulturist*, July 30, 1885, (reprinted from the *North Adams [Mass.] Transcript*).

[13] Noble, "A Noble Affair at 'Glen Arbor,'" *Noble Scraps*.

[14] Dennison, *Riverside Press and Horticulturist*, July 30, 1885.

[15] *The Undergraduate*, vol. IV, no. 2 (November 1, 1878), 28.

[16] *The Undergraduate*, vol. IV, no. 8 (May 1879), 118. *The Undergraduate* also reported that the Higleys entertained upper class students in their home where "everybody had an immensely nice time." Higley's direction of opera at the college earned high praise and was said to surpass anything in the entertainment line that Middlebury had seen in years. See: *The Undergraduate*, vol. II, no. 5 (February 1877), 75 and vol. II, no. 7 (April 1877), 108.

[17] Rt. Rev. Bishop Julius W. Atwood, "Autobiography of An Alumnus,"

Middlebury College News Letter, vol. XVIII, no. 2 (December 1943), 7.

[18] Dr. S. Orlo Jefferson, "Middlebury Memories," *Middlebury College News Letter*, vol. XVII, no. 3 (March 1943), 16.

[19] Billings, *An Address in Memory*, 6; *Middlebury Register*, May 12, 1916.

[20] Ward, "Edwin Hall Higley, An American Classicist," 81. Felix Mendelssohn founded the Leipzig Conservatory in 1843. Higley journeyed to Hamburg, Germany while on year's sabbatical in August 1906. In a letter to President Peabody, Higley offered his services while away if needed by the school. "I could interview crowned heads, anarchists or other prominent people," he sarcastically wrote. "The anarchists will probably have the crowned heads in a sack before long, so that I could see them all at one interview!" See: Letter, Higley to Peabody, August 26, 1906, Groton School Archives.

[21] Ibid., 81, 94.

[22] Dr. William Thayer in "History of St. Andrew's Church, Ayer, Groton, Forge Village: 50th Anniversary, 1892-1942," Groton School Archives, Groton, Massachusetts.

[23] Ward, "Edwin Hall Higley, An American Classicist," 93. Ashburn, as quoted by Ward, is from Ashburn's book, *Peabody of Groton* (Cambridge, MA: Riverside Press, 1944), n.135, p. 80.

[24] Letter, Franklin Roosevelt to his parents, October 3, 1897, September 25, 1898, December 18, 1898 in Elliott Roosevelt, *F.D.R. His Personal Letters: Early Years, Vol. I*, (New York: Duell, Sloan and Pearce, 1947), 124, 207, 247-248.

[25] Ibid., Letters of March 23, March 26 and March 28, 1899, pages 282-285.

[26] Billings, *An Address in Memory*, 6.

[27] *Acts and Resolves Passed by the General Court of Massachusetts in the Year 1889* (Boston: Secretary of the Commonwealth, Wright & Potter Printing Co., 1889), 1314. The decree for the name change was July 24, 1888. Census records suggest that Margaret Higley was born in 1887.

[28] "Recent Mysteries of Three Pretty Girls," *Denver Rocky Mountain News*, January 22, 1905.

[29] "Weds After Being Missing a Month," *New York Herald*, January 3, 1905, pg. 1.

[30] "Quits Gambling and Takes Bride," *Boston Herald*, January 4, 1905, pg. 4.

[31] David Walker Howe, "Classical Education in America," *Wilson Quarterly* (spring 2011), 31, 36.

[32] Ward, "Edwin Hall Higley, An American Classicist," 87.

[33] Edwin H. Higley, "The place of Geography and Biography in Elementary History," *Classical Association of New England Annual Bulletin*, Vol. 1 (1906), 32.

[34] Ward, "Edwin Hall Higley, An American Classicist," 89.

[35] Higley, "The place of Geography and Biography in Elementary History," 32.

[36] Marcus Tullius Cicero (106 BC - 43 BC), in *Pro Publio Sestio*.

[37] Endicott Peabody to unidentified friend, May 13, 1916, Groton School Archives.

[38] Billings, *An Address in Memory*, 6.

[39] Letter, Grafton Minot to the *Grotonian* magazine, May 31, 1916, Groton School Archives.

[40] Calvin Day Noble, "The Mountain Man," *Noble Scraps*, Riverside Metropolitan Museum.

[41] Ward, "Edwin Hall Higley, An American Classicist," 93.

About The Author

Upon receiving his Master's Degree in 1998, Richard Hanks was hired as a public historian and archivist for the *Riverside Local History Resource Center* and a year later he got the opportunity to lead this talented group of historians and archivists. It was there that he first read the collection of Civil War letters from Edwin H. Higley in the Samuel C. Evans papers. For the next decade he continued to work as an archivist for the RLHRC in Riverside, A.K. Smiley Public Library and the Lincoln Memorial Shrine in Redlands, California. In 2006 he earned a PhD in Native American History. He went on to teach American History and Native American Studies at various community colleges and in 2012 he published his dissertation: *This War Is For A Whole Life: The Culture of Resistance Among Southern California Indians, 1850-1866* with Ushkana Press of Banning, California.

In December 2013, Hanks retired to concentrate on his writing. He was asked to write a book based on the Higley letters, by the Riverside Metropolitan Museum which houses the collection. He and his wife Robin published their first book, *Senior Chief Turbo: Memoir of a Navy SEAL Canine*, through their fledgling company, Coyote Hill Press. This book is their second publication.

For more information about Coyote Hill Press go to http://www.coyotehillpress.com.

Bibliography

Books:

Abbott, A.O., *Prison Life in the South: At Richmond, Macon, Savannah, Charleston, Columbia, Charlotte, Raleigh, Goldsborough and Andersonville During the Years 1864 and 1865* (New York: Harper & Brothers, Publishers, 1865).

Acts and Resolves Passed by the General Court of Massachusetts in the Year 1889 (Boston: Secretary of the Commonwealth, Wright & Potter Printing Co., 1889).

American Civil War: The Definitive Encyclopedia and Document Collection, Spencer C. Tucker, (ed.), (Santa Barbara, CA: Abc-Clio Incorporated, 2013).

Appletons' Cyclopædia of American Biography, James Grant Wilson and John Fiske (eds.) (New York: D. Appleton and Company, 1888).

Ballard, Ted. *Battle of Ball's Bluff, Staff Ride Guide* (Washington: Center of Military History, United States Army, 2001).

Banks, Raymond H., *King of Louisiana, 1862-1865, and Other Government Work: a Biography of Major General Nathaniel Prentice Banks, Speaker of the U. S. House of Representatives,* (Las Vegas, Nevada: Privately Printed, 2005).

Benedict, George Grenville, *Vermont in the Civil War: A History of the Part Taken by the Vermont Soldiers and Sailors in the War for the Union, 1861-5,* Volume II, (Burlington, VT: The Free Press Association, 1888).

Block, Marguerite Beck, *The New Church in the New World: A Study of Swedenborgianism in America* (New York: Henry Holt and Company, Inc., 1932).

Boltwood, Lucius M., *History and Genealogy of the Family of Thomas Noble of Westfield, Massachusetts with Genealogical Notes of other families by the Name of Noble*, (Hartford, CT: Privately Printed, 1878).

Brooks, Noah, *Washington In Lincoln's Time*, (New York: The Century Company, 1895).

Burlingame, Michael, *Abraham Lincoln: A Life, Volume I*, (Baltimore: Johns Hopkins University Press, 2008).

Catalogue of the Officers and Students of Middlebury College in Middlebury, Vermont and of Others Who Have Received Degrees, 1800-1915, compiled by Edgar J. Wiley (Middlebury, VT: Middlebury College, 1917).

Collea, Joseph D., *The 1st Vermont Cavalry in the Civil War: A History* (Jefferson, NC: McFarland & Company, Inc., 2010).

Columbia Encyclopedia, Volumes I-V, William Bridgewater and Elizabeth J. Sherwood (eds.), (New York: Columbia University Press, 1958).

Donald, David Herbert, *Lincoln*, (New York, N.Y.: Simon & Schuster, 1995).

Dusinberre, William, *Them Dark Days: Slavery in the American Rice Swamps* (Oxford: Oxford University Press, 1996).

Eicher, John H. and David J. Eicher, *Civil War High Commands*. (Stanford, CA: Stanford University Press, 2001).

Emilio, Luis Fenollosa, *A Brave Black Regiment: History of the Fifty-Fourth Regiment of Massachusetts Volunteer Infantry, 1863-1865* (Boston: The Boston Book Company, 1894).

Enclyclopedia Americana, Frederick Converse Beach (ed.), (New York: The Americana Company, 1904).

Encyclopedia Britannica, Encyclopedia Britannica Online, Encyclopedia Britannica Inc., 2014. Web. 21 June 2014. http://www.britannica.com.

Foote, Shelby, *The Civil War, A Narrative: Fort Sumter to Perryville* (New York: Vantage Books, 1986).

____ *The Civil War, A Narrative: Fredericksburg to Meridian,* (New York: Vantage Books, 1986).

____ *The Civil War, A Narrative: Red River to Appomattox* (New York: Vantage Books, 1986).

Frothingham, Paul Revere, *Edward Everett, Orator and Statesman* (Boston: Houghton Mifflin, 1925).

Hamilton, Mabel Parker Clarke, *The Lantern,* no. 6 (Bryn Mawr College, June 1897).

Holmes, Elmer, *History of Riverside, California with Biographical Sketches of the Leading Men and Women of the County who have been Identified with its Growth and Development From the Early Days to the Present* (Los Angeles: Historic Record Company, 1912).

Howard, Tony, *Women as Hamlet: Performance and Interpretation in Theatre, Film and Fiction* (Cambridge: Cambridge University Press, 2007).

Ide, Horace K. and Elliott W. Hoffman (ed.), *History of the First Vermont Volunteers in the War of the Great Rebellion* (Baltimore: Butternut and Blue, 2000).

The Idea of Music in Victorian Fiction, Sophie Fuller and Nicky Losseff, (eds.), (Burlington, Vermont: Ashgate Publishing Company, 2004).

Jenkins, Helen Philleo, *The Congress of Women: Held in the Woman's Building, World's Columbian Exposition, Chicago, U.S.A., 1893, Mary Kavanaugh Oldham Eagle (ed.),* (Chicago, Ill: Monarch Book Company, 1894).

Johnson, Mary Coffin, *The Higleys And Their Ancestry: An Old Colonial Family* (New York: D. Appleton and Company, 1896).

Jones, Wilmer, *Generals in Blue and Gray*, Volume 1, (Mechanicsburg, PA: Stackpole Books, 2006).

Journal of the Sixteenth Annual Session of the Ohio Association of the New Church held at East Rockport, Ohio, Oct. 15-17, 1869 in *New Jerusalem Messenger Magazine, Vol 42* (Boston: C. A. Dunham, 1869).

Journal of the Sixteenth Annual Session of the Ohio Association of the New Church Held in Pomoroy, October 27-29, 1871 (Boston: John C. Regan & Co., Printers, 1872).

Keenan, Jerry, *Wilson's Cavalry Corps: Union Campaigns in the Western Theater, October 1864 Through the Spring 1865* (Jefferson, NC: McFarland & Company, Inc., 1998).

Kirsch, George B., *Baseball in Blue and Gray: The National Pastime During the Civil War* (Princeton: Princeton University Press, 2003).

Lee, W. Storrs, *Father Went to College: The Story of Middlebury* (New York: Wilson-Erickson, 1936).

Longacre, Edward G., *General John Buford: A Military Biography* (Cambridge, MA: De Capo Press, 2003).

Mackay, Constance D'Arcy, *Costume and Scenery for Amateurs: A Practical Working Handbook* (New York: Henry Holt and Co, 1915).

Mauro, Charles V., *Herndon: A Town and its History* (Charleston, SC: History Press, 2005).

McPherson, James, *Ordeal by Fire, the Civil War, Volume II* (New York: McGraw-Hill, 2001).

____ *Battle Cry of Freedom, The Civil War Era* (New York: Oxford University Press, 1988).

The New Jerusalem Magazine, Index to Volumes I-XLIV, 1827-1872
(Boston: The General Convention of the New Jerusalem Church in
the United States, June 1872)

New York in the War of the Rebellion, 1861-1865, compiled by
Frederick Phisterer, (Albany: J.B. Lyon Company, state printers,
1912).

Odhner, Rev. C. Th. and Rev. Dr. William Whitehead, *Annals of the
New Church, Volume II, 1851-1890* (S.I. : s. n., 1976).

O'Neill, Robert F., *Chasing Jeb Stuart and John Mosby: The Union
Cavalry in Northern Virginia from Second Manassas to Gettysburg,*
(Jefferson, N.C.: McFarland and Company, Inc., 2012).

Ortlieb, Patricia and Peter Economy, *Creating An Orange Utopia:
Eliza Lovell Tibbets and the Birth of California's Citrus Industry* (West
Chester, PA: Swedenborg Foundation Press, 2011).

Palovsky, Arnold M., *Riding in Circles, J.E.B. Stuart and the
Confederate Cavalry, 1861-1862* (Southhampton, N.J.: Published by
the author, 2010).

Patterson, Tom, *A Colony for California* (Riverside, CA: Press-
Enterprise Company, 1971).

Paver, John M., *What I Saw, From 1861 to 1864, Personal Recollections
of John M. Paver, 1st Lieutenant Company C and R.Q.M. 5th Ohio Vol.
Infantry* (Indianapolis: Scott-Miller company, n.d.).

Phillips, George Harwood, *Chiefs and Challengers: Indian Resistance
and Cooperation in Southern California* (Berkeley: University of
California Press, 1975).

Phillips, Jerry and Andrew Ladd, *Romanticism and
Transcendentalism, 1800-1860,* (New York: Infobase, 2006).

*Report of the Adjutant and Inspector General of the State of Vermont
from Oct. 1, 1864 to Oct. 1, 1865* (Montpelier: Walton's Steam
Printing Establishment, 1865).

The Reports of Committees of the House of Representatives for the 2ⁿᵈ Session of the Fifty-Third Congress, In Five Volumes, Volume 2 (Washington: Government Printing Office, 1893-1894).

Reminiscences of an Oldest Inhabitant: (A Nineteenth Century Chronicle), (Herndon Historical Society, 1976).

Revised Roster of Vermont Volunteers And Lists Of Vermonters Who Served In The Army And Navy Of The United States During The War Of The Rebellion, 1861-1866 (Montpelier, VT: Press of the Watchman Publishing Company, 1892).

Roosevelt, Elliott, *F.D.R. His Personal Letters: Early Years, Vol. I,* (New York: Duell, Sloan and Pearce, 1947).

Ryan, Thomas, *Recollections of an Old Musician*. NY: E.P. Dutton & Company, 1899).

Sears, Stephen, *Landscape Turned Red: The Battle of Antietam* (New Haven, CT: Popular Library, 1983).

Segars, Henry, *Andersonville: The Southern Perspective* (St. Petersburg, FL: Southern Heritage Press, 1995).

Sheppard, Elizabeth, *Charles Auchester, in Two Volumes, Volume I* (Chicago: A.C. McClurg and Company, 1891).

Shumann, Robert, *Shumann on Music: A Selection from his Writings,* Henry Pleasants, translator and ed., (Mineola, New York: Dover Publications, Inc., 1988).

Smith, Gene, *American Gothic: The Story of America's Legendary Theatrical Family* (New York: Simon and Schuster, 1992).

Sprouse, Edith, *Fairfax County in 1860: A Collective Biography,* (Historical Society of Fairfax County, 1996).

Starr, S. Frederick, *Louis Moreau Gottschalk (Music in American Life)* (Urbana-Champaign: University of Illinois Press, 2000).

Ullery, Jacob G. (complier), *Men of Vermont: An Illustrated Biographical History of Vermonters and Sons of Vermont,* Part III (Brattleboro, VT: Transcript Publishing Company, 1894).

Vermont History: Proceedings of the Vermont Historical Society For The Years, 1915-1916 (Vermont Historical Society, 1918).

Walt Whitman: Selected Poems, 1855-1892, Gary Schmidgall (ed.), (New York: St. Martin's Press, 1999).

The War of the Rebellion: a Compilation of the Official Records of the Union and Confederate Armies, (Washington, United States War Dept., 1880-1901).

The War of the People: Vermont Civil War Letters, Jeffrey D. Marshall (ed.) (Hanover: University Press of New England, 1999).

Welch, Linda M.F., *Families of Cavendish and the Black River Valley of Windsor County, Vermont, Vol. 3* (Cavendish, VT: Cavendish Historical Society, 1998).

Wert, Jeffry D., *Cavalryman of the Lost Cause: A Biography of J.E.B. Stuart* (New York: Simon & Schuster, 2008).

Willard, George Owen, *History of the Providence Stage, 1762-1891* (Providence: The Rhode Island News Company, 1891).

Williamson, James J., *Mosby's Rangers* (New York: Ralph B. Kenyon, 1896).

Williams, Rudolph, *The New Church and Chicago: A History* (Chicago: W. B. Conkey Company, 1906).

Wills, Garry, *Lincoln at Gettysburg: The Words That Remade America* (New York, N.Y.: Simon & Schuster, 1992).

Winkle, Kenneth J., *Lincoln's Citadel: The Civil War in Washington, D.C.,* (New York: W.W. Norton & Company, Inc., 2013).

Periodicals, Journals and Newsletters:

America's Civil War

The Atlantic Monthly

Civil War Times

Civil War Times Illustrated

Middlebury Campus

Middlebury College News Letter

The Musical Quarterly

New Advent Catholic Library

New-Church Messenger

New England Classical Journal

New Jerusalem Messenger

Paradigm

Scholar Commons

The Undergraduate

The Vermonter

Vermont History

Archives:

Riverside Metropolitan Museum, Riverside, California

Middlebury College, Middlebury, Vermont

Groton School, Groton, Massachusetts

Classical Association of New England, Providence, Rhode Island

Fairfax County Historical Society, Fairfax, Virginia

Herndon Historical Society, Herndon, Virginia

Index

Howe, David Walker, 238
Houston Telegraph, xiii, 199, 203
Huckaby, William, 229
Huntoon, Franklin, 43, 44, 45, 93, 94

Illinois Association of the New Church, 215

Jackson, Thomas "Stonewall", 9, 10, 11, 12, 14, 15, 17, 18, 19, 20, 92, 104, 149
James River, 8, 51, 127, 147
Jefferson, Orlo S., 232
Jewett, James, xiii, 207, 213
John Halifax, Gentleman, 58, 78, 96
Johnson, Andrew, 203
Johnson, William F., 111, 176
Jude's Ford, 128

Kautz, August, 163, 164
Kellogg, Brainerd, 74, 75, 102
Kellogg, George, 7, 15, 25, 34
Kelly's Ford, 43, 51, 67, 68, 78, 81
Kent, Evarts B., 126, 127, 132, 157, 161, 179, 186
Kilpatrick, Judson, xxii, 62, 65, 66, 67, 68, 71, 75, 87, 90, 92, 96, 97, 99, 106, 117, 120, 121, 122, 123, 124, 127, 128, 129, 131, 133, 134, 135, 136, 141, 142, 161, 183, 188
Kingsley, Charles, xii, 78, 102,

103, 106, 108, 175
Labaree, Benjamin, 142, 182, 196
Ladd, Andrew, xi, xii
Lake, Harry, 237
Lasell Seminary, 236
Lee, Fitzhugh, 43, 129, 154, 164, 165
Lee, Robert E., 17, 18, 20, 25, 29, 41, 57, 60, 65, 67, 68, 78, 81, 116, 131, 144, 147, 149, 153, 154, 158, 193
Lee, W. Storrs, 3, 6, 94, 155
Lewinsville, VA, 38, 39, 51
Leipzig Conservatory, 175, 233, 243
Lincoln, Abraham, xvii, xviii, xxi, 8, 15, 28, 29, 31, 33, 61, 91, 99, 103, 104, 120, 158, 178, 181, 193, 215, 222
Lincoln, Mary Todd, 172
Lincoln, Robert Todd, 98, 222
Lincoln, Tad, 193
Lindsay, Vachel, 215, 222
Longstreet, James, 20
Los Angeles, CA, 182, 224, 225, 242
Luray, VA, 9, 10, 17

Magruder, John Bankhead, 132, 180, 181
Malone, NY, 206, 217
Manassas, VA, 20, 21, 51, 60, 67
Manassas Gap Railroad, 12
Massanutten Mountain, 9, 10, 11, 12, 13, 17

Stone, Charles Pomeroy, 143, 183
Stoneman, George, 43, 93, 104, 143, 190
Stony Creek, VA, 165
Stoughton, Edwin, 44, 45, 46, 94
Strasburg, VA, 12, 14
Streeter, Amelia Noble, 221, 229
Streeter, Henry M., 229
Stuart, James Ewell "Jeb", 20, 40, 42, 68, 92, 149
Sturtevant, Ethan Allen, 30, 35
Summons, Daisy, 229
Swedenborg, Emanuel, xiii, 207, 208, 215, 222
Swedenborgian Church, 207, 209, 214, 215, 222, 223, 224, 229, 230
Swedenborgianism, ix, xiii, 208
Swift, Foster Elliott, 104, 213
Swift, Frances Emeline Noble, 104, 213

Taggart, Charles F., 46, 49, 50, 52, 53, 54, 56, 57, 94, 95
Thalberg, Sigismond, 122, 178
Thayer, William, 234
Thomas, John, 241
Thoreau, Henry David, xi
Tibbets, Eliza, 229
Tibbets, Nicey, 229
Tilden, William Calvin, 24, 34, 46, 109, 136
Timson, Samuel, 172
Todd, George Rogers Clark, 172, 190, 191

Tompkins, Charles, 12, 14, 25, 26, 31, 35, 95
Torbert, Alfred Thomas Archimedes, 141, 143, 183, 189

University of Vermont, 93, 155, 178, 182, 232
Upton, George, 7, 99

Vermont Brigade, 24, 94, 185
Vermont Record, xiii, 189, 193, 196, 218
Vestvali, Felicita, 120, 122, 123, 178
Vienna, VA, 51, 53, 54

Wallace, William Vincent, 122, 139, 178, 181
Waltham, MA, xiv, 210, 214, 223, 224
Walton, E. P., 55
Ward, Allen, xvi, 28, 35, 238, 239
Warren, Daniel, 52, 95
Warren, Gouverneur Kemble, 67, 69, 116, 118, 133, 156, 177
Washington, DC, 1-3, 15-18, 20, 24, 25, 30, 34, 36, 38, 41, 42, 43, 49, 51, 60, 63, 64, 70, 73, 81, 92, 99, 103, 104, 105, 111, 112, 124, 126, 166, 177, 178, 179, 184, 187, 188, 193, 203

Castleton April 17 1865

My dear Noble

I must "pray thee to
have me excused" for this week. Our
Middlebury friends, Lucy and Mrs.
Denison have been down here for
a few days and I have had little time
for anything besides visiting. Lucy went
back yesterday,—Mrs. D. stays a few days
longer.—Last evening we droove out to
Fairhaven to hear Maj. Copeland address
a meeting on the Washington tragedy. We
were will paid for the expedition.
I have no need, I am sure, to say anything about the sorrow which this shock
~~and sorrow~~ has brought to me. Your own
heart I know can tell you all about it.
To speak of the minor matters connected
with it,— it is some consolation to know

that Booth was an inferior artist. I
have heard him several times and was
at first pleased with him because – having
been brought up upon the stage; he was
perfectly familiar with all its tricks and
customs, has a fine figure and a good
share of his family natural ability. But
when he attempted great characters as Ham-
-let or Macbeth it was easy to see that
the soul was wanting. Where, in his
brother Edwin, there was deep and earnest
scholarly thought and study, together with
the most delicate appreciation and sym-
-pathy with every shade of the poets mean-
-ing, all thrown into the intense, passionate
impersonation of his character – with
this other it was all ranting affectation.
Mrs. Akers was especially disgusted with
him. – Curious that the last thing
which I heard him play was Mac-
-beth. – Heard him say
                    "This Duncan
Hath borne his faculties so meek, hath been

So clear in his great office, that his virtues
Will plead like angels, trumpet-tongued, against
The deep damnation of his taking off!"

Strange that a man who could
ever have been even slightly impressed
by such a powerful representation of the
terror that follows guilt, could ever have
dyed his hands with the "damned spots."

The books arrived safely.
I will send you something more in
time for next week.   I am greatly
gratiful for the commendatory words
which you have said because I dont
think you would say them if you
dednt mean them.

Allie & I ride horseback almost every-
-day. in your cav. co. I notice in the list of your
non. com. officers the name of Chas.
Wooley as corporal.   If you think
of it will you notice and tell me if
he can speak out loud. He lost
his voice when in the regiment.
                    Ever Yours
                            Ed.

www.ingramcontent.com/pod-product-compliance
Lightning Source LLC
Chambersburg PA
CBHW060008100426
42740CB00010B/1431